The
INNER
LIFE
of
MESTIZO
NATIONALISM

CULTURAL STUDIES OF THE AMERICAS

George Yúdice, Jean Franco, and Juan Flores, series editors

For more titles in the series, see page 242.

The
INNER
LIFE
of
MESTIZO
NATIONALISM

Estelle Tarica

Cultural Studies of the Americas
Volume 22

University of Minnesota Press
Minneapolis • London

A portion of a previous version of chapter 2 in was published as "Entering the Lettered City: Jesús Lara and the Formation of a Quechua Literary Patrimony in the Andes," in Morrison Library Inaugural Address Series 21 (Berkeley: Doe Library, University of California, 2001); copyright by the Regents of the University of California. A portion of a previous version of chapter 3 was published in Spanish as "El 'decir limpio' de Arguedas: La voz bilingüe, 1940–1958," in *José María Arguedas: Hacia una poética migrante*, ed. Sergio R. Franco (Pittsburgh: Instituto Internacional de Literatura Iberoamericana–Serie ACP, 2006), 23–38.

Published by the University of Minnesota Press
111 Third Avenue South, Suite 290
Minneapolis, MN 55401-2520
http://www.upress.umn.edu

Library of Congress Cataloging-in-Publication Data

Tarica, Estelle.
    The inner life of mestizo nationalism / Estelle Tarica.
        p. cm. – (Cultural studies of the americas series ; v. 22)
    Includes bibliographical references and index.
    ISBN 978-0-8166-5004-0 (hc : alk. paper) – ISBN 978-0-8166-5005-7 (pb : alk. paper)
    1. Latin American fiction–20th century–History and criticism. 2. Mestizaje in literature. 3. Nationalism in literature. I. Title.
PQ7082.N7T36 2008
863′.6093581–dc22

                                                                        2008008163

Printed in the United States of America on acid-free paper

The University of Minnesota is an equal-opportunity educator and employer.

15   14   13   12   11   10   09   08   10   9   8   7   6   5   4   3   2   1

To Ralph and Suzanne

Contents

Acknowledgments

Many people gave me guidance and support over the course of writing this book and helped make it possible.

For reading portions of the book in draft form and offering much-appreciated comments and formative advice, I am grateful to Dru Dougherty, Christina Gillis, William Hanks, Eduardo Kohn, Francine Masiello, Hugo Moreno, José Rabasa, William Rowe, and Cameron Scott. I am especially indebted to Marcia Stephenson, Michael Iarocci, José Luiz Passos, Laura García Moreno, and Jorge Coronado, who read and discussed my work with me and whose friendship and intellectual collaboration have been a source of strength. I am also lucky to have Robert McKee Irwin as a fellow traveler. Conversations with Richard Rosa, Anna Zalik, Jerry Craddock, Jiwon Shin, Martin Lienhard, Julio Ramos, Josefa Salmón, Natalia Brizuela, Fernando Unzueta, Hortensia Muñoz, María Eugenia Choque Quispe, Carlos Mamani Condori, Christian Gundermann, Guillermo Delgado, and Gordon Brotherston contributed much to the shaping of my ideas. In its earliest stages, Natalie Melas, Mary Roldán, and Edmundo Paz Soldán offered insight and encouragement that sustained the project. Rachel Weber and John Slocum gave me some crucial advice. I also thank the students in my graduate seminars "Indigenismo," "Memoria Andina," and "The Spanish-American Novel" for discussions that helped illuminate my own thinking.

This book owes a special debt to Luis Morató Peña, not only for his invaluable assistance with Quechua but also for his unstinting kindness and generosity as a teacher and friend as well as his guidance during my research stays in Bolivia. Ana Franco Martí was a formative intellectual presence during the course of my research, which owes much to our many long conversations. I am also particularly grateful to Debra Castillo, who has been a source of encouragement, critical insight, and inspiring intellectual guidance from the start.

Various institutions at the University of California–Berkeley provided generous support for the project. A Humanities Research Fellowship gave me precious time to write, as did a fellowship from the Doreen B. Townsend Center for the Humanities, with special thanks to Candace Slater. Teresa Stojkov and Harley Shaiken at the Center for Latin American Studies granted me summer research funds for this project and gave me a forum to present my work. UC Regents and UC–Berkeley Junior Faculty Fellowships also funded my research. I am indebted to Carlos Delgado and the Morrison Library for the opportunity to present and publish the early fruits of my research on this project. My colleagues in the Department of Spanish and Portuguese offered much supportive guidance over the years.

During research trips abroad I was fortunate to receive the generous assistance and hospitality of many people. I am especially beholden to Alcira Bascopé de Valverde, Adelina Morató Peña, Irma and Regi Rojo, and Celina Nogales and Antonio Fuentes for opening their homes to me and talking with me about their worlds. Iván Reyna and Rocío Ferreira were informative guides and companions in Lima. Cristina Soto de Cornejo, Gonzalo Cornejo Soto, and the Centro de Estudios Literarios Antonio Cornejo Polar greatly facilitated my research in Peru. In Mexico I was lucky to have the generous friendship of Gene Walsh, Luz Rangel, and Maríbel Díaz. I am indebted to my Quechua teachers at the Instituto de Idiomas Padres Maryknoll in Cochabamba, Víctor Carrasco Vega, Viviana Flores, Ana Franco, Inge Molina Rojas, Abraham Montoya, Roxana Pinto, and Fritzy Zambrana Padilla for sharing their perspectives with me. I gratefully acknowledge Carmen Lara del Barco and her family for granting me permission to examine Jesús Lara's personal archive.

I thank editor Richard Morrison at the University of Minnesota Press for his support of this book and John Eagleson for his careful work with it.

Jessica Basseches and Denise Tukenmez were a mainstay while I wrote, talking me through it and putting it all in perspective, along with Jessica Pitt, Bob Franklin, Bill Weinberg, Rebecca Egger, Liz Ozol, Andy Steckel, Nina Goldman, and Douglas Legg, who have been exceptional friends.

This book would not have been possible without the support and advice of my parents, Ralph and Suzanne Tarica, to which words can hardly do justice, and Brad Prager, my constant companion, whose love keeps me from losing my way.

Introduction

Intimate Indigenismo

What is indigenismo? One approach defines indigenismo as a discourse by non-Indians about Indians in Latin America, one that originated in the sixteenth century and continues into the present day. Such a definition emphasizes that indigenismo comes from a perspective that is external and alien to indigenous people themselves. This approach orients us toward the social relationship underlying indigenismo, a relationship between those who speak and those who are spoken about. It alerts us to the cultural differences and disparities in power that characterize that relationship and invites a meditation on the colonial foundations of Latin American societies. Indigenismo can be said to resemble Orientalism, because it is the product of the encounter and conflict between two groups and builds on the distinction between them to justify social hierarchy. It uses concepts of racial and cultural difference as instruments of domination (Said 2–3). Seen from this perspective, indigenismo is an exoticist and racist discourse that furthers colonial aims of exploiting, subordinating, and silencing Indians.[1]

Indigenismo has also been defined rather differently as "a current of thought favorable to Indians" (Favre 7), one that promotes a "sympathetic awareness of the Indian" (Stabb 405).[2] Its aims are anti-colonial, socially progressive, even revolutionary (Mariátegui 306). Seen from this alternative vantage point, indigenismo is a critical response to the conquest and colonization of indigenous peoples and the unjust societies that developed in their wake. It denounces the injustices to which Indians have been submitted and promotes some forms of Indians' resistance. Indigenista critiques of social injustice, still alive today, advance notions of common belonging and coexistence that cut across racial and ethnic lines.

These two contrasting approaches to indigenismo appear mutually exclusive, yet in fact they reflect distinct aspects of a single ideological phenomenon. Both must be taken into account in order to understand indigenismo. Modern indigenismo in Mexico, Bolivia, and Peru responds to entrenched and widespread structures of inequality and domination whose origins date back to the colonial period. Yet in an oblique and often hidden form, indigenista critiques of racism and socio-economic injustice, based on the discourses of interethnic sympathy and shared origin, shared destiny, shared space and language that constitute the mestizo nation, have also served to constrain and control indigenous people and perpetuate discriminatory attitudes about them.

Since the 1960s, fueled by a growing indigenous rights movement and by critiques of authoritarian nationalisms, a wealth of scholarly and activist work has been dedicated to demystifying indigenismo and the ideology of mestizo nationalism that it has served to consolidate. These approaches advance a view of indigenismo as the expression of a will to power that, under the guise of modernization-as-integration, secretly works to institute a new social hierarchy. Many of these critiques have stressed the problematic politics of representation that ensue when non-Indians claim to speak for Indians, a gesture that coopts, marginalizes, and ultimately silences indigenous voices while empowering indigenistas themselves. Partially as a result of these criticisms, the indigenista institutions that developed in the national-populist years of the mid-twentieth century have since weakened or disappeared. Yet increasing inequalities of wealth in the twenty-first century have given a renewed impetus to indigenista discourses, a resurgence that suggests that indigenismo's power may be both more subtle and more profound than has been acknowledged. Why has indigenismo historically been so appealing to non-Indians? How has it been woven into the fabric of modern nationalism in Mexico and the Andes? Why do indigenismo's nominally anti-racist elements so often end up working against indigenous people?

From the colonial period to the modernizing national-populism of the twentieth century, indigenista discourses have contributed to the consolidation of state power in Mexico and the Andes. Indigenismo has participated in transforming native populations into subjects of state control, an instrument of the broader historical project of exploiting indigenous labor, appropriating indigenous lands, and transforming indigenous cultures in order better to subordinate them to non-Indian rule. Yet indigenismo has fulfilled a very particular role in this endeavor. In its various manifestations across history, it has promoted a vision of Indians that is distinct from, and often antagonistic to, the vision promoted by colonial settlers and their descendants, who see Indians as objects of exploitation. From its inception in Bartolomé de las Casas's sixteenth-century defense of the Indians before the Spanish Crown, indigenismo has denounced the exploitation of indigenous people and has offered a sustained challenge to the discourse that links Indians to barbarism. Such a discourse was crucial to justifying the colonial enterprise and the civilizing mission of the postcolonial republics and modern nation-states. Indigenismo resisted the equation of Indians with barbarity. Yet in some ways it also continued to desire and justify the subordination of indigenous people.

In the sixteenth century and the twentieth century — the moments of its greatest strength in Mexico and the Andes — indigenismo contests the status quo while eventually becoming itself a source of considerable ideological force over both Indian and non-Indian subjects, but a force that is only imperfectly and unevenly implemented. Working primarily through discourses of Christian evangelization and, later, national identity, and almost always tied to the institutions of the state, indigenismo has set itself the task of humanizing Indians and rendering them familiars, and therefore of transforming the cultural and racial self-conception of Latin American subjects. The traces of these changing self-conceptions can be found in the indigenista text, particularly in autobiographical and fictional indigenismo, which serves as a rich archive through which to examine the rhetoric and ideology, the motives and limits, of the humanization and familiarization that indigenismo has historically sought to accomplish.

In 1938, Peruvian author José María Arguedas wrote, "Lo indígena está en lo más íntimo de toda la gente de la sierra del Perú" [Indianness is in the most intimate part of all the people of the Peruvian mountains] (*Canto kechwa* 13). The "intimate" of which Arguedas speaks, and around which this study is constructed, signals a new way of describing the regional and national self in the first half of the twentieth century. These words come from Arguedas's "Essay on the Creative Capacity of Indians and Mestizos." For Arguedas, this creative capacity involved a spiritual exercise of the highest order. The essay aimed to demonstrate to mestizos that their aesthetic expression — especially their music — emerges from an intimate, interior place where "Indianness" resides. Intimacy in this context does not refer primarily to sex or "carnal knowledge," nor is it limited to the idea of a private or domestic sphere of social relations.[3] Here, it refers to a kind of soulful communion between the individual self and a racialized time-space, the Andes, a time-space that regional intellectuals were then in the process of making symbolically coextensive with the nation itself. Naming the place of this communion "intimate," Arguedas implied the presence of a private self whose existence the public self might deny. He pointed to a sphere of deeply felt individual experience that both resists sharing and overspills the bounds of the self — it longs to sing, to create music. And he racialized it, thereby linking it to a particular history and geography that was collectively shared.

This book examines many such instances of personal, informal, and "intimate" expressions of indigenista sentiment, which emerged in Mexico and the Andes with modernization and social revolution in the early and mid-twentieth century. It seeks to understand indigenismo's hold over the national imagination and connection to less overt forms of state power and discusses its contribution to mestizo nationalism, of which indigenismo can properly be considered the parent discourse. It uses the autobiographical writings of influential indigenista thinkers such as Jesús Lara (1898–1980), José María Arguedas (1911–69), and Rosario Castellanos (1925–74) to develop an account of indigenismo's contradictory ideological nature. These three writers are often celebrated for having pioneered new forms of indigenista representation reflecting a more genuine, more intimate relationship to the Indians portrayed in their works, largely because of their use of "I" and their depiction of sympathetic relationships between Indians and non-Indians. Each author created a personal story built around these interethnic connections, a story that attests to the interpellating power of indigenismo, its capacity to change how people view themselves in racialized societies. As my analysis of these writers will demonstrate, however, indigenismo's contribution to modern self-transformations can be deeply problematic, for it works simultaneously to marginalize and disempower indigenous people before the law.

To examine this "intimate" discourse requires shifting the focus slightly in our understanding of indigenismo, to think about it not only in terms of its dialectical relationship to properly indigenous discourses, but also in terms of its dialectical relationship to other colonial and criollo discourses on race. That is, to think about it not only in terms of its relationship to its subject ("the Indian") but also in terms of its content and its relationship to its time. The task is a difficult one because the time of indigenismo has changed so dramatically over the course of the twentieth century. Simply put, indigenismo has gone from being oppositional and minoritarian to dominant and hegemonic. To appreciate this transformation, one has but to contrast the very different views on indigenismo advanced by two important Peruvian thinkers: José Carlos Mariátegui, writing in the 1920s, and Antonio Cornejo Polar, writing in the 1970s.

Peruvian socialist indigenista Mariátegui, in his widely influential 1928 *Siete ensayos de interpretación de la realidad peruana* (Seven Interpretative Essays on Peruvian Reality), insisted on the insurgent and revolutionary character of the Peruvian indigenista movement, as can be seen in his approach to indigenista literature. Mariátegui defined indigenista literature as literature about Indians produced by non-Indians, specifically mestizos, and insisted on the distinction between "indigenista" and "indígena" texts — indige*nist* and indige*nous* texts (306). Mariátegui was referring specifically to indigenista fiction and arguing against those who applied to it a realist concept of verisimilitude. The success of indigenista literature, he argued, should be measured with respect to the broader avant-garde political movement of which it was a part. Indigenista fiction does not represent indigenous lifeways realistically, nor should it try to. Instead, it represents the revolutionary spirit of the age (Mariátegui 306).

More recent approaches, however, have had to take into account a very different aspect of indigenismo, namely, its increasingly hegemonic status over the course of the twentieth century. The work of Peruvian literary scholar Antonio Cornejo Polar offers one of the most significant theorizations of indigenismo's hegemonic position. In the 1970s, Cornejo described indigenismo as "heterogeneous discourse," defined as a discourse in which the author and his referent belong to two distinct "socio-cultural" universes, i.e., indigenous and nonindigenous societies ("Indigenismo" 13). In his groundbreaking analysis of literary indigenismo, Cornejo argued that the most important feature of indigenista literature is its exterior position vis-à-vis the indigenous people it describes. This argument was directly inspired by Mariátegui's distinction between indige*nous* and indige*nist* texts. On the basis of this distinction, Cornejo modeled twentieth-century indigenista narrative on the chronicles of conquest written by the Spanish invaders in the sixteenth century. As a result of Cornejo's influence, what was for Mariátegui an attribute of indigenista literature has since come to be seen as the defining and essential element of indigenismo.[4] Its transitional or revolutionary character has been downplayed in order to highlight its colonial, Orientalist character.

If indigenismo is modeled on the discourse of the early Spanish colonizers, then the primary aim of indigenismo appears to be to dominate,
silence, exploit, enslave, or destroy indigenous people. While there is certainly much truth to this, it tells only part of the story because in fact
indigenismo has had other significant aims. One of these involves the
development of a juridical/theological discourse that demonstrates that
the exploitation of Indians is unjust and that Indians and Indianness
should not be stigmatized.[5] Another involves the development of notions
of collective belonging and individual selfhood that seek to undermine
established racial hierarchies. These aims need to be seriously examined
in conjunction with indigenismo's subordinating and oppressive effects.
What is the precise nature of the indigenista denunciation of indigenous
oppression? How and why does this denunciation become itself an instrument of oppression? Why does it seem to liberate those who enunciate it
but not those on whose behalf it is expressed?

To answer these questions, the basic premise of Cornejo's approach is
absolutely correct: to understand indigenismo, it is necessary to understand the contexts in which it is produced and circulates, and especially
to understand how indigenous people themselves have been marginalized or excluded from those contexts. However, my analysis of those
contexts is also substantially different from Cornejo's and has led me to
different conclusions about the ideology of indigenismo. Cornejo views
indigenismo through the dualist lens he inherited from Mariátegui, who
wrote extensively about the bisection of Peru into Indian and non-Indian
regions. But autobiographical indigenista texts tell a different story about
identity, a more complicated one. They point to the existence of multiple
ethno-racial categories often shading ambiguously into one another. They
reveal the relative porousness of racial boundaries, whether by showing
us the pathways that permit individuals to move "up" the social hierarchy toward a less-stigmatized condition, or by demonstrating how the
possession of particular attributes might bring an individual now closer,
now farther, to certain racial types. Thus, as the autobiographical texts
analyzed here repeatedly demonstrate, so often individuals find themselves straddling the divide — considered Indian and primitive in one
context, Hispanic and civilized in another.

The underlying duality of civilization vs. barbarism still remains, of
course, superimposed onto the far older distinction between Spaniards
and Indians, and the even older distinction between "Old Christians"

and "New Christians." Yet even if the fact of difference remains, the duality does not generate fixed and unchanging identity categories. These should be seen rather as composites, made up of a variety of attributes whose determining weight and significance can shift, depending on the historical moment, regional location, and social space. This shift is especially true during the modernizing period of the early and mid-twentieth century, when rural-urban migration and other forms of social mobility, combined with liberal concepts of education as a civilizing process, and, importantly, new concepts of national identity, destabilized established identity categories.

The circulation of ideas and changing political systems have also contributed to this destabilization: new social concepts and political ideas generated different ways of categorizing individuals and groups. Colonial categories of race were generally abolished when nation-states were formed in the nineteenth century. Yet these maintained a long half-life despite their disappearance from formal law, deeply embedded in social life. The categories that nominally replaced them, generally of a liberal order and greatly influenced by developments in European race thinking, were themselves continually revised over the course of the century in response to changing social and economic circumstances. Wars required participation of great numbers of indigenous soldiers, who were thus newly interpellated as citizens or nationalists.[6] Financial crises required reinstatement of Indian tribute (as happened in Bolivia) or other forms of colonial-era servitude, justified by recourse to colonial-era identity categories.[7] Changing social philosophies and regional power struggles involving all kinds of social actors have meant that concepts of "Indianness," indigeneity, and mestizaje have been the subject of conflict and debate. As many scholars have pointed out, at any given time, multiple and competing concepts of race and culture have coexisted.[8]

To take one particularly striking example: it is clear from his autobiography that Bolivian indigenista Jesús Lara did not consider himself to be an Indian as a child—he reserved that word for people of a lower social class, like the quasi-servant boy his mother hired to watch over him and his brother (*Paqarin* 7). Yet once in school, Lara found himself consistently linked to negative concepts of Indianness whenever he spoke Quechua, because it was widely held to be an inferior and primitive language—despite the fact that it was the maternal tongue of everyone in the room, teacher and students alike. Lara's indigenismo was, in part, an outgrowth of this deeply felt disjunction between a local sphere of identity

(e.g., home, village) and a broader, more national sphere (e.g., the municipal school). Paradoxically, in addition to establishing clearly demarcated
racial zones of belonging — Indians/Indianness do not belong in school —
this disjunction also created a lot of ambiguity: maybe the teacher was
right to assert that these students were, in some hitherto unacknowledged
way, Indians of a sort? From there it was but a short dialectic step to the
reversal of value enacted by Lara and other nationalist thinkers at the start
of the twentieth century, who proudly identified themselves, and Bolivia,
as Indian at the core — the key to establishing the nation as mestizo.

As the above reflections should make evident, the Latin American
situation contrasts strongly with how racial identities are defined and experienced in the United States. The United States is comparatively more
rigid in how individuals are assigned racial identities (e.g., the infamous
"one drop rule"), where "tightly bounded categories of black and white"
were created and have been preserved (Wade 38). Racial identifications in
Latin America are more malleable, without being *completely* malleable.
Many formal laws and informal norms existed to classify individuals into
ethno-racial categories in the colonial, republican, and national periods,
and there were numerous institutions established to regulate behavior
on the basis of these categories and police the resulting social boundaries. Nevertheless, ethno-racial identities in Mexico and the Andes have
always possessed a certain fluidity across time and place. Thus, as anthropologist Peter Wade has argued, "it is wrong to extrapolate from the
U.S. case to racial identification in general" (38).

Furthermore, Latin American racial identifications are not so centrally
focused on questions of phenotype and genetic inheritance as they are in
the United States. As historian Nancy Appelbaum argues, racial identity
in Latin America "has been as much about lineage, culture, and place
of origin within the nation as about phenotype or continental origin"
(Appelbaum 10). Ethno-racial identities in Latin America are designated
according to a wider variety of factors. The environment has played a particularly strong deterministic role in this regard, as I will discuss further in
chapter 1. But other factors, too, such as religion, language, accent, education, occupation, economic choices, and dress can all contribute, in one
way or another, to distinguishing among individuals in racial terms. For
example, the Spanish concept of "limpieza de sangre," "purity of blood,"
defined "purity" in part according to religious distinctions that have little
to do with nineteenth- and twentieth-century concepts of genetic or biological race. It was intimately connected to the categories "Old Christian"

and "New Christian," which, likewise, were not exclusively religious in the narrow sense of the word; they can also be considered racial designations because they were based on an individual's family ancestry. To be considered "of pure blood" or an "Old Christian," an individual had to prove that he or she was not descended from Jews, Moors, or heretics — and in the Americas, these designations inherently excluded Indians and Africans. Such concepts did not survive past the colonial period intact, yet in many ways the underlying moral framework persists. Arguedas, it is worth noting, continued to use the somewhat anachronistic dichotomy between "cristiano" and "indio" into the late 1960s: "Yo soy un peruano que orgullosamente, como un demonio feliz, habla en cristiano y en indio, en español y en quechua" ("No soy" 257) [I am a Peruvian who, like a cheerful demon, proudly speaks in Christian and in Indian, in Spanish and in Quechua ("I am not" 269)]. He did so in order to stress the almost theological nature of the distinctions made between Spanish and Quechua, to evoke and then transcend a set of longstanding associations about the war between believers and pagans, between a small minority of civilized people and the mass of savages, the saved and the damned, the known and the unknown.

It is worth pointing out, however, that despite these differences between the United States and Latin America, both societies are profoundly racialized. Recent scholarship in Mexican and Andean social history and ethnography has increasingly been devoted to understanding this aspect of social life. Above and beyond the presence of discrete racial categories and identities, it is necessary to speak of "racialization," the process whereby all Latin American subjects have been shaped by deeply embedded markings of human difference (Appelbaum et al. 2). Indigenista testimonies reveal this inescapability of race, its determining impact on all levels of social experience.

These factors make it more difficult to determine the site of indigenista enunciation as simply or straightforwardly "non-Indian," and thus to understand indigenismo as primarily a discourse about the Other.[9] Although Mariátegui and others are right to stress the persistence of colonial modes of thought in modern Latin America, the racialized social field from which indigenismo emerges is neither as dualistic nor as stable as Mariátegui's definition has been taken to suggest. However, this kind of shiftiness does not mean that questions of identity are so elusive as to become moot or unanswerable. On the contrary, it draws our attention to the highly charged nature of the rhetoric of identity, and to the relative power accorded to the individual voice. What does it mean to speak or write of oneself as Indian, or from a position "within" Indianness, as so many indigenista authors did? What made this apparently anti-racist rhetoric possible, even desirable, and what are its limits?

Not simply a cynical ploy or façade — though it is often that — the indigenista rhetoric of identity is the sign of the growing strength of the modernizing state, one in which the language of selfhood has been invested with a new power. Indigenismo participates in what Michel Foucault calls "the procedures of individualization by power" (*History* 59) because it provides an expression for the racialized subject. From this perspective, autobiographical and "intimate" indigenismo, a discourse emanating from the self, from a subjective position, is also a site of power, though its power may be of a different nature than indigenismo's more official and impersonal variants.

The "intimate" indigenismo I will analyze here refers to those strands of indigenista discourse that appeal to the existence of interior and subjective realms of interethnic affinity and sympathy. These instances of indigenista ideology involve a turn to an interior sphere of Indianness that non-Indians share with Indians, a sphere that forms the basis of mestizo nationality. Though indigenismo has always wielded notions of racial-cultural difference and has helped to cement those differences into institutionalized forms of inequality, it has also strongly affirmed the existence of an innate connection between Indians and non-Indians by calling on notions of collective space and history, most especially the nation form. In such intimate indigenista discourse, one confronts an indigenista rhetoric that aims, quite sincerely, to listen to an Indian voice rather than to silence it, and to evoke the affiliations between Indians and non-Indians rather than to reassert a hierarchical difference between them. This kind of indigenismo takes not only the Indian as its object but also those who repudiate the Indian. It rehabilitates not only the Indian but the Indian "within." For this reason, the archive of indigenista texts contains many examples in which indigenista action has been made personally significant for the writer as a kind of self-realization. One is struck by the almost religious faith in the promise of indigenismo, and the mestizo nation, that such texts exhibit. Peruvian writer José María Arguedas, whose life and work will be of central importance to my study, is perhaps the most famous exponent of this kind of intimate indigenista rhetoric. For him as well as others, indigenismo was a deeply personal, even spiritual, endeavor.

This turn to the Indianness within the nation and within national selves is a gesture characteristic of modernizing intellectuals who embraced a new vision of collective identity sometimes referred to as "the cult of mestizaje."[10] The glorification of mestizaje is most often associated with proud declarations of Latin America's unique cultural heritage on the world stage, especially vis-à-vis the United States. But the appeals to an interior, indigenous place that I will examine here are directed to a local audience and have a marked compensatory feel. In Arguedas's writings, as well as in the autobiographical writings of other indigenistas that I will address in this book, indigenismo takes on a special function: it connects individual aspirations to the collective mystique of nationalist thought and enables them to coalesce. At such times, indigenismo becomes a discourse of liberation and redemption, both individual and collective. Rather than aiming only at Indians themselves, it seeks to liberate and redeem non-Indians by insisting that they recognize and accept an inner connectedness to Indians.

In such indigenista discourse the ideal mestizo self is a noticeably self-conscious and searching subject, oriented toward the capture of an elusive interior dialogue. This indigenismo repeatedly invokes the practice of listening to the Other as a mode of listening to the self, an invocation first seriously examined by Mexican philosopher Luis Villoro, who developed a complex phenomenological account of indigenismo in 1950. Exploring the distinct currents of Mexican indigenista thought over the centuries, Villoro described its most contemporary instance as involving a process of self-encounter:

> El indio está en el seno del propio mestizo, unido a él indissoluble-mente. Captar al indígena será, por tanto, captar indirectamente una dimensión del propio ser. Así, la recuperación del indio significa, al propio tiempo, recuperación del propio Yo. (272)

> The Indian is at the heart of the mestizo self, indissolubly united with him. Thus, to grasp the Indian is to grasp, indirectly, a dimension of the mestizo's very self. In this way, the recovery of the Indian signifies simultaneously the recovery of the I itself.

Both Villoro and the indigenista thinkers whom he studied exalted this self-encounter as the truest expression of national belonging and as a form of liberation. Such enunciations can be found throughout the works of prominent nationalist thinkers in the Andes and Mexico, whether politically oppositional or allied to official power. All of them wielded a language of spirit and sentiment opposed to positivist and liberal notions of biological race circulating in the late nineteenth century and attempted to center national identity on what Bolivian poet Franz Tamayo described as "nuestra naturaleza íntima de mestizos" [our intimate mestizo nature] (145). Thus engaged, the national subject proclaims an intimate affinity with Indians — becomes, in effect, a new kind of mestizo: one whose Indianness is the source of his or her redemption. Marked by a strong introspective turn, this indigenismo expresses both a sense of marginalization and a sense of ascendant social power.

An appreciation of indigenismo's complex relationship to enduring power structures leads to a renewed awareness of its contradictory nature. Although indigenismo is an expression of the colonial domination over Indians, it competes with, but does not fully supplant, other discourses of colonial domination. Although indigenismo has always been the discourse of a dominant or rising class, it originates as a challenge to existing racial hierarchies — while also justifying new ones. Although indigenismo's main ideological effects over time have been the subordination or suppression of Indian voices and political aims, it has also acted to form non-Indian subjects by offering new understandings of what constitutes civilized humanity. Indigenismo is thus both a program of the colonial/criollo state and a program of opposition, both a colonial, racist discourse and a challenge to such discourses, both an attempt to better control Indians and an attempt to change how non-Indians view Indians and Indianness. Indigenismo is not only a discourse constructing the Other, but is also one of the sites of interaction and confrontation constituting modern interethnic relations (A. Ramos 5–7).[11]

The time of modern indigenismo is a time of historical transition, when the banner of modernization passes from oligarchic to middle-class hands, or comes to be shared by both. This transitional character gives indigenismo some of its contradictory ideological flavor, making it simultaneously a racist and an anti-racist discourse. Anti-racist, because it challenges some existing concepts of race; racist, because it also perpetuates some of these hierarchical concepts and/or introduces new ones. Because indigenismo competed with other racial discourses, which it generally did not succeed in displacing, it can be considered an example of a subordinate form of racism that coexists with more dominant forms. As anthropologist Marisol de la Cadena has shown, this subordinate racism

participates in the dominant racism's legitimation of certain kinds of social hierarchy, yet remains nevertheless distinct from it (de la Cadena
4–5). Seen in this light, indigenismo can be understood as a form of
racism wielded to combat another form of racism.

Starting from an awareness of these multiple aspects of indigenista
discourse, this book seeks to grasp indigenismo's contradictory nature,
to understand its challenge to the status quo and its enduring presence
within the status quo, its assertion both of Indian difference and of interethnic affinity and affiliation, its framing of an Indian object and its
search for a new kind of non-Indian subject. Drawing from autobiographical indigenista writings, my aim is to examine how indigenismo
has worked strongly from within, from the inside out, from the site of
the self that comes to awareness in the racialized space of the nation.
What is involved when the national subject — Mexican, Bolivian, or Peruvian — adopts a new pose, a listening pose attentive to indigenous
voices located somewhere within or at the boundaries of the self?

These constructions of a national mestizo"I" whose truth is said to
reside in a core that is both Indian and not Indian can be found in a
host of indigenista art and writing. The three autobiographical novels I
will examine here — Jesús Lara's *Surumi* (1943), José María Arguedas's
Los ríos profundos (The Deep Rivers) (1958), and Rosario Castellanos's
Balún Canán (Nine Guardians) (1957) — offer a particularly rich rhetorical and narratological elaboration. These examples of indigenista "relato
íntimo," intimate narrative, at the margins of fiction and autobiography,
are literary texts in which the indigenista will to power appears to have
been subverted by the presence of an affective repertoire of powerlessness — vulnerability, resentment, confession, and loss — and by the turn
to narrative forms that are subjectivist, fragmented, multi-voiced and
lyrical. These examples of "intimate" indigenista thought appear to run
counter to the kind of indigenista attitude one associates with state institutions, such as Mexico's Instituto Nacional Indigenista: top-down,
paternalist, positivist indigenista action oriented to an indigenous object that is framed as Other, as the inhabitant of a past time-space that
is alien to, and a problem for, the modern nation. Intimate indigenista
enunciations work from a sense of affinity rather than difference, from
a subjective position that seeks shared communication and experience
rather than an external, objective position vis-à-vis Indians.

But although such rhetoric is distinct from more paternalist or positivist indigenista tendencies, it cannot be truly separated from them. On

the contrary, the authors of intimate indigenista texts often straddled both of these tendencies — the objectifying, positivist outlook on the one hand, and the subjectivist, intimate outlook on the other — without perceiving a contradiction between them. What is the relationship between these two forms of indigenismo? Contrary to those who equate indigenismo with the top-down power of the state and/or elite social classes, I will suggest that paternalist-positivist indigenismo might be dependent on this more intimate variety, and explore the possibility that indigenismo is not the bearer of an exclusively repressive power operating externally or from above on those whom it takes as objects. "Intimate indigenismo" not only names a different kind of indigenismo existing alongside or within the more hegemonic indigenista discourse. It also indicates the ideological mechanisms by which indigenista discourse has influenced the racial and cultural construction of national selves in Mexico and the Andes by recognizing and promoting new kinds of subjectivity and social bonds. Indigenismo can be understood as ideological in the sense described by Althusser, as that "imaginary" through which individuals experience the conditions of their lives and become subjects.

This book explores how indigenismo has attempted to reconfigure the link between non-Indians and Indians by substituting, in place of a relationship built on hierarchy, opposition, and exclusion, one built on identification and shared affinity. My aim is not to extol indigenismo for this attempt, nor to suggest that it has been successful in the endeavor, but rather to open the door to an investigation of its constitutive elements and its effects. What is the productive power of indigenista myths in forming modern self-conceptions and providing a new language of subjectivity? The analysis of indigenista "relatos íntimos" suggests that indigenismo had the capacity to change modern Mexican and Andean self-conceptions. It appealed to a new kind of national "I" made possible, on the one hand, by the cracks in the existing system of racial hierarchies and by new forms of social mobility challenging oligarchic hegemony, and, on the other, by the existence of a longstanding philosophical, juridical, and aesthetic tradition in Latin America that offered a challenge to the discourse of civilization vs. barbarism.

The three novels at the core of my study — Jesús Lara's *Surumi,* José María Arguedas's *Los ríos profundos,* and Rosario Castellanos's *Balún Canán* — are set in modernizing nations whose oligarchies are on the verge of collapse. They are focalized, in part or in whole, through the point of view of narrators who find themselves situated ambiguously between the plantation and the schoolroom, spaces that have become symbolically charged as nodal points of conflict pitting regional oligarchies against an emergent middle class allied with other provincials who are experiencing a new degree of social mobility. These authors, tapping deeply into personal experience, produced "autobiographical fictions" (novels based on the author's life) rather than "fictional autobiographies" ("where a fictional narrator gives a retrospective account of his life"), to use Dorrit Cohn's distinction (30 note 24).

All three are known for having created an indigenista aesthetic that partially dispenses with the positivist representational apparatus necessary to frame and pathologize an indigenous Other. Their works have thus often been considered by critics to express an indigenista sensibility more authentically in tune with indigenous culture. Nevertheless, I believe the significance of this affective repertoire of powerlessness and affinity, and of the first-person voice created to channel it, warrants further scrutiny.

An important aspect of this first-person voice is that the narrative "I" of these novels is often difficult to distinguish from the "I" these authors used in their public speeches, private letters, and other more strictly autobiographical enunciations. The authors consciously encouraged the parallels between author and narrator in their self-projections. For example, in Lara's multi-volume autobiography, published when the author was already in his seventies, he explicitly stated that he had drawn from his own experiences at school in constructing his portrait of the Indian protagonist of *Surumi*. Lara himself, it should be made clear, was not officially classed as an Indian — his prerevolutionary national identity card listed him as "white." Yet he sought to frame an experience of national life that he believed to be shared by both Indians and non-Indians. Arguedas asserted even stronger parallels between his own life and the life of his fictional protagonist Ernesto of *Los ríos profundos*. Both Arguedas and his character suffered early banishment from the hacienda house by "cruel relatives," were subsequently adopted by a community of loving Indians, and spoke only Quechua in childhood. The result was the construction of a national subject — both fictional and autobiographical — who was tragically split between indigenous and Hispanic worlds, perfectly mirroring the dual and antagonistic nature of Peru's geography as it has been portrayed in the dominant national imaginary. Castellanos, too, drew parallels between her own childhood experiences and the experiences of the child narrator of *Balún Canán*: the traumatic death of the younger brother, the explicit devaluation of the surviving child because she is a girl, the painful solitude that ensued amid a family devastated by the loss, and the compounded catastrophe of the Cárdenas-era agrarian reforms, which entailed the loss of the family's lands in Chiapas. As a consequence of these similarities, the narrative "I" of these indigenista novels is difficult to separate from the "I" that the authors used when talking about themselves. These novels constructed a site of enunciation shared by author and narrator alike.

The confusion between novelistic and autobiographical "I" is further compounded because there are grounds to believe that in some cases these authors' personal life stories drew from their fiction, rather than the reverse. The autobiographical legends that circulated about these authors had their origin, in part, in their novelistic creations. For example, it appears that Arguedas was a fully bilingual Quechua–Spanish speaker as a child, not a monolingual Quechua speaker, a discrepancy I will address further in chapter 3. The idea of his Quechua monolingualism seems to have developed in the years he was writing *Los ríos profundos*, a novel thematizing the clash between Quechua and Spanish in ways that his previous works had not. Arguedas's self-identification as someone who had spoken only Quechua in childhood thus emerged in the process of novelizing his own life in *Los ríos profundos*. Regarding Castellanos, her self-identification as a Chiapan woman whose history was profoundly marked by the indigenista policies of the Cárdenas era did not become a part of her autobiographical enunciations until she began working on *Balún Canán*. Prior autobiographical statements and stories contained no reference to Mexican indigenismo and revolutionary politics. In the cases of both Arguedas and Castellanos, it appears that the authors developed their life stories in the process of creating the fictional lives of their novels' protagonists.

The novel and autobiography are already interlinked as literary genres, but the confusion between the authors and the narrators of *Surumi, Los ríos profundos*, and *Balún Canán* does more than underscore this historical connection. It also changes how we read these novels. While these narratives are indeed novels, they have lost a measure of stability and autonomy as aesthetic objects to take on some of the performative qualities of autobiography. Rather than expressing a preexisting subject, the speech act of autobiography creates one. Much like an autobiography, these novels participated in the invention of an embodied "I" with a life outside the page. And much like autobiographical narratives, these novels take on a flavor of contingency that brings questions of authorial intention to the foreground. Why did these authors choose to write in the narrative voice they did? Why did they choose, in the mode of intimate indigenismo, to emphasize the Indian nature of this first-person voice? How did they mark this nature as Indian, that is, what notions of Indianness were they working with and against? Why is this Indian-ized voice so unstable in these works, which tend to shift and slide between third- and first-person enunciation? How are these sites of narrative enunciation different from those which these writers had previously developed and then abandoned, and how do they exist in ongoing relationship to those other sites?

To answer these questions, I have used a kind of historical poetics to examine how the moment of the novel's writing has been taken up into the novel and made present there as a matter of form. In the experimental and at times inconsistent interplay of narrative voice and perspective, one can perceive, obliquely, the time and place of the authors' writing. However, a sociological and biographical approach to identifying that time-place of writing is of only limited use because writing as an event is not stable. Much like those Spanish American autobiographers who, as Sylvia Molloy has demonstrated, revised the story of their lives in light of changing circumstances in order to produce the most favorable self-images, these writers, especially Castellanos, appear to have revised their story in the very act of writing and to have left traces of these revisions — consciously or not — embedded in their novels. These are fictional texts markedly disturbed by their authors' "autobiographical unrest," to use Molloy's phrase (144), as if these novels, like the authors' life stories, were also works-in-progress.

Above all, one has the sense that these authors used the autobiographical inscription in their novels much as one would use the confessional: to free the present from the burdens of the past.[12] The author of a novel written from this site of enunciation would thus undergo a transformation over the course of writing it; would be, at the end of the novel, a different person from the one who began it. As I will argue, this difference, or the hope of this difference, is still faintly perceptible in the text itself. These three writers seem to have themselves been transformed by their writing over the course of writing it. Castellanos indeed expressed the conviction that writing operates "una modificación liberadora" [a liberating modification] ("Escrituras tempranas" 994), and early in her career speculated about the kind of confessions she would write, whether remorseful like St. Augustine's or stubborn like Rousseau's (*Cartas* 117). What is it that she imagined herself to be liberated from in writing her confession, and how might one perceive that modification in her work? The search for authorial presence that I have undertaken in my analysis of these novels is a search for the trace of the liberating modification Castellanos describes. What does liberation mean in this context?

Chapter 1 of this study will discuss, in general historical terms, modern indigenismo's intervention into an already racialized social field. It describes how indigenismo participates in redefining ethno-racial boundaries in order to create what Etienne Balibar terms the "fictive ethnicity" of the nation. Indigenista discourses build on and modify existing racial discourses to nationalize identity. My aim is bring out the underlying moral economy of race to which indigenismo was responding and which it sought to replace with another. By "moral economy of race," I refer to the fact that racial and cultural identities describe positions which define a subject's relative access to, or embodiment of, social virtue and authority. Central to the process of indigenista nationalization is the destigmatization of Indianness. Hence the importance of the discourse of interethnic intimacy and affinity, whose key rhetorical moves will be examined in this chapter. The rhetorical origins of modern indigenismo's response to racism, I argue, can be traced back to the sixteenth-century writings on the humanity of the colonized and to a racial logic understood in terms of innocence and guilt. The chapter concludes with a discussion of how an understanding of indigenismo as destigmatization provides an alternative to Cornejo's concept of indigenismo as "heterogeneous discourse."

Chapter 2 considers Bolivian indigenismo and the revolutionary nationalism of the 1940s, focusing on two texts by Jesús Lara, his novel *Surumi* (1943) and his bilingual essay-anthology *La poesía quechua* (Quechua Poetry) (1947). The chapter examines the rhetorical strategies contributing to the creation of a sense of mestizo nationality in Bolivia, such as the "double refusal" of the subject who "refuses to refuse" his Indian heritage, and who thus identifies as or with the Indian through the internalization of a moral imperative. I will also explore another rhetorical element central to nationalist discourses: the widespread populist story narrating how the Indian slave-thing is transformed into a man as a result of a revolutionary sentimental education. Finally, chapter 2 will examine how the experience of Quechua–Spanish bilingualism forms the emotional core of autobiographical indigenista discourse in the Andes.

Chapter 3 continues the analysis of Quechua–Spanish bilingualism by examining José María Arguedas's changing bilingual poetics, from his novel *Yawar fiesta* (1941) to *Los ríos profundos* (1958). There exists a substantial body of critical scholarship showing how the latter novel is the expression of a transculturated or mestizo subjectivity, one mediating between indigenous, rural, oral culture, and modern Western culture. In an extended dialogue with the work of literary scholar Angel Rama, my analysis focuses specifically on Arguedas's figurings of the mediator as a Quechua–Spanish bilingual in a diglossic society and demonstrates that Arguedas's construction of this bilingual mediator underwent a significant transformation between 1938 and 1958. Rather than "transculturation," I will emphasize the poetics of "translation" and "mistranslation." The chapter also brings out the quasi-religious idiom with which Arguedas spoke of Quechua, and demonstrates how, as a result, the bilingual becomes a privileged conduit or messenger for indigenous spirit. Through this spiritual idiom, Arguedas brought bilingualism into the service of other indigenista-nationalist discourses of modernization, while also strongly contributing to promoting a problematic connection between indigeneity and moral innocence.

Chapter 4 moves to Rosario Castellanos's novel *Balún Canán* (1957) to examine the experimental nature of her use of first- and third-person narrators. Here my interest will be to relate this experiment to the unresolved tensions involved in synchronizing the solitary "I" of the female author to narratives of Mexican indigenista nationalism. To this end, I have attempted to constitute a "prehistory" of *Balún Canán* using Castellanos's letters and poetry from the years immediately predating the novel. This prehistory, I argue, helps to explain Castellanos's turn to indigenismo as a response to the dilemmas faced by an intellectual woman in the context of 1950s Mexico and sheds light on the interplay between different narrative perspectives in the novel.

In each of the three chapters examining specific instances of the literary and autobiographical "I" of intimate indigenista narratives, my method has been to link the autobiographical novel to other sources of authorial autobiography and biography in order to demonstrate that these novels played a dynamic role in the authors' evolving ways of thinking about Indians and indigenismo — an evolution that is in turn symptomatic of changing concepts of racial and national identity. How do these changes manifest themselves at the level of narrative voice and language in the literary works under consideration?

In the late 1920s José Carlos Mariátegui referred to modern indigenista action as "la campaña pro-indígena" [the pro-indigenous campaign]. As I will argue throughout this book, indigenismo was also a campaign for promoting the national self, fostering new forms of identification through a nationalist discourse founded precisely on the ethno-racial *in*distinction of indigenista and indigenous voices. This indistinction derived in part from life stories organized around the shared experience, traumatic or uplifting, of the state's civilizing mission, and in part from the symbolic equation linking Indians to indigeneity more broadly conceived as the proper belonging to a given place, the national soil.

Mexican anthropologist Manuel Gamio, whose ideas were widely influential in the Andes, was clear on the necessity of asserting the slippage between "Indianness" and indigeneity: "La cultura indígena es la verdadera base de la nacionalidad en casi todos los países americanos" [Indigenous culture is the true base of nationality in almost all the American countries] (*Consideraciones* 8). This indigenismo thus aims to short-circuit the racial distinctions differentiating individual citizens and determining their place in a divided and hierarchical space by promoting an overriding collective mission embodied in the national mystique. And because the nation itself is understood as profoundly Indian, the characteristic statement made possible by intimate indigenismo, "my soul is indigenous," also declares "I am Mexican, Bolivian, Peruvian." This book is dedicated to examining the significance of such statements.

Chapter One

Anatomy of Indigenismo

Since the 1970s, scholarly accounts of indigenismo have focused on its status as a discourse of cultural and political domination of Indians, which is indeed a central and defining aspect of indigenista discourse. Although challenging existing racial hierarchies, indigenismo remains a kind of colonialism and a kind of racism, and has rarely been a friend to organized and self-identified Indian resistance movements, or to ideas of collective indigenous autonomy and self-determination. Despite its origins as a contestatory political discourse, indigenismo has perpetuated Indians' subordination to the state in the name of civilizing them. Furthermore, because in the latter half of the twentieth century indigenismo became the instrument of authoritarian regimes in Mexico, Peru, and Bolivia, which aggressively promoted mestizaje as a national ideal, it is difficult to uncouple indigenista policies from the repressive force of the state. Critiques of indigenismo, and especially of the mestizo nationalism that it sustains, have emphasized that, like other kinds of populist rhetoric, it is often little more than an empty charade, an illusion to mask a profoundly undemocratic reality. State indigenismo politically disempowers the people it continuously proclaims itself to be empowering. The fact that indigenismo tends to support the development of mestizo nationalism is particularly problematic, for in such cases, indigenista-oriented political regimes insist that Indian cultural assimilation to a mestizo ideal is the price of equal participation in national life. Thus indigenismo has either directly or indirectly promoted the disappearance of indigenous groups as collective entities in the name of fostering a homogeneous national culture.

One of the main indigenista strategies for the domination of Indians has been what anthropologist Johannes Fabian terms the "denial of coevalness," whereby the colonizer "assigns to the conquered populations a *different* Time" (Fabian 30, original emphasis).[1] The denial of coevalness is used to render Indian political claims illegitimate or invalid because it

1

posits indigenous cultures as archaic, primitive, premodern, out of step with history. An analysis of indigenista discourses from the early and mid-twentieth century shows how Indians are placed at the prehistorical origin of the nation, at its metaphorical roots. However, as I will further discuss, indigenismo is also responsible for creating a discourse of coevalness, for promoting an understanding of Indianness as lodged in the metaphorical gut, heart, tongue, soul, and blood of the nation and national selves; that is, it also promotes an awareness of "shared" time and space between Indians and non-Indians, the core of the mestizo nation. Keeping in mind that indigenismo wields both of these strategies, both denying and affirming Indians' coevalness, a new set of questions arises regarding the workings of indigenista ideology. Who wields these "affirmations of coevalness" and to what are they responding? How is the shared time-space that indigenistas invoke positioned with respect to that other time-space where Indians and Indianness are denied coevalness and considered backward or primitive? Does the indigenista affirmation of coevalness indeed empower indigenous claims?

Although indigenista discourse developed differently in Mexico, Bolivia, and Peru, in all three cases it became an instrument of revolutionary nationalism in the early twentieth century and thus shares a number of important characteristics. Indigenismo was the preferred discourse for responding to a general crisis in oligarchic regimes and for channeling the modernizing aspirations of rising social sectors. One of its primary aims was to "nationalize" Indians. It sought to rehabilitate the Indian from the position most often accorded it in the liberal and positivist thought of the mid-to-late nineteenth century: that of an alien and inferior being, one who is extraneous, if not dangerous, to the integrity of the nation-state.[2] In contrast to these views, modern indigenismo in Mexico and the Andes envisions the Indian as proper to the nation — as, in fact, its most valuable and integral asset, key to modern progress and prosperity. Seen from an economic perspective, the Indian becomes a potential labor force for nascent industry. Seen from a political and military perspective, the Indian becomes an ally in power struggles between oligarchic elites and a newly empowered urban middle-class. Seen from a symbolic perspective, the Indian becomes, as had already happened in the period of Spanish-American Independence, a sign of the distinct historical origin and cultural formations of Spanish-American nations: a sign of that which makes them unique with respect to the United States and Europe and hence possessed of their own destiny independent of the imperialist and neo-colonialist designs of such global powers.

At this historical point, the discourse of indigenismo intersects with, and becomes indispensable to, the discourse of mestizo nationalism in Mexico and the Andes, which projects the ideal national subject as one who harmoniously combines European and indigenous cultural traditions and makes modernity possible on "native" soil. Indigenistas in Mexico and the Andes established a new filiative principle for nationality, one grounded in what Nancy Stepan calls "constructive miscegenation," based on an inversion of the racial values common to influential strands of nineteenth-century European thought (147). Once despised and denied, the indigenous origin of the nation now became a source of pride.

In Mexico, Manuel Gamio, ethnologist and archeologist and one of the most influential ideologues of the Mexican Revolution, provided the clearest image of the mestizo nation to be constructed by the revolutionary state. In his now-classic 1916 book *Forjando patria,* he figured the nation as a statue whose pedestal is Indian and whose body is forged of all the races. He argued that the leaders of Spanish-American Independence had attempted to forge such a statue-nation, but that ultimately they failed to achieve their goal because they "forgot" the indigenous element and included only those "racial elements of Latin origin" (6). As a result, he writes, the Latin "statue" always remained weak and fragile, while the Indian "pedestal" continued to grow strong. The goal of the Mexican Revolution, as Gamio described it, should be to complete the work of Independence itself, to attain the liberated, strong nationality that Independence promised but could not deliver.[3]

In Bolivia, meanwhile, one can look to the revolutionary nationalism of the military government that assumed power in 1943. The president was Gualberto Villaroel, an officer in the Bolivian army and the visible member of an otherwise secret society of army men, a cabal named Razón de Patria. On taking power, RADEPA, as it was known, published a document that declared the following as their aim:

> poner fin a la anarquía que nos consume, reconstruyendo el alma nacional y creando el orgullo de bolivianidad, basándose en las glorias de la historia y la tradición nacionales, arrancadas de la grandeza del Incario y de nuestra estirpe India. (quoted in Céspedes, *El presidente colgado* 111)

to put an end to the anarchy consuming us, reconstructing the national soul and creating pride in Bolivianness, based on the glories of national history and tradition that stem from the greatness of the Inca Empire and our Indian lineage.

RADEPA was strongly allied with the Movimiento Nacional Revolucionario [National Revolutionary Movement], the political party that would later "win" the 1952 revolution, and that advanced very similar sentiments in its platforms and manifestos once it came to power (Salmón 125–30). These nationalists also drew from indigenista discourses of the preceding several decades, when thinkers of very different political stripes — Alcides Arguedas, Franz Tamayo, Carlos Medinaceli, and Jesús Lara, to name a few — echoed one another across Bolivia's fractious political landscape in their turn toward the nation's Indian heritage and in their insistence that Bolivians recognize it as "theirs," as a common cultural patrimony.[4]

In Peru, finally, indigenista thought developed as a response to reactionary "hispanistas" who had constructed a wholly negative iconography of "backward" Indians in the wake of Peru's 1883 defeat in the War of the Pacific against Chile; the Indians' alleged inability to understand themselves as national subjects was effectively blamed for the loss.[5] Indigenistas responded to their political opponents by declaring Indians to be the very essence of nationality. Manuel González Prada famously proclaimed, in 1888:

> No forman el verdadero Perú las agrupaciones de criollos i extranjeros que habitan la faja de tierra situada entre el Pacífico y los Andes; la nación está formada por las muchedumbres de indios diseminadas en la banda oriental de la cordillera. (66)

> The creole and foreign groups that inhabit the stretch of land between the Andes and the Pacific do not comprise the true Peru; the nation is comprised of the multitudes of Indians disseminated throughout the western strip of the mountains.

His words would later be taken up as fundamental by the indigenistas of the *Amauta* group, under the direction of José Carlos Mariátegui, exercising strong influence over subsequent political and aesthetic developments in Peru. Indigenismo became a potent instrument in regionalist attempts to assert political control against Lima's centralizing tendencies. In highland cities of the Andes such as Cuzco and Puno, indigenismo developed into a full-fledged movement of the avant-garde. Unlike in Mexico or Bolivia, however, Peruvian indigenismo would not become institutionalized in the integrating mechanisms of the state, such as school and the military, until much later in the twentieth century.[6]

But whenever indigenismo moved from being an oppositional to a state discourse, indigenistas construed contemporary Indians, as opposed to their illustrious ancestors, as an obstacle to modernization. Despite celebrating the nation's indigenous essence and origin, state forms of indigenismo advanced the view that present-day Indians were but the remains of an earlier great people — whether fallen and passive victims of a cruel history of oppression who required redemption, or stubborn premodern hold-outs who needed to be educated into the realities of the modern era. Indigenista discourses inserted Indians into a civilizing project directed by the state. Shoved firmly into the past, at the nation's origin, Indian identity became expressive, even in that prehistory, of the nation's distinct essence.[7] Present-day Indians, however, were still considered "primitive," held to be lacking in a number of essential features key to modern citizenship: knowledge of Spanish, capacity for reason, sense of national belonging, will to prosper and progress. The nation's past might be Indian, but its present and future were mestizo. Indians were denied coevalness in order that the nation might be brought into being as itself a relation of coevalness among individuals, a space of communication and "shared Time," as Fabian might say.

Yet denying that Indians are coeval to Western civilization and the modern nation is only one aspect of indigenista ideology, although it may be the dominant one. There is also a powerful trend within indigenismo that insists on the existence of a sphere of coeval relations with Indians, a sphere that exists, however, utterly innocent of power, and that is marginal to the worldly spheres of social life. Interior and often referred to as a kind of "soul," this time-space is one that Indians and non-Indians are said to share as intimates. In the mestizo nationalism of Gamio and RADEPA, among others, the Indian has been placed at the foot, at the root or origin. But in other examples of modern indigenismo one can see that the Indian has migrated symbolically to a new location in the national body, from the feet to the heart, the gut, or the tongue. As Villoro says, "El mestizo siente latir en él lo indígena, reviviéndolo en sí mismo" [The mestizo feels Indianness beating within him, reviving the Indian within him] (269). The choice to use the verb "latir" is significant: it is the verb that best expresses the motion of the heart, the circulation of the blood, the essence of life. Once Indianness is there, in the coeval location of the heart or the gut or the blood, it seems to become invested with language, with a voice of sorts, one that expresses a message to which one must listen in order to feel authentically national. This voice emanates from a location that has been made a site of nationality, but it is a nationality that is modeled on the soul, a soul marked by its vulnerable, interior, and individual condition.

Indigenismo appealed to the existence of this sphere using the language of intimate connection. The words of Peruvian author and ethnologist José María Arguedas provide a useful starting point for examining the contours of this kind of indigenista discourse. His work is filled with references to "intimacy," and he has indeed come to be known by his metropolitan readers as one of the most passionate and profound communicators of a special feeling of interethnic connection. In 1938 Arguedas published *Canto kechwa,* a collection of Quechua songs that he had translated into Spanish. He included as prologue a piece titled "Essay on the Creative Capacity of Indians and Mestizos," in which he explained that Indians and mestizos have created a musical form, the wayno, that is beloved by all Andeans, whatever their race or social position. And they love it, he argued, because it expresses something profound inside them:

> En su intimidad, toda la gente de la sierra siente el arte indio, a excepción, como he dicho, de esa minoría que hay en las ciudades grandes. Aunque lo nieguen, los mestizos, los principales de los pueblos chicos encuentran en el arte indio la expresión de sus sentimientos más hondos y propios. (*Canto kechwa* 11)

> In their intimate life, all the people of the mountain region feel Indian art, except, as I've already said, for that minority living in big cities. Although they might deny it, mestizos, the most important people in the small towns, find in Indian art the expression of their most profound and true-to-self feelings.

His essay argued that all Andean aesthetic expression, even when voiced by mestizos and criollos, comes from an interior place where "Indianness" resides. In a profoundly conciliatory spirit, he offers a figure for integration and balance between otherwise contesting forces. That figure is a national icon: the Peruvian attentive to the Indian within. At the most obvious level, this icon is a figure for integration itself, that is, for the hegemonic indigenista project of incorporating — and subordinating — Indians to the nation-state. Yet the image is not entirely reducible to a generic figure of the nation, for it is also meant to convey Arguedas's sense of the individual's unique existence. In invoking "the intimate," Arguedas calls on the language of private selfhood. And though the national figure he imagines is a racial one, it is constructed in such a way as to suggest that the divisions between individual and collective, interior and exterior, regional and national, might be more significant in shaping modern life than the divisions between Indians and non-Indians. Arguedas's words thus represent an attempt to render internal racial boundaries, if not immaterial, then secondary to other forms of division that reflect the individual's contradictory experience of modernity.

Arguedas's words sought to voice an experience that could be both individual and exemplary, private and shared, interior and spatially vast. Indianness as Arguedas conceived it in his essay, shades into, and ultimately merges with, broader and more inclusive categories of native belonging adopted by nationalist thought. Indianness and indigeneity become as one — "indigeneity" understood here as "being native to a place." Rather than marking a boundary or division within society, separating one subject from another on the basis of race and placing them in a hierarchical relationship, his notion of Indianness as indigeneity on the contrary speaks to an experience of regional belonging that appears to be racially inclusive: it pertains to "all the people" ("toda la gente") in the Peruvian Andes.

Arguedas's appeal to an inclusive, interior indigenous sphere attempts to undermine a vision of society divided into civilized vs. barbarian polarities. His ideas about race and culture were still deterministic but more loosely so than biological theories of race. Like other Latin American thinkers of this period, he gave strong weight to environmental or geographical factors.[8] In this, Arguedas was drawing from a political and aesthetic tradition of thought that points to a natural connection, of an almost sacred order, between the land and its inhabitants. Established by Independence and Romantic thinkers, it invokes the "American" land in order to justify the claims of "Americans" against the colonial state. When twentieth-century indigenistas turn to an indigenous or Indianized sphere, they do so in order to affirm a primordial connection to the regional or national space, a connection that is subjectively experienced and that becomes meaningful as a sublime experience of nationality.

Arguedas's intimate indigenismo is significant in large part because it shows how indigenismo attempts to nationalize subjectivity.

Etienne Balibar refers to national identity as a "fictive ethnicity," which is the ideological construct necessary for the configuration of a national "people." Fictive ethnicity binds individuals together as a people, naturalizes that binding, and makes of it "the basis and origin of political power" (Balibar 94). When Balibar says "fictive," he is not establishing a dichotomy between a "real" and an "imagined" ethnicity but rather underscoring that "every social community reproduced by the functioning of institutions is imaginary, that is to say, it is based on the projection of individual existence into the weft of a collective narrative, on the recognition of a common name and on the traditions lived as the trace of an immemorial past" (Balibar 93). The creation of a national "fictive ethnicity" allows for differences *within* the nation to be subordinated to national difference, to "the symbolic difference between 'ourselves' and 'foreigners'... which is lived as irreducible" (Balibar 94).[9]

Balibar points to two elements, language and race, that establish nationality as a "natural community" and define the borders between "us" and "them" (96–100). When speaking of the "fictive ethnicity" of nationality that emerged in the Americas, however, it becomes clear that a third element must be brought into play: land. Race has been strongly territorialized, or, put another way, land has been racialized. It is through the intertwining of land and race that nations were formed in the late colonial and postcolonial periods, although these national identities may have only sedimented initially in a small segment of the overall population. Bolivian historian Carlos Mamani calls this racialization of land "the necessity of nativism," which is characteristic of the "project of national construction" ("Restitución" 4). Also known as the "discourse of the autochthonous," it insists on the spiritual indivisibility and expressive powers of the national soil.[10] Twentieth-century indigenismo draws from the tellurism characteristic of nineteenth-century Romantic nationalisms, which developed a notion of indigeneity understood as a kind of "law of the land." One thinks here of Sarmiento's *pampa*, Gallegos's *llano*, and the "Andinismo" that swept both the Peruvian and Bolivian avant-gardes in the late 1920s. All of these spaces exert a force over their inhabitants, one that racializes them in particular ways. When seen as a positive force, this experience of indigeneity becomes literally and metaphorically the ground — both the physical territory and the ideological fundament — of nationality itself, the standard by which to judge that which is proper to the nation and that which is foreign to it.

The linkage between indigenous culture and indigeneity makes the Indian essentially a quality or an element of the land. Mestizo nationality draws on this principle of the "law of the land" which, although elaborated during the nineteenth century by diverse thinkers throughout Spanish America, does not become a dominant idea until the twentieth century in Mexico and the Andes. It establishes that indigeneity, the ground of nationality, is in fact Indian. Thus, to be Indian involves, essentially, to be of the national land, and vice versa: if one is of the land, then one is essentially Indian. Uriel García's words are emblematic in this respect. One of the first to develop a book-length account of Peru's mestizo identity, his 1930 *El nuevo indio* (The New Indian), he referred to "indianidad" as "ese ligamen beligerante del hombre con la tierra" [man's belligerent allegiance to the land] (87).

Indigenista nationalists in Mexico and the Andes invoke this equation in order to render subordinate, yet without eliminating, a more exclusive set of claims to the land personified in the regional oligarch or, as in Bolivia, the mining magnate. These last must come to seem unnatural and foreign, dividing and controlling what should be indivisible and shared. Mariátegui referred to these aspects of Peruvian society as feudal and colonial (49), to emphasize their fundamental otherness to a national state.[11] Only by invoking the more inclusive "law of the land" is the mystique of national belonging made possible, the "fictive ethnicity" of the national "we," that connection which is not really an ethnic relation at all but takes the form of one in order to assert a principle of common belonging over and above all forms of internal division within the social body — ethnic, racial, class, gender (Balibar 94). Even as mestizo nationalism, in the name of unity, seeks to eliminate indigenous cultural formations through reeducation and other kinds of assimilation, it retains the essential symbolic linkage: Indian-indigeneity-nationality.

Arguedas is probably the best known Andean thinker to have consistently articulated, over the course of his intellectual career, the existence of this kind of spiritual interethnic affiliation grounded in a common land and to have affirmed it as the basis for nationality. But he was not the first. Already in 1910, Bolivian poet Franz Tamayo had begun developing a very similar body of ideas. Like Arguedas, he was responding to those who considered Bolivia's indigenous heritage to be an obstacle to progress. He too anchored his polemic in a notion of race as "national character" formed predominantly by the physical environment. In his *Creación de la pedagogía nacional* (The Creation of a National Pedagogy) (1910) Tamayo understood race and nation as forged in a common experience of the land: "Esa tierra es ya una patria, en el sentido histórico.... La raza en cierto sentido es el producto del medio" [That land is already a nation, in the historic sense.... Race is, in a certain sense, a product of the environment] (159). Responding to the anti-mestizaje discourse of his contemporaries, he argued that Bolivia's ruling class should recognize and esteem its essential Indianness:

> Nuestros blancos que siguen viviendo una apariencia de vida europea, y como radicalmente divorciados de los indios, no se aperciben de que toda su vida a la europea tiene, en el fondo, un sabor tan aymara, que es como un matiz del todo indio en que se esfuma toda la actividad nacional. Música, literatura, arquitectura, maneras, políticas, costumbres, lo íntimo de lo íntimo, en nuestro blanco acusa ya la fuerza de la tierra y el genio del lugar. (149)

> Our whites, who continue to live the appearance of a European life, radically divorced from Indians, don't realize that their entire European lifestyle has a flavor that is so Aymara at its core, a flavor that is like an utterly Indian hue coloring all national activity. Music, literature, architecture, manners, politics, customs, the most intimate of the intimate — the strength of the land and the spirit of the place show their signs in our whites.

Like José María Arguedas, Tamayo proclaimed the importance of recognizing this fact as the foundation for a new program of nation-building — a national pedagogy — arguing that decolonization itself emanated from the Indian sensibility lodged within the mestizo heart:

> El mestizo, que sigue ciegamente siendo español de ideas, no lo es más de corazón.... El primer sentimiento trascendente libertario contra la metrópoli, no ha debido nacer en un pecho indio ni en uno español, sino en uno mestizo.... Si seguía pensando a la española, sentía ya como indio, y ese sentimiento y pensamiento combinados le hacían apto para tentar un día la empresa [de independizarse]. (144–45)

> The mestizo, who blindly continues to be Spanish in ideas, is no longer so at heart.... The first transcendent emancipatory feeling against the metropolis cannot have been born in an Indian or a Spanish breast, but in a mestizo's.... Though he continued to think like a Spaniard, he already felt like an Indian, and that combined feeling and thought made him able to venture [becoming independent].

Here Tamayo prefigures Manuel Gamio's words on the Mexican Revolution: that the Indian is at the root of national liberation but does not himself actualize it. Gamio had written, "El indio...no es quien ha hecho la revolución, no obstante que sus más hondas raíces germinaron y germinan todavía en la raza indígena" [The Indian...did not make the revolution, but its deepest roots germinated, and still germinate, in the Indian race] (*Forjando Patria* 93). But Tamayo goes much farther than Gamio, locating the very essence of liberty, of sovereignty, in the Bolivian Indian.

These kinds of indigenista enunciations focus on the phenomenological side of mestizo identity. Rather than approaching the mestizo as the embodied mixture of Western and non-Western races or cultures in the Americas, or as the sign for that ideal mixture, or even as a position in a continuum of cultural states of being ranging from the pure to the impure, these authors are referring to the mestizo as a form of subjectivity whose contours are national in character. This subjectivity is in part the product of the cultural politics of revolutionary nationalism, of a state-centric project of national consolidation involving its own "moral and intellectual education," as Luis Tapia has argued (n.p.). Though it is as historically contingent as any other kind of identity, it is experienced as ahistorical or nonpolitical, as a form of collective belonging akin to family or religion, as Benedict Anderson suggests national identities are experienced (5). Therefore one might speak of mestizo *nationality* and *subjectivity* rather than mestizo culture, and to aspects of the *nationalization of identity,* rather than cultural homogenization, transculturation, heterogeneity, or cultural mestizaje. Though the nationalization of identity in colonial and postcolonial Spanish America has a history that intersects with the longer and broader history of mestizo cultural formations, it is nevertheless distinct from it, and involves its own institutions, discursive moves, political conflicts, and negotiations.

As regards Mexican discourses of mestizaje, José Vasconcelos's *La raza cósmica* (The Cosmic Race) is obviously the paradigmatic example, yet Vasconcelos speaks of a collective racial mission that he rarely if ever centers on the individual. Lesser-known Mexican indigenistas are far more eloquent on this score. Consider the words of Yucatec writer Antonio Mediz Bolio, one of the Mexican translators of the Maya *Book of Chilam Balam*. In the following text from 1934, he speaks of the national self as inhabited by the lament of Indian ancestors:

> Como a la mujer bíblica, solemos decirle a la patria: "Dos naciones hay en tu seno." Se habla de la redención política del indio, pero no de su redención espiritual; quiero decir: de su incorporación, explicada y aceptada, como elemento formativo de nuestra alma actual, con ser esto una tarea indispensable y previa a la política, como lo es la idea con respecto a la acción. Todas esas voces oscuras, de abuelos indios, que lloran en nuestro corazón, no han tenido desahogo. (Reyes 10)[12]

> Just as we say to the biblical woman, we say to the patria: "Your heart holds two nations." We speak of the political redemption of the Indian, but not of his spiritual redemption, that is, of his incorporation, explained and accepted, as a formative element of our present-day soul. That task is necessary and prior to politics, just as ideas are prior to action. All those obscure voices of Indian grandparents, crying in our heart, have felt no relief.

In Mediz Bolio's sentimental invocation, Indian and mestizo become confused: he advocates the spiritual redemption of the Indian, yet in fact it is those who have the Indian in their hearts and souls who must be made to see the truth in order to feel existential relief.

Novelist Agustín Yáñez, in his introduction to the collection *Mitos indígenas* (Indigenous Myths, 1942), also advocates a turn to the Indian soul, pointing out that, in any case, it is useless to deny its presence:

> Bajo la influencia de cuatro siglos ... el mexicano de hoy aún siente no sé qué misterioso aire — subterráneo y familiar — ... contra cuyo poder más o menos oculto se han mellado los esfuerzos de aniquilamiento. Allí perdura el alma indígena con sus herencias, e infructuoso error ha sido el querer desconocerla y el obrar negándole beligerancia. Sus vicios han resultado así más peligrosos,

y sus virtudes quedan como fuerzas perdidas, estancadas, en la historia del país. Ha llegado a padecerse un cierto género de absurda vergüenza por lo indígena, signo de una de nuestras mayores miserias y de ignorancia en cuanto lo indígena fué y es; en cuanto subsiste dentro del alma nacional. (xxiv–xxv)

Influenced by four centuries . . . the Mexican of today still senses an unknown, mysterious air — subterranean and familiar — . . . whose more or less hidden power has undermined all efforts to destroy it. There, the indigenous soul endures with its heritage, and it has been a fruitless error to pretend it doesn't exist and to deny its power as an opponent. Its vices have thus become more dangerous, and its virtues have remained like wasted resources stagnating in the country's history. We have reached the point of suffering a certain kind of absurd shame for Indianness, the sign of one of our greatest misfortunes and of our ignorance regarding what Indianness was and is, and how it survives in the national soul.

Like Mediz Bolio, Tamayo, and Arguedas, Yáñez is more concerned with the indigenous soul of mestizos than the soul of Indians. It is mestizos who must resist feeling "absurd shame" toward their own Indianness, for without it they are not Mexicans.

Taken together, these recurring references to a shared "soul," to the communion, via the racialized time and space of the nation, of Indian and non-Indian, point to an alternative indigenista archive. Rather than approach Indians as a problem to be solved, this indigenismo approaches them as bearers of an inner voice lodged within national subjects, one to which national subjects must listen to recover their own identity.

Indigenismo as Destigmatization

The repeated references to shame in the intimate indigenista enunciations I have considered above suggest that indigenista nationalism responds to a particular moral economy of race whose alienating effects are experienced by a wide variety of subjects. David Lloyd has argued for the need to pay attention to the "psychic impact of domination in the cultural and political dynamic through which the emergence and formation of nationalist movements takes place" ("Nationalisms" 176). The solidarity of nationalism "is not based merely in ideological manipulation of the masses but to some extent at least in the common experience of domination" ("Nationalisms" 176), that is, in the phenomenology of racism. Indeed, the perception that Indians and non-Indians share a common experience of racism is a strong feature of the indigenista rhetoric I examined above.

Clearly, that perception is a problematic one. Indians and non-Indians did not share identical experiences or degrees of racism. However, I would argue that the existence of some degree of overlapping terrain between these experiences and the existence of zones of identitarian ambiguity provided fertile ground for "intimate indigenismo" and allowed it to take root. The authors of intimate indigenista rhetoric were subjected to some of the punitive effects of the racist discourse of Indian barbarity. They were made to feel ashamed for their attachment to things identified as Indian, to particular languages, kinfolk, landscapes, behaviors, or art forms. Indigenista "relatos íntimos," such as the fragments I have analyzed above and the more extended narratives I will analyze in subsequent chapters, describe how subjects are forced to come to terms with features which are obstacles to participation in the hegemonic public sphere as decent, upstanding citizens. These narratives are thus versions of what Erving Goffman, in his study of social stigma, calls the "moral career" (32). The moral career recounts the steps taken by those who are coming to grips with their stigmatized identities and who, in the process of doing so, resist the attribution of stigma and call certain stigmatizing notions into question.

In response to an oppressive racial discipline, indigenistas promoted forms of national identification that were designed to be morally cleansing, to restore dignity to an otherwise shameful condition. The indigenista enunciations I have described above, by Franz Tamayo, José María Arguedas, Agustín Yáñez, and others, are instances of the "moral career." They are aimed at those who have internalized the racial and cultural stigma associated with Indianness, those who are not Indian yet suffer guilt by association. They hold that Indianness is not a taint but rather the most profound sign of an individual's humanity. More than anything else, these writers are responding to the denial of Indianness, the denial of non-Indians' affinity with Indians. The persistence of stigma associated with Indianness confounds and frustrates them. Arguedas asks, "Why this shame?" (*Canto kechwa* 13). If only people would see that Indians are not inferior:

> Lo indígena no es inferior.... La vergüenza a lo indio, creada por los encomenderos y mantenida por los herederos de éstos hasta hoy,

será quebrantada, cuando los que dirigen el país comprendan que la muralla que el egoísmo y el interés han levantado para impedir la superación del pueblo indígena, el libre desborde de su alma, debe ser derrumbada en beneficio del Perú. (13)

Indianness is not inferior.... The shame of Indianness, created by the encomenderos and maintained by their descendants until today, will be destroyed once those who run the country understand that the wall raised by egotism and self-interest to block the betterment of the Indian people, the boundless overflowing of their soul, must be brought down to the benefit of Peru.

Arguedas's psychological idiom is imbued with confessional tones. He speaks of the need to be cleansed of one's shame, to transform inherited guilt into innocence. He links shame of Indianness to self-negation: the denial of Indianness is a denial of self, and, furthermore, a denial of the nation. Thus embedded into the language of nationality, pride and shame become the predominant factors defining the social worth of racialized subjects, making racial origin a matter of interior, affective management, rather than birth or biological inheritance, and converting the nationalist sentimental education into an instrument strong enough to combat the feeling of social illegitimacy.[13]

Marisol de la Cadena, in her study of Cuzco indigenismo, shows that indigenistas attempted to divorce Indianness from its stigmatized qualities. Indigenismo sought "the reinvention of indigenous culture stripped of stigmatized Indianness that the elites assigned it since colonial times" (de la Cadena 7). In so doing, modern indigenismo challenged the basis for oligarchic social hierarchies. Indigenistas insisted that race and culture are not vessels of immanent qualities but rather of transferable, mobile qualities, which individuals can assume or cast off as they move through society.[14] They rejected the idea that Indians as a group are distinguished by certain innate qualities, and that "cultures [are] vessels of immanent inequalities of reason that legitimate — and naturalize — hierarchies among human groups" (de la Cadena 4). Modern indigenismo focuses instead on individuals' "Indianness," their position along a scale of cultural identification that can be of greater or lesser intensity depending on their social location, which is in turn a function of their individual achievement. By dint of their own effort, especially through education, individuals can leave their stigmatized condition behind.

But the indigenista rhetoric I have examined also suggests that dignity can be achieved along another avenue — not by abandoning certain features that are considered uncivilized but almost religiously, through a self-accepting inward turn that transcends stigmatizing discourse altogether in favor of universalism. This idealistic nationalism proclaims the existence of a higher order that has been interiorized in the heart and the soul, one governed by laws that are at odds with the laws of traditional oligarchic societies. This inner self is held to be capable of transcending social distinctions; it is universalist. What is most significant about this universalism is that it is so thoroughly associated with Indianness. Intimate indigenista rhetoric not only humanizes Indians in order to destigmatize them; it also posits that the inner, indigenous self of the national "I" represents the *most human* aspect of the individual.

In the twentieth century (and in the twenty-first century as well, I would argue), "humanness" is conceived in terms that respond negatively to capitalist modernization. Indians are considered innocent of materialism. They are associated with those arenas of social experience imagined to be farthest from the corrupting influence of market relations and the instrumental reason of industrialized life (e.g., the aesthetic, the spiritual, the pastoral-rural, the wild).[15] But humanness also continues to be conceived through a much older paradigm. The intimate indigenismo of the modern period reactivates the indigenista discourse dating to the early years of Spanish colonialism, when the difference between humans and barbarians was determined according to an underlying distinction between innocence and guilt.

The turn to the intimate sphere of the "Indian within" characteristic of modern indigenismo became linked to national hegemony only in the past century, but to understand why indigenistas rhetorically entered that sphere and the effects of doing so, it is necessary to keep in mind Bartolomé de Las Casas's mid-sixteenth century attempt to prove the humanity of the colonized Indians. Modern indigenismo bears the traces of Las Casas, whether directly influenced by him or not. Mexican indigenistas were more directly influenced by him than their Andean counterparts; Mariátegui explicitly repudiated Las Casas, as will become clear below. Yet all can be said to have drawn on the rhetorical and philosophical legacy that came to be embedded in the colonial Laws of the Indies as a direct consequence of Las Casas's writings. It is true that modern indigenistas did not share the same site of enunciation as Las Casas. Las Casas did not feel himself to have been interpellated by the discourse of barbarism he was attacking (as modern indigenistas often did), and he did not write from the perspective of a national subject, that is, he appealed to different kinds of moral and geographic bonds and boundaries to frame his arguments. Yet despite these differences, modern indigenistas advanced many arguments similar to his.

Las Casas argued that Indians were fully human, rather than barbarians, because they were innocent of the inherited stains — racial and religious — carried by other infidel populations dominated by Spain, such as Jews and Moors. The stigma of Indianness that modern indigenistas attempt to cleanse from Indians and from themselves carries the trace of these original debates about the nature of those who resisted Catholic Spain's imperial ideologies. In order to destigmatize Indians, Las Casas had to show that Indians were innocent of that resistance, that is, he had to demonstrate that they were willing and able to submit to evangelization. Determining the humanity of colonized subjects became inextricable from questions about their moral innocence. Las Casas's *Brevísima relación de la destrucción de las Indias* (The Devastation of the Indies: A Brief Account) (1552), his most widely read work, went even further, because Las Casas's rhetoric conveyed the idea that Indians are the most innocent of people — and hence, by extension, the most human. Modern ideas about racial difference operate within a moral economy whose origins are colonial, and modern indigenismo responds, in part, to concepts of innocence and guilt that are racially determined.

The Racial Logic of Innocence and Guilt

Las Casas's *Brevísima relación* is a short, intense denunciation of the violence suffered by indigenous people at the hands of the Spanish encomenderos.[16] It questions *how* colonial power is being exercised and to what ends, as well as the moral and legal framework justifying it. But firmly convinced of the need for Spanish missionary endeavors — the conquest of the soul — Las Casas did not question the validity of the colonial enterprise overall so long as its goal was Christianization. Las Casas's description of indigenous people was underwritten by a discourse of anthropological difference that he adopted through his readings of Columbus, of whom he was a great champion, as copyist and editor of Columbus's travel diaries (his copy of the diary of the first voyage in 1492 is the only one extant). Beatriz Pastor has argued that this denial is based on the semantic construction of the natives' savagery, which lies in their nakedness ("desnudez"), their defenselessness ("sin armas," "indefensión"), and their generosity, recurring tropes in Columbus. In Columbus's First Diary, Pastor shows, these terms constitute a discourse of civilization vs. savagery, for they are employed by Columbus in order to differentiate the natives both from himself and from the grand Asian civilizations he was expecting to encounter, and from there, to justify his decision to treat the Indians as commercial products (Pastor 55–57).[17]

When these terms — nakedness, defenselessness, generosity — are taken into Las Casas's text, however, they also come to connote something else: the natives' innocence of worldly matters, their tender compliance ("tiernas en complisión"), and their radical inability to defend themselves from their aggressors.[18] The qualities that, for Columbus, indicated the natives' inhumanity, become for Las Casas rather the proof of their shared humanity, even as they serve, in the first instance, to distinguish Indians from the European colonizers.

This resemanticization of Columbus's discourse has as one of its effects the authorization of a new subject, Las Casas himself, who speaks *to* the sovereign, *against* those colonizers who commit injustices, and *for* — in place of — the indigenous people against whom injustice has been committed. Fundamental to this complex discursive triangulation is the presumption that those on whose behalf Las Casas claims to speak before the law, and hence to exercise power in the realm of the state, cannot do so for themselves — not because they have been barred from such a dialogue or otherwise silenced, but because they are so good and docile that they are innocent of it. Las Casas denies the Indians' coevalness, not in order the better to exploit them but in order better to defend them against the "tyranny" of encomendero rule. By focusing on their docility, decency, humility, patience, and pacific nature, Las Casas could better affirm that the Indians were willing and able to be Christianized. Thus, he argued, they should not be considered barbarians and did not require enslavement and military conquest in order to be subjected (that is, Christianized).[19]

The denial of Indians' coevalness, in Las Casas's *Brevísima relación*, rests on constructing a sphere of human attributes that is "outside" political power. However, this sphere, though used here in the service of a culturally othering discourse, is not one in which *only* Indians reside. It is also at the root of Las Casas's humanism, the universalist aspect of his

Christian discourse which held that "there was no natural difference in the creation of men" (cited in Hanke 96). As he says in the *Brevísima relación,* the Indians were made in the image of God and redeemed by his blood (128). The missionary spirit that animated the conquest, he argued, must continue to infuse the conquerors. The *Brevísima relación* takes the form an injunction to the Crown that Spanish colonialism not forget its raison d'être as civilizing mission. As with most instances of indigenista discourse since then, it operates as a reminder to a governing class that their domination of Indians is justified only when it operates with missionary intent, as a form of spiritual salvation, not just of the Indians, but also of those who govern them. Thus, he accuses the encomenderos of acting with "infernal tyranny" (78) and "diabolical greed" (112), turning the Conquest into the Devil's work rather than God's. The strength of that missionary project means that the othering that underwrites the violence of colonial domination, coexists with an idea of shared origin and destiny in a sphere delineated by God, one in which, to the extent that it has a temporality, Indians and non-Indians *are* coeval.

Las Casas rendered the Indians innocent of earthly power, but this was not a "natural" innocence of the kind to be found in Rousseau's image of the state of nature, innocence understood as ignorance of good and evil. It is, rather, innocence from inherited sin. Indians, unlike other targets of Christian evangelization and material conquest — such as Moors and Jews — were not stained with the sin of refusing Christianity. They manifest this innocence by their compliant and submissive behavior, which are essential to the Sacraments, especially confession. In effect, Las Casas was saying that the Indians were just as willing and able to enter the confessional sphere — and emerge from it cleansed — as the "Old Christians" were.[20] Their humanity and, as a consequence, their rights, derived from their proven aptitude for the Sacraments.

As a result of these discursive moves, the confessional became racialized in colonial Spanish America. It became an instrument used to demonstrate the barbarity or not of the conquered populations. This instrumentalization of the confessional reveals the tension between, on the one hand, the universalist pretensions of the civilizing mission and, on the other, the necessity of instituting a complex social taxonomy for the long-term management of the imperialist venture.[21]

When Las Casas first made his claims about the humanity of the colonized, they were deeply controversial.[22] Indian servitude in the colonies was justified by recourse to prevailing notions of "limpieza de sangre." As anthropologist Claudio Lomnitz writes, "the converted Indians, Jews, Moslems, and Africans were supposed to be spiritually unreliable and were therefore legitimately subordinated to the Spaniards" (*Exits* 264). Indians, as New Christians of a sort, were thought to have accrued a spiritual debt from their centuries of faithlessness, which made them untrustworthy (hence "infidels"); this debt had to be paid through servitude.[23] But Las Casas, argues Lomnitz, "did not support the transformation of spiritual debts into perpetual serfdom" (*Exits* 264). In other words, sin in the one sphere did not justify violent subordination and territorial dispossession in the other. Las Casas was attempting to undo the link between spiritual debt and earthly subordination. And with respect to their spiritual debts, within the confessional sphere, Indians and non-Indians are more similar than different. Indeed, in the late sixteenth century, Franciscan missionaries explicitly sought to forge this similarity by imposing the confessional narrative on indigenous self-descriptions, normalizing and standardizing indigenous autobiographies according to its ideal in order to create "vidas simples y similares unas a las otras" [simple lives similar to one another] (cited in Klor de Alva 73). This standardization, argues Jorge Klor de Alva, must be understood as a technique of colonial control. It suggests that confession among the Nahuas functioned as a form of discipline and consolation as well as a way of destroying Nahua concepts of self and the cultural context they developed within (Klor de Alva 68).

Las Casas's vision of the Indians' humanity was incorporated into the colonial state apparatus, in the Laws of the Indies; yet it never fully displaced the dominant racism of those who, like Sepúlveda, justified the forced labor of the Indians by creating "an image of a half-man creature whose world was the very reverse of the 'human' world" of the Europeans (Pagden 118). Indeed, in Peru, opposition to the New Laws of the Indies and the moral economy underpinning them sparked a civil war among the most powerful colonizers. The perniciously racist and reactionary nature of Hispanist thought in Peru, still active today, owes much to the memory of this sixteenth-century event. In effect, the "nación criolla" [creole nation] developed in Peru around the heroic figure of the rebellious Gonzalo Pizarro, as Luis Millones has argued (vi–vii), and thus remained closely tied to the assertion of the rights of encomenderos over their subhuman indigenous laborers.[24]

The "intimate indigenista" affirmation of Indian coevalness — of their shared humanity — rests in part on a notion of their innocence before God and the law, which is proven by their willingness to submit to the civilizing mission and which thus directly contradicts the views held by encomenderos and oligarchs. The indigenista destigmatization of Indians originates in a moral concept of race and culture. Rosario Castellanos was able to bring this legacy of Las Casas fully into the present without altering the fundamental moral structure of his discourse. She wrote an article on the occasion of the four-hundredth anniversary of Las Casas's death and celebrated his legacy in contemporary Mexico. She also made explicit the equation between humanity and innocence that underlay his work. Castellanos wrote: "Un indio es, esencialmente, un hombre y su desarrollo pudo haber sido favorecido o retardado por las circunstancias y de la adversidad de ellas *no se infiere la culpa de él* ni se deduce la justificación de una forma abusiva del trato" [An Indian is essentially a man and his development may have been favored or hindered by circumstances, and from the adversity of these *we cannot infer his guilt* nor find a justification for abusive forms of treating him] ("El Padre Las Casas" 145, my emphasis). Modern indigenistas' turn to a coeval space shared by Indians and non-Indians — a space in which the category of the human overrides other forms of social distinction — responds to the same desire to destigmatize Indians as Las Casas's.

But it also includes a new component: a need to destigmatize Indian*ness* — that is, those cultural or racial characteristics that the dominant racism insists can stain even those who cannot be officially classed as Indian. It appears that some indigenista writers modeled the nation on the shared time-space of the confessional that Las Casas promoted and sought in it the same kind of legitimacy and dignity for themselves that Las Casas sought for the colonized Indians. Intimate indigenismo emerges from modern phenomenologies of race in Mexico and the Andes.

Indigenismo has sometimes been understood as "a discursive gesture of a European-oriented elite" (Stepan 146). But the indigenista enunciations I have thus far described, and the indigenista "relatos íntimos" that I will examine in the following three chapters, demonstrate the extent to which indigenista racial and cultural discourses respond to regionally specific and historically mutable moral economies in which indigenistas themselves were participants and which they had interests in reforming. Intimate indigenismo proclaimed a certain kind of Indianness — a "native" connection to the national space, a sensibility uncorrupted by the more alienating aspects of modernization yet still willing to be perfected — but only once it destigmatized Indianness by dissociating it from notions of intractability and imperfectibility.

Keeping this context in mind, it seems that the destigmatization of Indianness was a necessary step in recognizing "mestizo" as a *legitimate* identity. It is worth remembering the extent to which mestizo identities, though they now appear at the cornerstone of hegemonic political projects, were previously considered transgressive before the law — though it must be stressed that this was a profitable transgression. Mestizos, though unlawful, nevertheless historically enjoyed substantial social power vis-à-vis Indians, and at the expense of Indians.[25] Nevertheless, mestizos were often understood to be unlawful or transgressive by their very being, whether seen from the perspective of the dominant Eurocentric culture or from indigenous communitarianism.[26] Centering modernization on the figure of the mestizo, mestizo nationalism turns a condition to which stigma, shame, and suspicion have always been attached, into one of normalcy, pride, and innocence. Thus José Vasconcelos, in his prologue to *La raza cósmica,* understood mestizaje to be the herald of a more egalitarian doctrine of political rights: "Vuelve, pues, la doctrina política reinante a reconocer la legitimidad de los mestizajes y con ello siente las bases de una fusión interracial reconocida por el Derecho" [Thus the reigning political doctrine recognizes once again the legitimacy of processes of racial mixture and lays the groundwork for an interracial fusion recognized by Law] (83). When mestizo nationalism is institutionalized, it extends official recognition — state recognition — to a social position otherwise considered unlawful, although in a curious condition of unlawfulness, as I have already said, since it has invariably led to greater political and economic power, at the expense primarily of indigenous people. Mestizo nationalism aimed to rewrite the law, and thus to certify, to destigmatize, specific kinds of experience. It has the effect of authorizing subjects who were previously transgressive, or partially transgressive, before the law. In redeeming Indians, indigenistas were often redeeming themselves.

As the colonial history repeatedly demonstrates, in redeeming Indians from stigma, indigenismo also subjected them to new forms of control. How does the attribution of innocence — this *insistence* on Indians' innocence — contribute to discriminatory discourses against Indians? It ratifies an important element of anti-liberal nationalist thought in Latin

America, namely, the belief that Indians as a group are incapable of, and uninterested in, the rational exercise of power. This belief serves to justify and reassert Indians' subordination in economic and political life. Appeals to a universal sphere of humanity and an understanding of racial characteristics as mutable rather than permanent thus coexist with notions of racial-cultural hierarchy.[27]

The "intimate indigenista" assertion of Indians' incapacity for the rational exercise of power is indirect and implicit and tends to be wrapped up with claims of respect, love, solidarity, and affinity for Indians. It is an essential aspect of indigenistas' defense of Indians against their detractors and colonizers and cannot be extricated from indigenistas' claims about the Indians' humanity, their nonbarbarian status. Yet it ultimately works to constrain indigenous voices by linking their humanity to their innocence and their innocence to docility. They are considered human equals but only while docile, only when they correspond to that ideal or image of human perfectibility that all people are held to carry within.

Indigenismo asserted interracial or intercultural identifications while still maintaining and exploiting racial-cultural distinctions. Affirming the innocence of Indians served not only to defend them against stigmatizing notions of race but also to solidify disinterested paternalism as the most appropriate attitude toward them by those in power. Indigenista thought challenges the idea that Indians are inherently inferior, which is the central tenet of "dominant racism." But it nevertheless continues to justify social hierarchies within the nation by reference to racial-religious distinctions whose origins date back to the colonial era.

The indigenismo I have been examining seeks to replace one moral discourse with another. How distant these sentiments are from Mariátegui! He rested the merits of his revolutionary indigenista approach on its repudiation of Las Casas:

> Quienes desde puntos de vista socialistas estudiamos y definimos el problema del indio, empezamos por declarar absolutamente superados los puntos de vista humanitarios o filantrópicos, en que, como una prolongación de la apostólica batalla del padre de Las Casas, se apoyaba la antigua campaña pro-indígena. (46)

> Those who, from socialist points of view, examine and define the problem of the Indian, declare to be absolutely superseded those humanitarian or philanthropic points of view on which, like an

extension of Father Las Casas's apostolic battle, the old pro-Indian campaign was based.

It is precisely the strand of indigenismo explicitly rejected by Mariátegui that becomes most meaningful to the authors whom I will examine in the chapters that follow. It provides a language to describe the racialized character of their social experience and to project an ideal nation that will erase the marks of stigma.

Indigenismo beyond Heterogeneity

Indigenista literature, particularly the indigenista novel of the twentieth century, has been a privileged site in which to examine the ideological aims and effects of nationalist indigenista discourse since Mariátegui's famous "Proceso de la literatura" [The Trial of Literature], one of the essays collected in his *Siete ensayos de interpretación de la realidad peruana,* and more recently, since the pioneering work of literary critics Joseph Sommers, Angel Rama, and Antonio Cornejo Polar. In terms of contemporary literary-cultural criticism in the United States and Latin America, Peruvian scholar Cornejo Polar has arguably exerted the most influence in this field through his work on indigenismo as "heterogeneous discourse," as I discussed earlier. Although my approach to indigenismo moves away from Cornejo's in some respects, it also builds significantly on his approach and is a product of the same complex history of Latin American literary criticism.

Cornejo's theory of "heterogeneous discourse," of which indigenista literature is but one example, emerged in the mid-1970s as an intervention into debates about Latin Americanism circulating among literary intellectuals in the wake of the commercial "boom" of the novel and as a response to the critical bankruptcy of the term "mestizaje" as a means to understand the logic of cultural transformation in the Americas.[28] Using an idiom drawn from Mariátegui, Cornejo centered the main current of Latin American literature on those narratives that best reflected the "nonorganic nationality" of the region's societies, their "disintegrated" status deriving from their colonial heritage ("Indigenismo" 8, 21). He was referring to Peru's failure to constitute a singular national history, its fracture into two mutually opposing regions and cultural systems locked in a hierarchical relation dating back to the Conquest: occidental and indigenous, coastal and Andean, Spanish and Quechua, written and oral.

Cornejo significantly deepened the historicism that had dominated accounts of indigenista literature (involving endless typologies: romantic indianismo, neoindigenismo, ethnographic indigenismo, etc), while moving the discussion of indigenista literature beyond debates about its aesthetic merits vis-à-vis the "nueva narrativa" of the 1950s and 1960s.[29] Aesthetic achievement, in this context, had meant judging indigenismo by its ability to represent the indigenous world "realistically." This realism was defined either according to ethnographic standards, or, as in Mario Vargas Llosa's tendentious and self-congratulatory literary history, as a direct function of character development, narrative complexity, and moral ambiguity (1288).[30] Cornejo insisted instead on returning the aesthetic field, and aesthetic interpretation, to the specific character of Latin American modernity.

Though Cornejo's "heterogeneous literature" is a political reading of indigenismo, it is not of the consciousness-raising sort advocated by Mariátegui in the late 1920s. The politics of the indigenista text operates for Cornejo quite a bit like the political unconscious does for Fredric Jameson: "It is in detecting the traces of that uninterrupted narrative, in restoring to the surface of the text the repressed and buried reality of this fundamental history, that the doctrine of a political unconscious finds its function and its necessity" (Jameson 20). The "uninterrupted narrative" and the "fundamental history" whose reality Jameson proposes to restore to the surface, however, cannot be the same as the ones that Cornejo aims to restore, for Jameson has just quoted a passage from *The Communist Manifesto* and is referring directly to class struggle. Cornejo, meanwhile, following in Mariátegui's footsteps, arrives at a narrative of history driven by factors *other* than the relations of modes of production, namely, the colonial history, one that is not really a singular narrative or reality at all. Rather, it provides, as Gayatri Chakravorty Spivak writes, "a story of a series of interruptions, a repeated tearing of time that cannot be sutured" (*Critique* 208). For Cornejo, this underlying narrative is given in the failure of the national form. This failure is itself constitutive of Peru as a nation, nonidentical to itself yet tragically self-aware of itself as split. Thus one arrives at indigenista literature, an example of heterogeneous literature, literature of the fracture, of the failure of the dominant half of Peruvian society — its urban, coastal, lettered, Spanish-speaking, occidental half — to provide an undistorted and realistic account of the subordinate half of the country — its rural, Andean, oral, Quechua-speaking, indigenous half.

My own approach is indebted to Cornejo's work in several ways: it holds that to understand indigenismo's ideological significance, one must understand the context of its production and circulation; it places indigenista literature of the twentieth century into a discursive framework whose origins date back to the colony; and it views non-Indian expressions of solidarity and affinity with Indians with a strong degree of suspicion. However, there are some problematic aspects of Cornejo's legacy that need to be addressed.

First, as I discussed earlier, in focusing exclusively on the distinction between non-Indian and Indian worlds, Cornejo obscures the extent to which racial discourses establish boundaries that can be fluid and change over time. Second, Cornejo tends to reify the association of orality with Indianness. In his initial elaborations of the concept of heterogeneous literature, he emphasized that it is the indigenista textual "mode of production" that separates it from indigenous discourse proper ("Indigenismo" 18). His later modifications of the concept, though downplaying the question of textual "mode of production," still preserved the underlying connection between Indianness and orality. Cornejo understood the distinction between writing and orality to be at the symbolic heart of colonial and postcolonial ideas of difference.[31] Although Cornejo's indexing of literacy to power has the very important merit of pointing out that literature in specific and "letras" in general have been central categories in consolidating and perpetuating political power in exclusionary, state-centric institutions over the course of centuries, it falsely suggests that writing is essentially alien to indigenous modes of thought. In this, it echoes, if distantly, a notion of cultural authenticity put forward by Valcárcel and other Andean indigenistas in the 1920s and 1930s, namely, that literate Indians can no longer be considered authentically Indians but are rather mestizos. Valcárcel would write, in 1927, that Indians who received an education degraded themselves in the process and became "degenerate" mestizos and "common shysters" who contributed to the continued oppression of the Indian (*Tempestad* 39–40). Forty years later, Fausto Reinaga, founder of the Partido Indio in Bolivia, found himself having to confront the same deeply ingrained prejudice. Reinaga felt so excluded from all forms of national debate that he was compelled to appeal to a higher authority. He registered a complaint with the secretary general of the United Nations, in a letter charging his compatriots with racism. He wrote, "Es que en Bolivia, nadie admite que un indio escriba..." [It's just that in Bolivia, no one accepts that an Indian can write...] (8, original ellipsis).[32]

Third, Cornejo's critical method places indigenista literature in an odd position with respect to the wider field of indigenista policies and aims, because Cornejo effectively separated indigenista literature from indigenista populism and revolutionary nationalism. He was a vocal critic of the populist indigenista state, which in Peru reached its fullest expression in the military regime of Velasco (1968–75), yet he celebrated indigenista literary production, promoting writers such as Ciro Alegría and José María Arguedas and insisting on the enduring value of indigenista works. The indigenista novel was for him far more representative of the reality of Peru, and of Latin America in general, than most of the more-celebrated novels emerging in the 1960s and 1970s. However, rather than seeing indigenista literature as the expression of the wider aims of indigenista political movements and institutions, Cornejo posited that the indigenista novel offers a challenge and an alternative to them. It subtly or unconsciously reveals the fissures and contradictions in a discourse of national unity that projects an otherwise powerfully coherent self-image. These fissures are revealed, not in the content of any given indigenista text, but in their linguistic materiality, in the fact that they are written. This means that for Cornejo the apparently pro-Indian politics of indigenismo are strongly offset, if not canceled out, by the very enunciation of indigenismo itself. From this perspective, it matters little if indigenista literature depicts the oppression of the Indian in order to denounce it; this denunciation is inherently antagonistic to those it seeks to defend. It will tend to reinforce, rather than to transcend, the divisions inaugurated by the Conquest, and thus it cannot bridge the underlying fracture of nationality.[33] The failure of indigenista referentiality is, according to Cornejo, its most profound truth.

If indigenista novels offer a vision of the nation that runs counter to the vision promoted by national-populism, how to explain the fact that the creators of these fictions so often embraced and worked within the state's indigenista institutions? That they believed the state's indigenismo to hold the potential to transform society? Why does their writing, when understood as an example of "heterogeneous discourse," so directly contradict their own political trajectories? To value indigenista writers and writing for the challenges they posed to the indigenista politics of the national-populist state, as Cornejo proposed, has had the perverse consequence of robbing them of the value they themselves saw in their work —

a value that is inseparable from the revolutionary national-populism that animated indigenismo throughout the twentieth century.

I seek to understand the intentionality of the mestizo gesture embedded in the indigenista text and to understand its links to nationalist discourses and to the underlying moral economies animating its enunciation. These reveal the emergence of a new experience of national belonging made possible by the destigmatization of certain aspects of Indianness. These stigmatized aspects are, concretely, the link between the Quechua language and barbarity, to the refutation of which both Lara and Arguedas dedicated a considerable amount of effort, as I will show in chapters 2 and 3, and the link between indigeneity, femininity, and barbarity, which Castellanos attempted to undo in her early work, as I argue in chapter 4.

In asserting the existence of an "intimate indigenismo," I aim to stress the changing nature of the distance or difference between Indians and non-Indians, both over time and across socio-geographic spaces and institutions. This kind of nuance is necessary if one is to account for Reinaga's political critique of the Bolivian elite, or the indigenismo of a writer like Jesús Lara. Though officially "white," Lara sometimes classified himself as Indian (Capdevilla 65), and, under certain state definitions of identity categories, would have had to be considered the son of an Indian, because his mother spoke only Quechua.[34] Lara offers an example of an indigenista subject who challenges the underlying definition of indigenismo as a discourse about Indians produced by non-Indians. What is the "non-Indian" status of a writer such as Lara? What happens when someone such as Lara — not an Indian, yet not fully not-Indian either, given his indigenous mother tongue — adopts indigenista conventions and writes about an other to whom he declares himself similar if not identical? Above and beyond our objections to Lara's performance of populist authenticity, the question takes on a particular significance when we consider that Lara wrested this posture from the state itself, for that is how all speakers of Quechua were interpellated at school — or at least, this is the story Lara himself tells, obliquely, in order to explain his Indianness.

In Lara's shifting identifications, one can sense both a genuine subjective confusion as well as a deliberate and rebellious misrecognition and misidentification of his own ethno-racial identity. If we understand that identity as a position in the moral economy — ethno-racial identity as determining an individual's relative social virtue — then Lara's trajectory demonstrates how unstable such an economy can be. Thus, in the

chapters that follow, before correcting this confused or rebellious subjective position by submitting it to a process of objective corroboration
according to uniform standards, I propose first to examine its characteristic rhetoric and to explore the underlying transformations in the moral
economy of modern nationality that it signals — to ask why and how
Jesús Lara, José María Arguedas, and Rosario Castellanos adopted an
Indian voice in order to explain their experience of national life.

Chapter Two

The Voice of the Son
in Jesús Lara's *Surumi*

En toda mi obra, a partir de *Harawiy, harawiko,* ha habido un hilo conductor permanente: mi propósito de escribir como un hijo de mi raza.

In all my work, beginning with *Harawiy, harawiko,* there has been a constant thread: my resolve to write like a son of my race.

— Jesús Lara, *Tapuy Jayniy*

Close to eighty years old, Jesús Lara looks back on his life and sees continuity, a "guiding thread" to his life. This thread is a certain kind of writing, writing as identity: he writes as someone in particular, the son of the Indian race. The statement is itself a proclamation of identity: "I am mestizo." As such, it might initially appear self-evident: if Lara *is* a mestizo, how *else* could he write, since mestizo identity implies, by definition, that one has Indian ancestry? Borges once asked this question about writing and identity but ingenuously so, in order to underscore its banality, its status as a "pseudo-problem": what else could an Argentine's writing be, but Argentine (426)? Nevertheless, it would be a mistake to approach Lara's statement in the manner of Borges, with such matter-of-factness about the stability of one's given identity. Lara refers, implicitly, to a society in which the pressure to be or to become *other* than Indian was — is — almost inescapable. His statement raises the possibility of its negative, of a mestizo who refuses to be the son of the Indian race. His life's work, Lara thus implicitly tells us, has been undertaken to refuse that refusal.

Bolivian historian Silvia Rivera Cusicanqui suggests that double refusals such as this one — the refusal of a refusal of a name — may in fact be typical of all will-to-power in a society in which the power to name, profoundly differentiating, has always provided the justification of hierarchy (because the power to name so insistently refers us, by way of 1492, to the foundations of colonialism). Names are fundamental, not incidental, to colonial hierarchies, which give rise to their own peculiar phenomenologies built around the question, "Am I that name?"[1] The simple refusal of certain names — "indio," "cholo," "pongo" — is not enough, for it demonstrates the self-interiorization of the negative image.[2] It is thus not a true refusal, because it accepts the underlying social hierarchy as natural. In order to challenge such terms, Rivera argues, one must "go through the looking glass" and claim the bad name as one's own: "romper o atravesar este espejo para reencontrar un sentido afirmativo a lo que en principio no es sino un insulto o prejuicio racista y etnocéntrico" [shatter or go through the mirror in order to find an affirmative meaning to what is in principle nothing but an insult or a racist and ethnocentric prejudice] ("La raíz" 57). The double refusal aims to become, finally, a decolonizing affirmation and to vanquish the dialectics of recognition that make social identities unstable and provisional.

Looking at Lara's novel *Surumi* (1943) and the first edition of his anthology of Quechua literature, *La poesía quechua* (1947), this chapter will examine one such double refusal within the context of the construction of progressive indigenismo and populist nationalism in Bolivia during the 1940s. The double refusal is, I would argue, one of the most significant rhetorical elements of Bolivian mestizo nationalism. Rivera, writing in the 1990s, offers the practice of double refusal as one that resists the dominance of mestizo ideology, the pressure to negate one's indigeneity. Nevertheless, as I will show here, analysis of Lara's work suggests that in the 1940s this practice was itself instrumental to forging the ideology of the mestizo nation. For Lara and other nationalist thinkers, this passage was a crucial component of a notion of autonomy — both individual and national — concentrating modern liberation on the form of the sovereign first person who lies "beyond the looking glass."

Lara was one of Franz Tamayo's youngest followers; still in his early twenties, he moved from Cochabamba to Oruro to work with Tamayo on the journal *El hombre libre*. A few years later, in 1927, he would publish the first fruits of his apprenticeship to Tamayo's "national pedagogy." This was an account of his journey to the Inca ruins of Incallajta, in the Cochabamba provinces.[3] It is his earliest indigenista text, his first turn to his own mestizo soul, constructed as a narrative of emancipation from slavery:

Todo es consecuencia de un mal común nuestro, de este incurable mal que nos aplasta desde hace cuatrocientos años: la esclavitud. Aún no somos libres. Nuestra libertad está en la forma de nuestras leyes y acaso también en la forma de nuestra vida. Nada más. Nuestro espíritu se encuentra todavía ajeno a sí mismo; todavía corre detrás del amo pretérito; todavía se desvive por imitar a él en todo.... Somos aún *mitayos* del alma. (*Viaje a Incallajta* 2–3)

Everything is a result of our common illness, this incurable illness that's been crushing us for four hundred years: slavery. We are still not free. Our freedom is in the form of our laws and perhaps also in the form of our life. Nothing more. Our spirit still finds itself alien to itself; it still follows behind its old master; it is still devoted to imitating him in everything.... We are still *mitayos* of the soul.

Lara's figurative use of the term "mitayo" is significant here: mitayo refers to a form of Indian draft labor in the mines, first under the Incas, then under the Spaniards in the colonial period (Klein 22). A "mitayo of the soul," as Lara proposes, is thus someone whose soul has been enslaved, yet whose body is free. Taking up forced labor as a metaphor and as the name for a condition of the psyche, Lara attempts to bring together under one linguistic roof two very different kinds of experience: the Indian experience of forced labor and the mestizo or cholo experience of modern alienation. Through this elision, Lara and others of his generation launched the most serious critique of Bolivia's modernizing process and set the course of a revolutionary nationalist path.

Surumi takes up the search for emancipation from slavery and focalizes it through an Indian character who escapes his destiny as a slave laborer by entering school. The novel returns the mitayo metaphor to its literal home in the forced labor of Bolivia's hacienda Indians. *Surumi* was Jesús Lara's first major novel, though it does not rank among his most widely known and translated realist novels, such as *Yanakuna* (1952) and the Agrarian Reform trilogy (1959–65).[4] Like Arguedas's *Los ríos profundos* and Castellanos's *Balún Canán*, it is an indigenista novel composed in different narrative voices. The presence of an Indian "I," sandwiched here between omniscient narrators, makes this novel an exemplary instance of intimate indigenismo. Why did Lara choose to write in an indigenous first-person voice, and why did he deliberately blur the distinction between this voice and his own mestizo voice? The answer lies in the development of revolutionary mestizo nationalism, in the phenomenology of forced labor in first decades of the twentieth century, and in the tremendous value that Lara accorded to writing as a destigmatizing and self-transforming practice.

Set in the first three decades of the twentieth century, in a historical sweep coterminous with Lara's own life up to then, *Surumi* starts with a denunciatory account of life on a Cochabamba hacienda; its protagonists are two "colonos," Ramu and Surumi, and their story is told in the third person.[5] Their son, Wáskar Puma, becomes the focus of subsequent sections. Using the first-person voice, this character recounts his experiences at school in the city. Then the novel switches back to the third person to narrate his participation in the Chaco War and the social upheavals of the 1930s, as well as his final coming-to-consciousness as a revolutionary leader. The novel's first-person section, in which Wáskar describes his life at school, serves dramatically to establish his life's development at the center of the novel. It shifts the emphasis away from the fate of the indigenous hacienda laborers and onto their son and his experience of assimilation — or, as the novel has it, his emancipation from slavery.

How did Lara mark the continuities and discontinuities of the transition in narrative perspective from third to first person and of the historical transition from serf to free man? How is Lara's elision of literal and figurative slavery made present in the text? In the rhetorical construction of this narrative, including its play with voice and perspective and its temporal complexity and uncertainty, is a lesson about the kind of alliance politics forged between war veterans, teachers, union leaders, urban intellectuals and indigenous peasants, in the last years of oligarchic liberalism in Bolivia. What kind of stories did nationalists recount in order to render that experience common across race and class?

Surumi, Lara stated, is a novela de tesis, intent to prove that birth is no determinant of social worth or status. Like the progressive indigenistas of Mexican revolutionary nationalism, Lara believed that the Indians' "backwardness" was a product of their history of oppression, rather than an innate characteristic of the "race," and so they could be "bettered."[6] But whereas many of his contemporaries advocated "bettering" Indians by subjecting them to regimes of bodily discipline so as to render them more docile participants of a modern national hegemony, as Marcia Stephenson has shown, Lara construed this "betterment" on more Hegelian grounds: the development of self-consciousness and independent thought, through a sentimental education of the mind primordially shaped by the dialectical logic of recognition.[7] *Surumi* is, in this sense, Bolivia's first universalizing, revolutionary indigenista novel.

Precisely because of its universalizing thrust, it may seem perverse to bring mestizo nationalism in line with Rivera's decolonizing "passage through the looking glass." Rivera advocates this passage in order to establish a nondialectical notion of difference that emphasizes the strength of Indian cultural survival over the past five centuries. This view posits an Indian refusal, a "no" that is simultaneously a "yes" of cultural pride and collective self-determination. It is the Aymara "janiwa," which, as Josefa Salmón points out, continues to serve as a potent symbol of race war among mestizo and criollo sectors of La Paz (Salmón 26). Lara's double refusal, however, altogether rejects the idea of indigenous cultural difference existing *within* the nation.

It is for this reason that, from the perspective of those who have been mobilized by Indian social movements of the past thirty years, Lara would be another figure in a long line of mestizo intellectuals intent on remaking Bolivians in their own image. In Bolivia, writes Stephenson, "hegemonic discourses have anxiously reiterated a desire for the self-same throughout the twentieth century" (2). Josefa Salmón argues a similar point: "la imagen indígena proyectada resulta construida a semejanza del criollo, mestizo o ladino" [the indigenous image that has been projected turns out to be constructed in the image of the creole, the mestizo, or the ladino] (16). Nationalist thought of the 1940s and beyond articulated the passage to authenticity to a narrative of individual social ascension and cultural assimilation whose terms were defined within the overall "civilizing mission" of modernization. The passage to first-person authenticity — humanization and liberation themselves — becomes a passage to civilization, the overcoming of the primitive, and it happens in and through the nation form. René Zavaleta Mercado, in his seminal *Bolivia: El desarrollo de la conciencia nacional* (Bolivia: The Development of a National Consciousness) (1967), the book that, after Carlos Montenegro's *Nacionalismo y coloniaje* (Nationalism and Colonialism) (1943), best expresses the precepts of revolutionary nationalism, argues that the individual "yo" [I] can be realized only within the nation: "El yo individual, en efecto, está incompleto y sin sosiego, frustrado y preso cuando no se realiza el yo nacional" [The individual I is effectively incomplete and uneasy, frustrated and confined, so long as the national I is not achieved] (Zavaleta 51).

The passage to authenticity and belonging that Bolivian revolutionary nationalism describes has a strong historical resonance: it is the transformation from slave-thing to man, and so it articulates the struggle of Bolivian Indians to the world-historical story of the universal realization of freedom. As a narrative of emancipation, it is inseparably linked to the story Bolivian nationalist intellectuals tell about the revolutionary struggle for the nation. Montenegro incorporated it into his 1943 screed, pointedly contrasting Bolivia to Chile: "Chile que quiere ser Chile, tiende a afirmarse como nación. . . . Bolivia, bajo la tuición suicida y alevosa del espíritu colonial, tiende a no ser Bolivia" [Chile, which wants to be Chile, tends toward affirming itself as a nation. . . . Bolivia, under the suicidal and arrogant control of the colonial spirit, tends toward not being Bolivia] (171). Bolivia denies itself, a negative that must be overcome. Even into the 1960s, this double refusal was a marked feature of progressive nationalism, as these words by Zavaleta demonstrate:

> Frente al acoso, en el pasado, las clases nacionales no habían hecho sino resistir rechazando. Se identifican en la movilización militar y se reconocen como combatientes y se aperciben entonces de que ser no es solamente resistir sino que también es necesario elegirse. Es el tránsito de la nación fáctica a la nación para sí misma y del país resistente al país histórico en un proceso por el cual, después de haber resistido a la negación de la nación, las clases que la contienen, *niegan la negación de la nación* y tratan de realizar un Estado nacional, en sustitución de las semiformas estatales creadas por las clases extranjeras. (63, emphasis mine)

> When attacked, in the past, the national classes resisted solely by refusing. They take on an identity during military mobilization and recognize themselves as combatants, and then they realize that being is not only resisting, that it is also necessary to choose oneself. It is the transition from the nation in itself to the nation for itself, from the resisting nation to the historical nation, in a process through which, after having resisted the negation of the nation, its classes *negate the negation of the nation* and try to achieve a national state that replaces the semi-forms of the state created by foreign classes.

Zavaleta makes the double negation the heart of his historical vision of national liberation.

Despite his remaining at the political margins of the revolutionary-nationalist hegemony, the rhetorical construction of Lara's double refusal echoed those of the nationalists who shaped oppositional progressive movements in the 1940s and beyond and contributed to forging the cultural and political hegemony — however precarious — of Bolivian revolutionary nationalism across its various incarnations.[8] Their double refusal, however, remained couched in a civilizing language that later indigenous thinkers would reject.[9] It is thus necessary to affirm that Lara's double refusal — his mestizo affirmation — operated simultaneously as the negation of a specifically Indian double refusal. In other words, it was not just a negation of neo-colonialism and Bolivia's Eurocentric "Rosca" (its mining-oligarchic elites) but also of subaltern resistance to internal colonialism.

However, it is also necessary to understand the regional context that shaped Lara's political views. In Bolivia, as elsewhere in the Andes, the existence of distinct regional economies of ethno-racial difference must be taken into account when analyzing the forms taken by decolonizing discourses. The difference is especially marked when comparing Cochabamba to the highlands of La Paz. Without oversimplifying regionalist distinctions, in the Cochabamba valleys, in contrast to La Paz, the stakes of subaltern resistance have never been clearly articulated in the name of indigenous cultural survival. There is no Cochabamba-regional, Quechua-language equivalent to the Aymara "janiwa." In Cochabamba, the "no" of subaltern responses to the hegemonic aims of criollo elites is not a straightforwardly Indian "no." If anything, it is closer to the "no" historically pronounced by Bolivia's miners across the twentieth century, and in fact revolutionary mobilization in the Cochabamba valleys was strongly linked to the miners' unions.[10]

The narrative of humanization with which this chapter will be primarily concerned emanates from an intellectual and "letrado," a person of letters. Yet variants of it were taken up by the popular leaders of the revolution of 1952 in such a way as to confuse its source in a particular class or ethnicity. As Jorge Dandler and Juan Torrico document in the oral histories they collected about this period, Indian accounts of their emancipation from forced labor and other abuses take shape as narratives of humanization. Their passage to freedom transforms animals into men. In the words of one Indian leader: "People treated us like pongos and animals. After everything, [in spite of] what we heard about these decrees and promises, no one helped us, and, by order of the patrón, we were treated more cruelly than ever. . . . But by this time we were beginning to defend ourselves like men" (Dandler and Torrico 339; original ellipsis). The narrative of the passage from slave to man was perhaps already embedded in popular culture, however, as these words from a Cochabamba song collected and translated by Lara suggest:

> Mamayqa wachakuwasqa   Mi madre me trajo al mundo
> "Qharisituchari" nispa,   diciendo: "Será varón."
> tatayri waqariskusqa   Y mi padre: "Será obero
> "Llank'ay yana jamun" nispa.   y esclavo," dijo, y lloró.
> (*Poesía popular quechua* 51)

> My mother brought me into the world
> Saying, "He'll be a man."
> And my father: "He'll be a worker
> and a slave," he said, and cried.

These narratives are a form of biography: popular and popu*list* life stories shaping the "yo individual" within the "yo nacional." The populist biography Lara advances in *Surumi* and, in veiled form, in his essay-anthology *La poesía quechua*, constitutes a prerevolutionary record defining what constitutes freedom and the horizons of national liberation, providing a narrative that would later be echoed by those who passed through the revolution as if it were the looking glass. Lara established this political common ground by focusing on experiences of alienation and self-negation that seemed to apply to a wide range of subjects, both subaltern and intermediary, provincial and metropolitan.[11] This chapter will first consider the historical significance of Lara's commitment to Indian social mobility and then turn to an analysis of *Surumi* and *La poesía quechua* and the phenomenology of racism that animates the first-person inscriptions of these texts. Examining these narratives constructed around scenes of self-negation, self-recrimination, guilt, and stigma, this chapter reflects on the difficulty of constructing an exemplary biography of the Bolivian subject.

Revolutionary Indigenismo

Were it not for its first-person middle section, *Surumi* would not stand out from Lara's other fiction, or indeed from the Andean indigenista literary tradition more broadly. Similar to late nineteenth and early twentieth century indigenista texts by authors such as Clorinda Matto de Turner or Alcides Arguedas, Lara's novel appealed to his readers' sense of moral outrage, using heavy narrative irony to reveal the hypocrisy and corruption of Bolivia's ruling class and its greedy middle strata. And like these older novelists, he also appealed to his readers' sentimental identification with his victimized Indian characters by staging their oppression as family dramas involving greed, lust, envy, and love, both romantic and filial. Lara made use of well-established Romantic tropes that played on what Ana Peluffo calls "el poder de las lágrimas" [the power of tears]: sentimentality deployed as political force.[12] Lara also drew on longstanding indigenista aesthetic representations of Indian men and women along the twin axis desirability-vulnerability, in that disturbing combination of piety-arousing erotics characteristic of many indigenista novels. From Matto de Turner's *Aves sin nido* to Arguedas's *Raza de bronce* to Lara's *Surumi* and his subsequent *Yanakuna*, Indian struggles against injustice, their strong desire to be free — free to follow their hearts' desires, as often as not — transformed these victims into heroes and heroines. In this sense, Lara used the novel as a pedagogical instrument in an ongoing national "sentimental education," using aesthetic representation to convert Indians into objects of desire and identification.

Yet *Surumi*, unlike other examples of Andean literary indigenismo, used pietism and sentimentality in the service of a new denunciation: Lara was arguing against the idea of an Indian "essence" or "timelessness" linked to rural ways of life. Lara once told an interviewer that with *Surumi* his intention was to write "una novela de tesis...que demostrara que la cultura iguala a los hombres y borra las fronteras que hay entre las clases sociales" [a novel with a thesis...demonstrating that culture equalizes men and erases the boundaries between social classes] (Lara and Antezana 14). His social vision, in other words, was far more radical than that of his nationalist contemporaries. More than any other Bolivian text up that point, Lara's is an attempt to normalize or naturalize the *historical* nature of Indian identity.

Hence the fundamental importance of the theme of social mobility in the novel. *Surumi* is an account of how its protagonists exploit the means available to them in the liberal-oligarchic and then military-populist years to cross the internal boundaries of prerevolutionary Bolivian society. What Silvia Rivera calls "la paradoja de la oferta liberal de ciudadanía" [the paradox of the liberal offer of citizenship] is fully laid out in the novel, a paradox constituted by liberal openings that are also exclusionary: "los mecanismos integradores por excelencia del horizonte ciudadano — el mercado, la escuela, el cuartel, el sindicato — han generado nuevas y más sútiles formas de exclusión, y es en torno a ellas que se recomponen las identidades cholas e indígenas como demanda y desafío de coherencia hacia la sociedad" [the quintessential integrating mechanisms of the citizen's horizon — the market, the school, the military barracks, the trade union — have generated new and more subtle forms of exclusion, and it is around these exclusions that cholo and indigenous identities reconstitute themselves as a coherent demand and challenge to society] ("La raíz" 78). *Surumi* develops around all of these "integrating mechanisms" that remain nonetheless exclusionary.

The novel's part 1 is dedicated to an account of the life of Wáskar's parents, Ramu and Surumi, focusing on their suffering as hacienda colonos and their difficult entry into regional markets of the Cochabamba valleys, working on their own, "cueste lo que cueste" [whatever the costs], in addition to the work demanded of them by the hacienda's cruel "mayordomo" (overseer). This allows them to amass enough capital to send their son to school, "para que vaya a comprar su libertad con el estudio" [so that he can buy his liberty with study] (*Surumi* 69).[13] Despite their amassment of these "extra" resources, they remain subservient to the hacienda and its laws throughout, in a situation they repeatedly liken to slavery (69). The novel's part 2 is devoted entirely to an account of Wáskar's experiences at the Colegio Bolívar in Cochabamba. Wáskar's entry into the "lettered city" effectively assimilates him, converting him into a member of the urban lower-middle class. Yet he is still grossly marginalized. Thus he does not abandon a consciousness of the peasant struggles for freedom that landed him there. His experiences on the front lines of the Chaco War, narrated in part 3, further radicalize him, but now collectively, as a member of ex-combatants' associations and, eventually, a new political party. By the end of the novel, an appreciation of his mother's long struggles as an Indian peasant incites him to return to the countryside, now as a political organizer. Lara made it clear in *Surumi* that, although his protagonist's mobility leads to a reconfiguration of internal social boundaries, this is not an end goal in itself but rather a stage in a longer process. As a result of the path taken by Wáskar and others like him, new relationships emerge which become the basis for oppositional political action. The novel ends with a view toward the still-distant revolutionary horizon: "El panorama de la lucha se extiende inmenso y arduo como el suelo boliviano" [the panorama of struggle extends immense and arduous like the Bolivian soil] (*Surumi* 250).

Lara belonged to a generation of intellectuals who found their voice in the years following the Chaco War against Paraguay, in a period of increasing challenges to liberalism through middle-class and popular mobilizations. It is a period of nascent populism as well as of new coalitions linking together middle-class indigenista intellectuals with indigenous movements in the highlands and valleys and with union movements of teachers and students (Rivera, *Oprimidos* 59). Many letrados served in the war, and their experiences on the frontlines — which served as the raw material for numerous books in the subsequent decade — lent a renewed urgency to ongoing criticisms of Bolivia's oligarchy and to the populist military regimes with which they were often allied in this period.[14] Their arrogance, lack of foresight, and gross mismanagement were held responsible not only for the war's disastrous losses but for the nation's overall lack of progress. This generation of intellectuals was instrumental in the social transformations that would eventually culminate, in 1952, with the Bolivian Revolution. *Surumi* thus has an oracular quality, for it gestured toward the formation of a revolutionary class in the Cochabamba valleys and towns that would in fact be, ten years after the novel's publication, instrumental in the takeover of the state, and that was effectively hegemonic from 1952 until the institution of neo-liberalism in the mid-1980s. Lara was writing *about* the prelude to the Bolivian Revolution during the years that would in fact, with historical hindsight, *become* the prelude to the Revolution.

Given the extent of *Surumi*'s participation in the ideological convergence of progressive nationalisms, it may be difficult to appreciate the extent to which the novel offered an oppositional view at the time of its publication.[15] Though *Surumi* is to a large degree a novel about an Indian's education, it is not a novel about "Indian education" in the way this topic had historically been discussed by Bolivian elites. The novel did not ask, "Can Indians be educated?" or "Should they be educated?" or "How should they be educated," along the lines of so many social reformers.[16] This is an individual's story; that is precisely the point of his education, in fact: the construction of a self-conscious, skeptical, desiring subject utterly uprooted from his original community, except for the sentimental ties that bind him to his mother — Surumi herself — ties which in turn become the basis for the nation-in-the-making he will forge in struggle with his peers.

The novel offers a view of the education of the most marginalized social sectors as a redemptive yet painful process spawning equal measures of pride and resentment, key ingredients to political mobilization. Though this argument would be central to the hegemony of indigenista nationalism of post-Revolution Bolivia, in the early 1940s it flew in the face of prevailing indigenista discourses, all influenced by tellurism to greater or lesser degrees, and thus anchored by the equation Indian = land/nature. The idea of a *mobile* Indian subject could not be computed by indigenistas of any political stripe. This inability apparently led to at least one publisher's rejection of the manuscript. Antonio Zamora, of Editorial Claridad in Buenos Aires, wrote in his rejection letter that *Surumi* would have been a marketable novel were it not for its concern with the veterans of the Chaco War (Zamora). The novel was not indigenista *enough* to be of general interest.

Though the enduring contradictions of his mobile Indian subject remained largely suppressed in *Surumi,* because Wáskar's uprooting and assimilation are painted in far too redemptive tones, Lara's vision of national belonging was not built around a notion of authenticity as rootedness, distinguishing him from both other progressive nationalists and from reactionary sectors. Following from the deterministic national psychology of Franz Tamayo in *Creación de una pedagogía nacional* (1910) and the host of other discourses based on the supremacy of certain enduring "characters" over others, and repudiating the biological determinism of Alcides Arguedas in *Pueblo enfermo* (Sick Nation) (1909), the progressive nationalisms of the 1940s were grounded in the distinction between authentic and inauthentic indigeneity. This distinction was used, among other things, as a political weapon to delegitimize reigning economic elites, especially in mining, for being "foreign" (Salmón 96). But this distinction was also wielded politically by more reactionary oligarchic sectors. In effect, Marisol de la Cadena argues that in the 1930s and 1940s, the complex dynamics of identity formation in the Andes were ideologically reduced into a simplified binary between two opposing forces: illiterate, hence innocent, Indian agriculturalists and the corrupt landed sectors that oppress them (de la Cadena 87). This simplification corresponds to the emergence, in both Bolivia and Peru, of politically progressive, even populist governments intent on modernizing, that nevertheless retained strong allegiances to conservative oligarchic social sectors. Within this historical conjunction, Indian identity was rigidly redefined as *inherently* other to rational political processes (de la Cadena

115). Efforts at state consolidation and expansion aimed to incorporate Indians, but in Bolivia at least, to do so without disturbing their "natural" belonging to the rural environment. Within this conjunction, the presence of educated Indian activists, who in Bolivia in this period formed unstable and provisional alliances with populist military governments, provoked a range of anxieties among the ruling classes that, as Laura Gotkowitz argues, "conjured up a whole set of long-standing assumptions about purity and danger; about the innocence of Indians versus the nefarious interference (or abuse) by mestizos and eventually also labor organizers or communists; about the sanctity of rural society versus the contaminating effects of cities" (Gotkowitz 201). This premise was nothing if not a politically expedient way to ignore peasant demands against the oligarchy, attributing them to forces supposedly foreign to the peasantry: mestizos, communists, labor leaders, city people, etc.[17] The "modernizing ethos" of the populist 1940s regime of Gualberto Villaroel paradoxically "sought to keep Indians on the land, shielded in protective and productive rural environments," Gotkowitz argues (222), showing that "to modernize in many way was still to civilize, to preserve and protect, not radical integration, culturally or politically" (224). Referring to the important Congreso Nacional Indígena held in 1945, she writes, "The official program of the congress thus displayed the limits of the government's own integrationist views; it searched for and inscribed an authentic, untainted, uncorrupted Indian — just as it sought to modernize and incorporate Indians into one legal, cultural, and institutional universe" (169). Indian education was, as often as not, a question of preserving that rural "innocence," and authentic indigeneity remained circumscribed to the rural sphere.

Mercedes Anaya de Urquidi's seminal book *Indianismo* (1947), literally required reading for the nation's indigenista educators, included several "Plegarias Indígenas" [Indian Prayers] that she recommended be taught to Indian schoolchildren. Each proclaimed the supplicants' desire to be recognized as "like other men": "Señor, la raza indígena reclama un sitial en el mundo; reclama sus derechos de hombre sano, fuerte y libre. Señor, haz que los civilizados comprendan nuestra vida; que también somos gentes como todos los hombres" [Lord, the indigenous race demands a place in the world; demands the rights of healthy, strong, free men. Lord, make the civilized people understand our life, for we are people just like other men] (111). Yet the phrase "like other men" is misleading, for underlying these prayers is a vison of social space naturalizing existing divisions:

> Señor, Tú, que conoces nuestro corazón, aliéntalo en sus faenas cotidianas; confórtalo en sus recónditas penas. Haz que sintamos las dulzuras de la paz y la ventura en el hogar campestre.... Y que así plácidamente aclamemos tu nombre y cantemos tu gloria en montes y collados, los valles y las sierras; en la roca, en el agua, en el viento y la luz, con emoción sublime, con intenso fervor. (112)

> Lord, you who know our heart, encourage it in its daily tasks, comfort it of its hidden sorrows. Let us feel the sweetness of peace and happiness in the rural home.... And thus we calmly praise your name and sing your glory in mountains and passes, in valleys and plains; in the rock, in the water, in the wind and the light, with sublime emotion, with intense fervor.

By this view, to each race corresponds a natural location.

Although Lara was not a member of the rapidly growing nationalist party and did not subscribe to all of its platforms, he did share some of the same nationalist concerns. He was not above criticizing writers like Franz Tamayo and Ricardo Jaimes Freyre for not being Bolivian enough: "en virtud de su predilección por motivos ajenos al medio, no nos han dado sino calidad, una gran calidad, mas no hacen obra bo-liviana" [By virtue of their fondness for themes that are alien to this environment, they've only given us quality, great quality, but they do not create Bolivian works] ("Bolivia tiene" 3). But the question of authenticity was not for him a telluric one; it had nothing to do with land as an existential or ontological category, with indigeneity as an experience of the sublime, as occurs in Anaya's "Indian prayer." Though "the Indian" lay at the heart of Lara's conception of Bolivianness, he criticized the metonymic association of Indians with the earth as one more ideological tool of their oppression. In his novel *Yanakuna* (1952), Lara drew from current events in order to depict the judicial trial against the leaders of an indigenous rebellion in the Cochabamba highlands. In his vision of these events, Lara has the prosecution at the trial argue on behalf of the oligarchy that, "El indio era parte constitutiva de la tierra y por tanto su persona pertenecía de modo irrestricto al propietario" [The Indian was a constitutive part of the land, and thus his person belonged completely to the landowner] (341).[18] It is precisely this equation that Lara's

works of this period strongly denounce. The political salvation of Bolivia's Indians, the novel shows, lies squarely in the city, with precisely
those socially uprooted sectors deemed unsavory or scandalous by the
oligarchy and its supporters. Wáskar Puma's trajectory in *Surumi* was of
a nature calculated to inflame what Gotkowitz calls the "distress about
the transgression of racial boundaries, the rural/urban, Indian/mestizo
divide" (204). Lara, perhaps better than any of his non-Indian contemporaries, had a specific talent for narrating the range of vicious practices
such transgressions could provoke and for asserting that only a social
revolution could provide the ultimate undoing of such injustice.

The Road to Freedom

In his populist novel-biography, Lara focused particularly on figures who
were both inside and outside slavery: the hero of *Surumi* is a slave and a
student; his parents are hacienda colonos and small-scale entrepreneurs.
This mixed economy of subjection and mobility, alienation and self-
determination, is sustained by a number of destabilizing social forces.
The first among these that Lara presents is *sexual desire*. The master's
sexual desire for his/her slave—the mayordomo's desire for Surumi, the
mistress's desire for Ramu—is the axis on which the dialectic of recognition turns. After having been seduced by his mistress, Ramu begins to
intuit, still obscurely, that she might be dependent on him, rather than the
reverse. A few days later, he discovers in himself a new orientation toward
the future: "Se trata de una fuerza extraña, vestida de enigmas, cuya virtud parece ensanchar el horizonte que le rodea y arrancar luces extrañas
de los maizales, de los cerros, de las nubes" [It's a strange force, clothed
in enigmas, whose virtue seems to broaden the horizon that surrounds
him and bring out strange lights from the cornfields, the mountains, the
clouds] (*Surumi* 47). Acting now within this newly widened horizon, he
begins to make plans to allow his son to escape his fate as a slave.

The second among these destabilizing forces depicted in the novel, and
central to its narrative of emancipation, is the regional market, particularly in "chicha."[19] Lara does not valorize it as an end in itself, but rather,
as with sexual relations, for its capacity to shift the balance of power.
The market signifies new connections, movement across distinct social
geographies. It is the two colonos' entry into the regional market—Surumi as a "muk'era," the lowliest rung in the chicha economy, Ramu as
small-scale trader, exchanging valley produce for highland wool—that

allows them to amass enough surplus cash to send their son to school where he can then "buy" his freedom with study.[20] But the market is ambivalent in *Surumi*. It is also an alienating force, almost as dangerous as the oligarchic labor institutions themselves. A popular Cochabamba refrain makes the connection between the city and the conversion of humans into products:

> Amalayas ñawpa tiempo,   ¡Que buenos los tiempos de antes!
> sipas aycha phatallapi   Carne de joven [muchacha] valía medio,
> kay supaypaq llaqtanpitaq en esta [ciudad] del diablo,
> paya aycha uj sarapi.   carne vieja y vale un peso.
> (Sichra et al. 142)[21]

> How good things were in the past!
> Young meat was worth five cents,
> In this city of the devil,
> Old meat is worth eighty cents.

This commodifying aspect of market relations becomes explicit in the latter portion of Lara's novel, ironically exposed by the author in the words of one urban character: "No hay ni tata ni mama cuando viene un sueldo fijo cada mes" [Neither father nor mother exist when a fixed salary arrives every month] (245).

But most important of all these socially mobile figures is the student, to whose emergence and development Lara dedicates an entire section of the novel. Education operates alongside the destabilizing forces of desire, the market and, later in the novel, the Chaco War; but it is accorded far greater transformative power. Lara assigns overwhelming importance to script literacy — alphabetic writing — for providing a non-market, nonviolent form of social mobility. Even more important, it is the best means of transforming stigma and shame into legitimacy and pride. Wáskar's trajectory in *Surumi* illustrates this, as does Lara's own autobiography, which contains the following reflection on how its author came to consciousness of himself as mestizo:

> Garcilaso [el Inca] y los otros me habían lanzado al encuentro de mi raza, de mi sangre indígena, del espíritu de mi pueblo; me habían impelido a reconocerme en el indio de hoy y a remover en el fondo de mi ser mi sensibilidad indígena adormecida desde hacía cuatro centurias. (*Wichay Uray* 154)

the Inca Garcilaso and others had launched me on the encounter with my race, with my Indian blood, with the spirit of my people. They had compelled me to recognize myself in the present-day Indian and stir up, in the depths of my being, my indigenous sensibility, asleep for four centuries.

Indeed, it was in the archive — the Municipal Library in Cochabamba, which Lara directed for many years — that Lara would find the ideological sustenance to assume this heritage as his birthright and liberate himself from shame. In *Surumi,* this trajectory takes on an added element, for it is now not only a passage to liberation from shame but also to freedom from forced labor.

The voice of *Surumi*'s part 2 alternates between slavery and freedom, as Lara charts his hero's process of social ascension in a story of prolonged emotional transformation. His education is above all the sentimental education of modern subjectivity. At its heart *Surumi* contains an intimate narrative, built around the experience of an intensely lived inner life, and designed to communicate the depth, the architectonic interiority, of a modern subject who finds himself — in the double sense of self-discovery and consignment — on the social margins. This intimate narrative offers a story of the individual's emancipation, one that parallels, up to a certain point, the story told by those who, a decade later, passed through the revolution, the story of the passage from pongo-animal-slave to human.

Salvador Vázquez, a former peasant leader in the Cochabamba valleys, emphasized this trajectory in his oral account of the prerevolutionary period. "Nosotros hemos nacido esclavos desde los tatarabuelos" [We were born slaves since our great-grandparents], he says, explaining his attachment to the populist military leaders of the 1930s and 1940s, Germán Busch and Gualberto Villaroel, who understood this fact and fought for liberation (Gordillo 69). The passage to freedom was also, however, a passage to civilization. Vázquez explains:

> Ya en aquella época yo les dije a mis compañeros que se había acabado la esclavitud, que no teníamos por qué seguir trabajando para la hacienda, que se habían acabado los servicios, que ahora nosotros éramos los dueños, los presidentes de nuestra familia, de nuestro hogar, ahora nosotros debíamos procurar para que nuestros hijos sean profesionales, ya sea profesores, o ingenieros agrónomos con capacidad, yo les dije que ahora nosotros teníamos

que velar por nuestros hijos, que nadie los va a hacer profesionales, ningún Gobierno. Que teníamos que llegar a la civilización. (Gordillo 116)

Already back then I told my companions that slavery was over, that there was no reason why we had to keep working for the hacienda, that our service was over, that now we were the owners, the presidents of our family, our home, now we had to endeavor that our children might be professionals, capable professors or agricultural engineers, I told them now we have to watch out for our children, that no one will make them professionals, no Government. That we had to attain civilization.

Lara's narrative, however, is not quite as straightforward as Vázquez's recollection. It does not motor directly to civilization, like a train reaching its point of arrival. What does it mean to be human and civilized in this novel? It does not mean abandoning the name "pongo" nor the name "Indian" for the title of "president" or "professional," but rather, as per Rivera's "through the looking glass" formulation, a double refusal. Paradoxically enough, Lara's protagonist authorizes himself as slave.

Three elements of Lara's discourse of emancipation will be underscored here. One, freedom is in fact a kind of subjection, the subjection to one's own desires, desires that are nothing other than the individual's internalization of the mandates of what Althusser would call "the ideological state apparatus," i.e., school. Lara figured Wáskar Puma's emancipation from pongo servitude as a new subjectivization and a new subjection, a process staged through scenes of naming very much like the staging of interpellation that Althusser described to understand the formation of subjects: hailed by a policeman, the anonymous individual turns toward the voice of authority, demonstrating that he recognizes himself to have been identified, and that he is impelled to submit, whether he wants to or not, to the call of the state (Althusser 174). As I will argue, Lara's novel provides an insight into the uneven workings of interpellation when the "ideological state apparatuses" are committed to the reproduction of forced labor, rather than the creation of modern subjects. But it also suggests the end of this situation in its representation of the oligarchic state *in crisis,* a crisis made apparent by the fact that a slave can become a subject by passing through the state's own institutions. Two, this subjectivity is biographical in nature; the individual stands at the center of his life, itself composed of the sum of his past experience. Autonomy as Lara understands it is in large part a matter of being able to remember, and actively claim as one's own, the archive of one's life. And third, as Lara has it, this process of remembering is achieved exclusively through the technology of writing.

School and Subjection

In moving from part 1 to part 2 of *Surumi*, the reader confronts the tremendous discontinuity between the distanced, ironic, "objective" and linear narration of hacienda life (part 1), and the intensely subjective, emotionally earnest account of school life (part 2), with its multi-layered temporality. Lara presents Wáskar's experiences at school in terms of an intense inner life, narrated entirely subjectively and utterly excessive in its representation of adolescent emotionality. This narrative is continuously punctuated by crises around naming. Leaving the plantation for school and escaping the life of his parents, this hero is assigned a proliferation of names as he moves across stringently policed internal social boundaries. All these names are initially alien to him; some of them he eventually comes to accept as his own. In other words, it is a narrative about the mechanisms of self-recognition; about how these are materialized, primarily in writing; and how they are the effects of assimilation to the nation-state. The first-person narrative in *Surumi* demonstrates that the stakes of progressive indigenista nationalism, as Lara saw them, involved creating subjects out of those who previously were nonsubjects, and then having them take over the state.

Arguably the most important recurring verbal phrase of this section is "Yo me sentía..." [I felt...]. Feeling is the action of the novel as it unfolds in these pages, the self-palpation of feeling. This process of self-reflection and, crucially, self-expression is meant to be understood as confusing and uncontrolled — not just for the narrating subject himself, who often speaks of the "desconcierto" [sense of being disconcerted] that besets him in the city, but for his interlocutors as well, including the novel's readers. *Surumi*'s part 2 starts in medias res, signaling its rupture with the previous narration and illustrating the aporetic nature of its narrative. It leaves the hacienda and its colonos behind to focus on a new story: the story of how "I" left home and came to school. Who this "I" is, and what its relation to the previous narration, will remain a mystery for several pages.

Once this complex staging of his authorial presence has been established, Wáskar will go on to recount the details of his four years at school. Wáskar's transgressions, and the backlash against him, are the backbone of this section. But transgression tells only half the story. Wáskar's ascension occurs through education, through the "ideological state apparatus" of school, and so it is also about living within the terms of the law. It is worth remembering that *Surumi*'s narrative is oriented to the capture of the state as its end goal, not the overturning of the law. Wáskar's father hopes his son will "buy" his own freedom with study and so escape his parents' fate as slaves (69). Thus education is figured as an entry into the liberal economy, and freedom is a commodity: self-knowledge.

The bulk of part 2 concerns Wáskar's response to the various attempts to kick him out and keep him down because he is an Indian. Scenes of public humiliation, followed by increasingly affirmative demonstrations of his determination and resiliency, form the heart of this narrative. It is also the narrative of his displacement away from the hacienda, which is in itself a form of social transgression for which he is repeatedly punished at school. But Wáskar has also ceased to be a part of his family's community. The confusion about who Wáskar is, and is becoming, is played out over the course of this section in terms of his proliferating names. At school he has been given the name "Pongo Puma," when the students find out that he is not exempt from this form of domestic forced labor. At home, meanwhile, his parents refuse to let him work alongside them; they now care for him as if he were "un objeto de lujo" [a luxury item] and contemplate him like an idol (96). His father begins to call him "niñuy," a diminutive used by hacienda colonos for young masters; other colonos refer to him simply as "Patrón." Wáskar strenuously protests this treatment, which is for him a form of misrecognition: "Oprimido de vergüenza le rogaba que me llamase como a su hijo, no como a su amo" [oppressed by shame I pleaded with him to call me as he would his son, not his master] (90). By the end of his narrative, however, these conflicts over names, and the questions concerning Wáskar's social place and status, have been largely resolved: Wáskar has learned by then how to name himself through acts of self-narration. Self-authorized and yet still attached sentimentally to his family of origin, he has become an ideal antagonist to oligarchic liberalism.

However, this narrative of social ascension does not follow an easy line toward emancipation and self-determination. Perhaps most significant in this regard is the fact that this arc from object-hood to subject-hood is narrated as a story of incorporation to the state, meaning that in *Surumi,* subjectivization is not understood as freedom in an absolute sense; it is also a form of subjection. The freedom the son buys with his studies might seem at first to be the freedom to exist for himself rather than for the master. He has finally found his own voice and with it the ability to control his destiny. These notions contain a kernel of liberal thinking, for subject-hood, freedom, and private property are intertwined (he buys himself freedom by amassing his own inner capital, so to speak). Yet Wáskar is not the sovereign subject of liberation. His self-consciousness is figured as a subjection to himself: he will find himself "subjugated" by his own desire to write of himself: "me siento subyugado por un deseo que a ratos me aguija con fuerza incontenible" [I find myself subjugated by a desire that stings me at times with uncontainable force] (88). And this self-consciousness does not develop in a purely dialogic form, as a consciousness *for* oneself *of* oneself as other; it develops through a far more complex social theater, staged primarily at school, in which the state plays a leading role. The desire that subjugates him is the desire to finish the writing assignment imposed by his literature professor: "terminar de volcar este universo que hormiguea dentro de mí" [to finish pouring out this universe swarming within me] (88). It is the desire to take up the unfinished work of the state as his. This subjection to himself is thus the result of his new subjection to the state and is intimately bound up with writing.

Lara's portrayal of subjectivization as subjection is strikingly conso-nant with Althusser's argument that the subject is an effect of ideology, and that it is through ideology — through subject effects — that we are bound into social relations of power that serve to reproduce the state (Althusser 170–73). In this the novel is amazingly forthright about the political stakes of indigenismo: to take control of the state by creat-ing new Indian subjects. Like other progressive modernizers, Lara thus positioned Indians within a narrative of progress that frames their exis-tence, prior to the state's interpellation of them, as not fully subjectivized ("primitive," in the language of a slightly older discourse than Lara's).

Wáskar's emancipation from slavery occurs through his interpellation by "ideological state apparatuses," notably school, which is why part 2 is constructed around public scenes of humiliation; as in Althusser, engage-ment by the state is a theater of naming and self-naming that presumes the subject's constitution through guilt. Part 2 opens with scenes of public self-display, all in some ways a version of the "theoretical scene" of hailing described by Althusser. Each is embedded within the other, as text within text, in a mutual entanglement that becomes one element among several signaling the difficulty of narrating Wáskar's transformation from slave to man.

The narrative starts with the description of a literature professor, an unquestionably authoritative man: "Ejerce un dominio absoluto sobre todos sus alumnos. Todos nos esforzamos por seguir sus exposiciones y por cumplir las tareas que nos asigna" [He holds absolute power over his students. We all exert ourselves to follow his lectures and complete the tasks he assigns us] (79). The professor has required the students to compose, in prose or verse, "una reminiscencia de cualquier época de su vida" [a reminiscence from any period of your life]. The narrative then abruptly shifts to this written assignment, a text-within-the-text, thus introducing another layer of first-person narration. The "narrating we" immediately becomes a "written I."

Like all scenes of interpellation, this one contains, in the words of Judith Butler, "a demand to align oneself with the law, a turning around (to face the law, to find a face for the law?), and an entrance into the language of self-ascription — 'Here I am' — through the appropriation of guilt" (*Psychic* 107). The student, still unnamed, in effect decides to write about the experience of being an Indian at school, which is for him an experience of stigma. In his composition we encounter the first scene of humiliating public self-display: "Desde el primer momento me vi aislado y menospreciado. [Mis compañeros de clase] pasaban por mi lado mirándome de pies a cabeza y riéndose.... Yo era indio y llevaba el estigma en la cara, en el lenguaje, en el traje de casinete mal cosido y en los zapatos de cuero burdo" [From the very first moment I found myself isolated and despised. My schoolmates would walk by, regarding me from head to toe and laughing... I was Indian and I carried the stigma on my face, in my language, in my badly sewn clothes and in my rough leather shoes] (83). This student's "Here I am" for the agent of the state — his professor — is thus the self-ascription of a subject who recognizes himself as guilty of being himself. It is also a sign of his recognition that, as Butler writes, " 'Submission' to the rules of the dominant ideology might then be understood as a submission to the necessity to prove innocence in the face of accusation" (*Psychic* 118). The student writes "I" as if before the tribunal, as if a witness in his own defense.

In fact he *has* been placed before such a tribunal, a scene he vividly recounts in closing his composition. Yet rather than serving as an exemplary instance of state interpellation, the tribunal scene demonstrates an instance of noninterpellation. The author is brought before the school tribunal for having struck a fellow student, unfortunately for him the son of a family of notable "decentes." The autobiographical narrative explains that, though his violence was a clear case of self-defense in a fistfight initiated by the other, the author is given no chance to defend himself. He is ordered to apologize publicly to the offended "decente." Fear paralyzes him at the public interpellation, as he recounts in this scene from his homework assignment:

> —¡Hable! — me impuso el rector.
>
> Esa voz me hirió como un arma desconocida. Yo estaba obligado a hablar. Algo tenía que decir. Pero mi cerebro se debatía en un pesado caos y no aparecía por ninguna parte una palabra. Mi silencio se estiraba sobre mi angustia de plomo y el suelo empezaba a socavarse bajo mis plantas.
>
> —¡Hable, indio!' — repitió como un eco de puñales el caballero de Astorquiza.
>
> Ahondábase el vacío de mis plantas y mis rodillas se rendían …me abandonó la voluntad y fui aplastado por una inmensa montaña… (87, final ellipsis in the original).

> "Speak!" the rector demanded.
>
> His voice wounded me like an unknown weapon. I was being forced to speak. I had to say something. But my brain was struggling in a heavy chaos and no word appeared anywhere. My silence stretched over my leaden despair and the ground began to give way beneath my feet.
>
> "Speak, Indian!" the gentleman from Astorquiza repeated, like the sound of fists.
>
> The emptiness at my feet deepened and my knees gave way. …my will abandoned me and I was crushed by an immense mountain… (final ellipsis in the original)

What happens when the oligarchic state in some sense refuses to interpellate this student, as is repeatedly the case, because he is an Indian? Or when it tries and fails, because it does so in a way that blocks his entrance into language? There is something wrong with the mechanism of interpellation as the student describes it in this scene. If its primary purpose is to create the effect of subjectivity, then it fails to achieve its goal: it flattens the subject out so hard that he disappears. The "writing I" has described a kind of temporary implosion of the subject; the call was too violent and intense to engage him. Butler underscores that interpellation involves an entrance into the language of self-ascription: "Here I am." But in this scene, as it is described in the school essay, the response to the call cannot be articulated in language: the student is wounded by the voice, feels paralyzed by emotion, and faints. It is a moment of non-self-recognition, exactly the opposite effect described by Althusser's scene. The student's nonlinguistic signs, if they can be read as such, suggest that he is responding to the call by resisting the "Here I am," communicating instead a thorough "Not me," in a performance of "I am not here."

Interpellation as an Indian is, in this scene and in others in *Surumi*, not interpellation at all, in the strict sense of the term. Its effects are not subject effects. It enslaves, to use the vocabulary of the novel, in order to perpetuate the labor regime of pongueaje. Wáskar is cruelly given the name "Pongo Puma" when his classmates discover that he is not exempt from this labor, even as a student, and someone sees him hauling trash from his mistress's house in the city. True to the Hegelian paradigm, the subjective experience of forced labor is emphasized in descriptions of its utterly alienating components. While working as a pongo, Wáskar notes, "Yo me movía como un autómata. Habíanme resultado suficientes dos días por hundirme, para desaparecer dentro de mi condición de pongo" [I moved around like a robot. All it took was two days to destroy me, for me to disappear into my pongo condition] (112). When, on returning to school, he is greeted by his classmates with the words "¡Pongo Puma!" (116), he is thrust back into this alienated mode of consciousness: "Como en la casa de la patrona se paralizó mi pensamiento. Mi voluntad y mi rebeldía de otrora sufrían una inercia irremediable. Mi sensibilidad parecía haber fugado de mi cuerpo. Me juzgaba un ser del todo ajeno a mi mismo y al mundo que me rodeaba" [Just as in the mistress's house my thinking was paralyzed. The will and rebelliousness of my past suffered an irreparable inertia. Feeling appeared to have fled my body. I judged myself to be utterly alien to myself and to the world around me] (116). These descriptions of the soul-killing, self-disappearing effects of forced labor highlight the loss of humanity, and particularly of subjectivity as self-experience. Feeling, thought, will, self-identity, and collective belonging all vanish. He has been reduced to an object who exists only for the master.[22]

In each of these cases, interpellation as such has failed. But this failure is not one that the novel celebrates as a sign of indigenous resistance to domination, the perverse resistance of the "bad subject." On the contrary, Lara suggests that the mechanism has been purposefully designed to fail when it takes an Indian as its object. Responding to the hailing — to use Althusser's word — with an inarticulate performance of "I am not here," Wáskar becomes a more perfect servant. It is important to underscore this point, and to remember that *Surumi*'s narrative has a national revolution as its end goal: the capture of the state, not its undoing. The denunciation that Lara effects with these scenes of slavery, is not a denunciation of interpellation per se, but rather of the kind of failed, improper interpellation that the oligarchic state stages in order to reproduce a class of slave labor.

This investment in more modern regimes of labor perhaps explains why the extended underlying metaphor in Wáskar's account of the experience does not turn on the opposition human-animal, as an older indigenista discourse might have done but rather on the opposition human-machine. Consider the contrast, for example, with the following description of the base condition of the pongo, from an 1869 text reproduced by Alcides Arguedas in his *Historia general de Bolivia* (A General History of Bolivia) (1922):

> Un pongo es el ser más parecido al hombre, es casi una persona, pero pocas veces, hace el oficio de tal, generalmente es una cosa. Es algo menos de lo que los romanos llamaban "res." El pongo camina sobre dos pies, porque no le han mandado que lo haga de cuatro, habla, ríe, come, y, más que todo, obedece; no estoy seguro si piensa. . . . Pongo es sinónimo de obediencia, es el más activo, más humilde, más sucio y glotón de todos los animales de la creación. (cited in A. Arguedas 300)

> A pongo is the being most like a man, is almost a person, but he plays this role infrequently, generally he/it is a thing. He/it is something less than what the Romans called "res." The pongo walks on two feet, because he hasn't been ordered to walk on all fours; he talks, laughs, eats, and, above all, obeys; I'm not sure if he

> thinks.... Pongo is synonymous with obedience, is the most active, most humble, dirtiest, and most gluttonous of all the animals in creation.

The category of "thing" is underscored, but it remains nevertheless a position within a hierarchical realm of natural relations. Lara's description retains the central element from the older discourse, pointing to the threat to individual subjectivity. But the nature of this utterly alienating experience is couched in an extended metaphor that simultaneously riffs on the perils of modern industrial culture: the pongo is like a robot. This significant change from the rhetoric of the nineteenth century means that Lara understood the pongo as a manifestation of modern society but an aberrant one; he is dominated but cannot become a subject. This interpellation gone awry is precisely what maintains oligarchic power.

History, Memory, Autobiography: The Pongo as Subject

Looking over unpublished drafts and early editions of the novel, we see clearly that Lara made a very conscious decision to make pongueaje a mechanical rather than a bestial experience, but that he did so for reasons that were no longer apparent by the time of the novel's second edition in 1950. One aspect of slavery that Lara had initially meant to underscore in his subjective account of pongueaje was the extent to which it had converted Wáskar into a kind of recording machine. As a pongo, Wáskar found himself an unwilling eavesdropper on violent, intimate scenes between master and mistress. Their harsh words then became indelibly inscribed on him. It was this process of inscription, to which the pongo submitted, involuntarily, horrified and robot-like, that Lara emphasized in the versions of the novel prior to 1950. These two earlier versions each dwell on that experience of inscription, showing the extent to which, as a pongo in the house of his masters, he had become a kind of automatic recording device of the cruelty and moral decay of the oligarchy.

In the first of these earlier versions, a handwritten draft of *Surumi* (no date), Lara had crafted the following scene describing Wáskar's self-alienation as a pongo, in which he must listen to his master and mistress exchange insults:

> "¡Te odio, chola!"
> "¡Te desprecio, chancho!"
> No he perdido ni una sola palabra de las que oí aquella mañana.
> Todas ellas se grabaron en mi cerebro como en granito.... Yo me
> movía como un autómata. (*Surumi* ms. n.p.)

> "I hate you, chola!"
> "I despise you, pig!"
> I haven't lost a single word of what I heard that morning. Each
> word was engraved on my brain as if on stone.... I moved around
> like a robot.

This version underscores the process of traumatic and impersonal inscription (he is like a stone), though not its mechanistic aspect. Yet in his
own hand Lara crossed out several of the lines after "chancho," moving
immediately to describe Wáskar as "autómata," thus emphasizing the
mechanical nature of this unfeeling experience above all else.

However, in the novel's first edition, published in 1943, a new line was
added, one that reaffirmed the mechanical nature of the experience while
also bringing back in the association with recording: "Captaba las palabras del mismo modo que una máquina calcadora de sonido" [I grasped
these words in the same way as would a sound recording machine] (118,
first edition). This line was cut from all subsequent editions, yet its trace
can still be perceived in the narrative that remained. That is to say, even
in the subsequent editions, after all references to recording devices had
been eliminated, Lara continued to chart the passage from pongo-slave-
machine to human in terms that contrast the free individual with the
recording machine. For the slave to become a man, it is necessary that
he produce his own memory of the past.

The truth of a man, Wáskar will say, can be found in the recovery
of his own personal memory, exteriorized and shaped creatively in writing, and organized, furthermore, into a narrative that differentiates past,
present, and future. Reflecting on the newfound pleasures of writing,
Wáskar notes:

> Un extraño sentimiento acaba de nacer en mí y me dice que no
> hago mal en descubrir la verdad de mi vida, porque nada significa
> la rechifla de las gentes. En efecto, un hombre que aspira a una vida
> sencillamente humana, no tiene nada que ocultar. Jamás ocultaré
> mi origen, ni la miseria de mis padres, ni el dolor de mis derrotas.

Ese mismo sentimiento me lleva a explorar las más diversas rutas en la selva de mi espíritu. Me invita a meditar en mi vida de ayer y en la de mañana. (88)

A strange feeling has just been born inside me, and it tells me that I don't do wrong to discover the truth of my life, because people's jeers mean nothing. In effect, a man who aspires to a simple human life has nothing to hide. I will never hide my origin, nor the poverty of my parents, nor the pain of my defeats. That same feeling leads me to explore the most diverse pathways in the forest of my spirit. It invites me to meditate on my past life and on my future.

To live as a *human,* one must know one's past, share it with the world, and yet continue to know it *as* past (rather than present or future). The transformation of passive memory — the mind as recording device — into living memory activated by "I," and the integration of this memory into a chronological biography, are thus a central feature of the passage from slave to subject that *Surumi* narrates.

One of the odder elements of this overcoming is that it involves accepting the name "Pongo Puma" as his own. By the time the words "Pongo Puma" appear as graffiti all over the city, and etched one day on his door, they work as a true form of ideological interpellation, through the appropriation of guilt: "Huí como culpable de un crimen monstruoso.... Mi culpa estaba en mi nacimiento, era culpa heredada, culpa de raza, una culpa que llevaba el indio desde que una cruz de falsa piedad extendió sus brazos ávidos sobre las entrañas de oro de los Andes" [I fled like someone guilty of a monstruous crime.... My guilt was in my birth, it was inherited guilt, the guilt of the race, a guilt that the Indian has carried ever since a cross of false piety extended its avid arms over the gold entrails of the Andes] (119–20). Thus when Wáskar recounts how, over time, he comes to accept the name "Pongo Puma" with diminishing degrees of pain, we are perhaps less surprised, remembering that it is an ideologically productive naming. He has internalized the history of the race as his own; he now *has* a history. One day he realizes that his classmates now utter the words with "good humor" and that he has become so accustomed to it that he barely notices it, even though it remains inscribed on the city's walls: "De tanto oir y leer esas palabras, me iba acostumbrando de ellas como a las campanas, como a los petardos de las fiestas" [Having heard and read these words so often, I was getting as used to them as church bells, as fireworks on festival days] (120). His "slave" name is indistinguishable from the sounds of the "ideological state apparatus" and indistinguishable from his "real" name. He admits, "Yo ya no establecía diferencia entre mi nombre y mi sobrenombre... imperceptiblemente y sin cicatrices habíase injertado en mi vida" [I no longer distinguished between my name and my nickname... imperceptibly and without a scar it had inserted itself in my life] (135).

The Self as Archive

To the extent that it is possible to derive Lara's changing intentions over the course of the various rewritings of the pongo scene, it would seem that, while he consistently understood the essence of the pongo's dehumanization to lie in the reduction of person to machine, the machine in question was in his original conception not a labor machine but a recording machine. Wáskar felt himself to have become an automaton at that moment when he became a site of forcible inscription, a passive, mute testimony to oligarchic decadence. This witnessing, rather than leading to greater self-consciousness — as it did in the earlier draft of the novel, when it awakens his mind to the morally debased and hence illegitimate nature of elite power — leads instead to self-alienation. The element of passivity, of loss of will — "I felt like an automaton" — comes about as a result of this inscription, for in the face of this recording process he remains utterly helpless. At this moment, he becomes half-dead, an archive-*object*, in the sense described by Derrida: "the archive, consignation, the documentary or monumental apparatus as *hypomnema*, mnemotechnical supplement or representative, auxiliary or memorandum. Because the archive... will never be either memory or anamnesis as spontaneous, alive and internal experience" (Derrida 11). His transformation from slave-machine to human agent thus involves returning memory to its condition of aliveness, not only to bring the memory to life, but to bring himself to memory as an act of living again, as an act of self-determination.

In describing Wáskar's new subjectivity, Lara turned repeatedly to the language of interior spaces, in which knowledge and experience are housed. Derrida reminds us that the Greek root of "archive" is *arkheion*:

> initially a house, a domicile, an address, the residence of the superior magistrates, the *archons*, those who commanded. The citizens

who thus held and signified political power were considered to possess the right to make or to represent the law. On account of their publicly recognized authority, it is at their home, in that *place* which is their house (private house, family house, or employee's house), that official documents are filed. The archons are first of all the documents' guardians. (2)

To become human, in *Surumi,* is to open the door and enter into one's own house, the inner place where memory and experience reside; to take control of one's archive and become the *archon* to oneself, as it were, revealing and interpreting its contents oneself, rather than remain a mute, self-alienated repository, "una máquina calcadora de sonido" [a sound recording machine].

In bringing in the idea of memory as key to self-determination, Lara articulated his narrative to an ongoing critique of state censorship, of efforts to seal the archives shut, of which Lara had previously felt himself to be a particular target. It is worth recalling, for instance, that *Repete,* Lara's earlier book, had been censored by the military authorities after it was published. Although it received widespread recognition, having won a literary prize, the military had copies of it burned in the street. Lara considered the national archive to have been purposefully distorted through the systematic destruction of information. In particular, it refused to house information about indigenous history and experience, such as the staggeringly high percentage of Indian casualties in the Chaco War, a fact that *Repete* documented.

The importance of opening the national archive became a veritable theme for the author.[23] Following *Surumi,* he published *La poesía quechua,* his Quechua poetry anthology (1947), which he specifically construed as a response to those Bolivians who, like the colonizers of old, continued to believe that Indians were "without history" (*Poesía quechua* 14). Here too, as with *Repete,* the full extent of the truth was kept hidden by illegitimate *archons.* Lara provides a detailed account of the trouble he encountered on trying to gain access to a private archive of Quechua poetry. Its *archon,* a respected man of letters, refused to let him in:

> Hermético y desconfiado, no quería mostrarnos los documentos. '¿Para qué?' nos dijo cierto día. 'Es muy difícil su lectura.' Las veces que nuestra visita era admitida no cesábamos de rogarle que tradujera o publicara algunos trozos. Ante nuestra insistencia el

ilustre patricio movía la cabeza con una sonrisa enigmática. (*Poesía quechua* 64)

Hermetic and suspicious, he didn't want to show us the documents. 'What for?' he asked one day. 'It's very hard to read them.' When he did let us visit him we never stopped begging him to translate or publish some fragments. Faced with our insistence the illustrious patrician would shake his head with an enigmatic smile.

Finally, Lara recounts, the *archon* lets him in, whereupon Lara must confront another grave obstacle. As the archivist had indeed warned, the texts are almost impossible to decipher: "Se desdoblaron ante nuestros ojos páginas amarillentas en que parecían enredarse en loca vorágine miriadas de patas de araña, largas, estriadas, trágicamente mudas" [Before our very eyes the yellowed pages unfolded, in which there seemed to be entangled, in a crazy maelstrom, myriad spiders' legs, long, striated, tragically mute] (64). Lara goes on to say — to summarize briefly the rest of the anecdote — that he was able to decipher a few pieces, including some poems by Wallparrimachi, an eighteenth-century poet from Potosí hitherto unknown to him, and was permitted to copy these down, along with a few other items of Incan origin, but only after a long struggle with their "cruel possessor." For political reasons Lara was unable to review the collection again; a few years later its owner died intestate, and his "treasure" disappeared without a trace (64).

Lara constructed the archive episode primarily to highlight the issue of archival authority: who controls the archive, what secrets are kept there, and how can they be deciphered and disseminated? The episode took place in 1922. When Lara wrote *Surumi,* some twenty years later, he was already quite familiar with the suppression of archives testifying to Indian achievements (in literature, on the battlefield), filled with a historical knowledge that, were it accessible, could be used to legitimate their inclusion in national life.

As the above episode demonstrates, embedded within the issue of archival authority is the issue of writing as the most authoritative form of testimony. Perhaps unconsciously, the episode alludes to a foundational moment for Andean history in which writing is shown to be an instrument of conquest that the colonized must learn to master. In describing the indecipherable words on the parchment page as insect-like, Lara's text mimics a widely performed popular play reenacting the death of the Inca Atahualpa at Cajamarca in 1532: "La muerte de Atahualpa," or

"Atahualpa Wañuntin," as the play is called in Quechua [The Death of Atahualpa].[24] In the Quechua poetry anthology he published three years after *Surumi,* Lara translates and cites one of the best known passages from this play. Here, Atahualpa attempts to read a message sent to him by Pizarro, but cannot make out the writing. Puzzled, he passes it to his advisor Waylla Wiksa, who says the following:

> No sé qué dice aquí, quizá nunca lo sepa. Mirando de este lado parecen hormigas que se mueven. Mirando de este otro, son como las señales que dejan los pájaros sobre el lodo de las orillas de los ríos. Mirando de aquí parecen *tarucas* con la cabeza abajo y las delgadas patas al aire. Y, si vemos así, son como llamas cabizbajas y como cuernos de *taruca*. No puedo comprender. (*Poesía quechua* 110)

> I don't know what it says here, perhaps I'll never know. On this side it looks like moving ants. On the other side, they're like the tracks left by birds on muddy river banks. From here they look like upside-down *tarucas* with legs in the air. And, if we look at it this way, they're like upside-down llamas and *taruca* horns. I cannot understand.

The moral of this particular tragi-comic fragment, which can be found in all versions of the play, is that Atahualpa was in some sense defeated by his own illiteracy. Lara's incomprehension before the Quechua archive could not more closely parallel the Inca's attitude on encountering his first example of alphabetic writing. He has in effect put himself in the place of the Inca, linking his powerlessness to his incomprehension before the written text. Gaining access to the archive and deciphering its secrets becomes a political imperative.

However, it is worth pointing out that, unlike Lara, the play "Atahualpa Wañuntin" does not fetishize reading above all other forms of interpretation but rather dramatizes multiple attempts by advisors and ancestors to make sense of confusing signs. In most versions of the play writing is only one textuality among others in need of decipherment. It competes, for example, with the prophetic powers of Atahualpa's dream of the conquest, whose difficult interpretation is as excessively staged as are the scenes around the "papelito blanco" [little piece of white paper].

Furthermore, unlike Lara, Atahualpa in the play almost always ends up "rejecting" writing — throwing the piece of paper, in some cases the

Bible itself—down to the ground and saying, with royal disdain, "Take this away":

> Ima yana unuwan ch'aqchusqachari kay chhallachaqa. Manam manam unanchayta ni watuyta atinichu. Itukapuy apakapuy.

> ¿Con qué agua negra estará asperjada esta hojita? No puedo, no puedo adivinar ni preguntar. Alzatela, llévatela. (Beyersdorff 333)

> What kind of black water is sprinkled on this little leaf? I cannot, I cannot find the answer or ask the question. Take it, take it away.

Lara says, rather, "Bring this closer to me. I must have it!" Writing is the key to power. Although Lara's anecdote operates a symbolic reversal of this defeat, by having the key text be in Quechua rather than Spanish, it leaves the authority of writing intact.

In Wáskar's school composition, we find a passage where the "writing I" comments on his writing in the act of writing. In the present of narration, he reports that the professor's requirement fills him with a new pleasure: "El mandato de mi maestro viene a regalarme un goce nuevo, pues encuentro que volcar los recuerdos sobre el papel es mucho más bello y más real que contemplarlos entre las bóvedas interiores. Voy sintiendo que escribir es como construir un edificio, como levantar una montaña" [My teacher's command gives me the gift of a new pleasure, since I find that pouring out memories on the page is much more beautiful and more real than contemplating them amid interior vaults. I'm coming to feel that writing is like constructing a building, like raising mountains] (79). Writing is a self-authorizing practice: objectifying what is housed in his "interior vaults" by displaying them on paper makes them "more beautiful" and "more real." The narrator communicates here a sense of the visuality and materiality of writing, an aesthetic appreciation of the intimate flow of self-consciousness that the technology of writing achieves. Neither the act of remembering alone, the inner self-examination, nor the communicative act in and of itself, are sufficient to arrive at this appreciation. What is needed is "volcar...sobre el papel" [to pour out on paper].

Wáskar's composition has the status of a survivor's text, for its very existence proves that the silenced "indio" of the story he recounts survived his humiliation to write about it. This is how writing becomes a personally redemptive practice. It is like "raising mountains," he says in his school essay, whereas public humiliation is like being squashed by mountains: "fui aplastado por una inmensa montaña" [I was crushed by an immense mountain], he had written, to describe the experience of losing consciousness; it is likened to being flattened out. To "raise mountains" is thus to liberate himself from the weight of shame, and regain consciousness, understood here as interiority. In effect, he has learned to hail himself; these are nothing if not scenes of self-authorization. This is how Wáskar manages eventually to overcome the enslaving effects of the state's hailings, even though the insults intensify over the course of the days, rather than dissipate, an effective instrument for the "upstanding sons" of the school against the upstart. Wáskar is able to resist, however, by calling on *interior* reserves: "La indigencia de mi espíritu no duró muchos días. Mi entereza comenzó a alzarse sobre mi derrota como se alza el trigo nuevo sobre el rastrojo arrasado" [The poverty of my spirit did not last many days. My strength of mind began to rise above my defeat like new wheat rising above the razed stubble] (116). His *spirit is rich,* not indigent; and his *mind is strong.* He has enough interior capital to keep buying himself freedom.

Ultimately, *Surumi* measures the distance between slave and human, parents and son, in terms of the capacity for self-knowledge derived primarily, if not exclusively, from writing. Wáskar's father, Ramu, his interior life figured as a region of a dark fog illuminated by occasional flashes of light, will always remain a slave: "En realidad, Ramu no alcanza a comprender lo que le pasa. Sin duda, él también se nota cambiado, pero el cambio no puede clarificarse entre las brumas de su inteligencia. Siente extrañas inquietudes, deseos imprecisos, impulsos que reclaman actitudes no conocidas" [In reality, Ramu can't understand what's happening to him. Surely he too notices he's changed, but the change doesn't become clear amid the fog of his intelligence. He feels strange anxieties, vague desires, impulses that require unknown attitudes] (47). An earlier scene is even blunter: "El no es más que un indio.... El no conoce los caminos de la defensa porque siempre vivió a oscuras" [He is nothing but an Indian.... He doesn't know the path to self-defense because he's always lived in the dark] (39). Though these kinds of sentiments have an element of ironic double voicing — the phrase "he is nothing but an Indian" voices both the racist view and its tragic internalization by its victim — they strongly assert Lara's view of the colono's intellectual helplessness.

Unable to imagine that there might be forms of self-objectifying representation — or of consciousness-raising — other than writing, the novel partakes of what Martin Lienhard calls the "fetishization" of writing, which was endemic to the colonial enterprise and often attributed, by mestizo intellectuals, to indigenous people themselves (25–32). Lara may have derived this view from the Inca Garcilaso, whose influence on this novel can definitely be felt in the hero's name.[25] Writing is made out to be the key to authoritative self-projection, not just for success in the dominant society, but *tout court* as a precondition to full self-awareness. I have already discussed the extent to which Lara's view, in *Surumi,* of the importance of Indian education differed tremendously from other non-Indian social reformers, who in the 1940s were by and large advocating educational programs that would keep Indians in the countryside because that is where they "naturally" belonged. But it is also important to underscore how Lara's view on the importance of education — of writing, more precisely — differed from indigenous discourses contemporary to it. In the first half of the twentieth century, education had become an active demand of indigenous communities, which mobilized repeatedly to bring in schools. This was one element of the struggle to defend communal lands against hacienda encroachment (Choque et al. 41–78). But in *Surumi,* education in general, and writing in particular, is presented as a technology solely for the individual's success, rather than as a key to *collective* self-projection. In this, Lara reproduced some aspects of the "racial ideology" of the populist state, as Gotkowitz describes it, filled with "images of unruly, upstart mestizo-cholos, and victimized, downtrodden Indians," which were replays of liberal-oligarchic discourse (264). In focusing on the plight of hacienda colonos and making the pongo the emblem of Indian servitude, Lara reflected the tendency of the governments of those years to give less attention to the struggles of Indian comuneros (members of free Indian communities) to maintain control over their collective land.

The Son's Debt to His Race

The familial story recounted in *Surumi,* concerning the legacy Wáskar's parents bequeath him and Wáskar's subsequent filial sentimentality, marks social change both temporally and spatially: the passing of the generations, the rural-urban migration of the student. Wáskar's world is not the same as that of his parents. A close reading of the novel reveals, however, that Lara was not sure how to position his protagonist vis-à-vis this transformation. The biographical timeline of the novel contains a serious temporal fracture, in all likelihood a mistake by the author, but a significant one, for it involves a question about how the assimilated, emancipated son should relate to his nonassimilated, enslaved parents, most particularly his mother. Should he celebrate his education and social advancement as freedom, or mourn the distance that it has created between him and his parents?

This error in the construction of the novel's part 2 occurs amid the confusing temporalities of text within text, memory within memory, that characterize its opening pages. Lara opens part 2 by throwing out two arcs of remembrance. First, the recent memory of being in the classroom and told to write a memory, in a series of sentences that establish that this narration is happening within a day of the events recounted. Second, the more distant arc of memory cast by the school composition itself, which describes the events that brought the narrator to the classroom in the first place. The present is the same for both arcs: in the early days of his life at school, the narrator looks back at formative events, some more recent than others.

But then Lara seems to have made a mistake. Not long after the student composition has come to a close, he introduces a voice who is remembering these events from a much greater distance, after several years have passed: "Ahora que tengo unos años más de sufrimiento y de inquietud, se me humedecen los ojos cuando considero que en el silencio de aquellas lágrimas [mi madre] volcaba sobre mis hombros diez meses de angustia y de esperanza" [Now that I'm older by a few more years of suffering and anxiety, my eyes mist when I think that in the silence of her tears, my mother poured onto my shoulders ten months of despair and hope] (96). The net effect is hopelessly to confuse the temporal grounding of the narrative. The present time established by the episode around the composition is clearly the first months of school, in those key moments when the desire to write grasps him and thrusts him through "the open door" of his mind, as he says (88). Yet the present time established by the subsequent present-tense moment — "Now that I'm older by a few more years . . . " — is clearly a much later one, inhabited by an older Wáskar looking back on his younger self and, significantly, paying homage to the sacrifices of his mother rather than focusing on his own inner discoveries.[26] When is the "now," the "moment in which I write these lines"? And why is the confusion surrounding it linked to sentimental memories of his mother?

The temporal fracture in *Surumi* is all the more significant when one considers that the writing of history itself had become a site of nationalist debate. In 1943, Carlos Montenegro attacked the dominant current of Bolivian historiography for what he termed its willful "destruction of the past." Its aim, he argued, was to eliminate in the people any notion that they have a history, and hence to deny them their status *as* a people (Montenegro 16). He accused its historians of negating the strong currents of national history, of seeing only external and superficial elements — foreign elements. He compared national history to a river, one whose deep currents Bolivian historians refused to investigate. The result of these negations was a chaotic, nonsensical history verging on the insane: "creaciones dislocadas, bruscas, arbitrarias y truncas de una extraña demencia" [nonsense creations, abrupt, arbitrary and truncated, strangely demented] (70). Its ultimate effect was therefore colonialist and "anti-Bolivian," because it failed to reflect the truth of Bolivia and the Bolivian *people,* namely, that the nation is nothing but its history, a continuous, evolutionary history that is internally coherent, possessed of a "solid organic interior" (74). Thus Montenegro understood his populist historiography to be decolonizing, the bedrock of national independence, integrity, and authenticity: "La evidenciación vitalista del pasado constituye...no menos que el gran baluarte en que los destinos auténticos de Bolivia pueden atrincherarse para contrarrestar y repeler la invasión que ha facilitado...la psicología colonialista creadora del sentir anti-boliviano" [The vitalistic explanation of the past constitutes...nothing less than the great bastion in which to entrench the authentic destiny of Bolivia in order to counteract and repel the invasion made possible by...the colonialist psychology which creates anti-Bolivian feeling] (17).[27]

Lara's *Surumi* was published in the same year as Montenegro's *Nacionalismo y coloniaje.* Not surprisingly, it enfolds these same ideas of populist historiography into the novelistic biography that forms the heart of its narrative. That a person's life is the sum of his past experience, much like the nation — the people — is composed of its history; that this past belongs to him, is his to remember and claim; that such claims are acts of recovery, making whole what was truncated; and that, in the face of widespread discrimination by elites ("anti-Bolivianism" in Montenegro's parlance), such acts are tinged with heroism — these are all features of the narrative of education-as-emancipation recounted in *Surumi*. Like Montenegro, Lara considered this kind of historical remembering to be a form of social virtue; it is the bedrock of authenticity, and authenticity is akin to heroic action: it leads to freedom. To know your past and hence to know yourself and your people — your family, your community, your nation — signals courage, strength, presence of mind, independence of spirit; to ignore or deny the past, to repudiate yourself and your people, the vilest servility. *Surumi* is in large part the story of one person's refusal to repudiate his past, and to make of that refusal the cornerstone of his honor and freedom.

Robert Albro has described a certain affinity for biography flourishing in Cochabamba towns, a genre that pays homage to local notables who are "hijo d'algo," ("son of something") and yet whose foremothers re-main anonymous Andean women (310). How do men who do not have notable lineage construct "something" from which to be descended? In this the figure of Surumi is of paramount interest. Lara turns toward the powerful fiction of transgenerational continuity materialized in the mother's body and in her child's sentimental attachment to it: "Su madre es una voz que le habla de un deber, una mano que le señala un rumbo, un calor de sol que pronto hará germinar la simiente que ella misma de-positó en el surco de su espíritu allá en los años de esfuerzo y esperanza" [His mother is a voice that speaks to him of duty, a hand that points him to a path, a sun's warmth that will soon make germinate the seed that she herself placed in the furrow of his spirit, back in the years of effort and hope] (192). Bearing the name of a local Virgin and kept as the novel's title despite criticisms from early readers, Surumi bears an uncommon symbolic weight to make this a novel about "the son."[28] Consonant with the rhetoric of mestizo nationalism, this symbolism principally accrues to the Indian mother as origin, as past, a past that is especially significant with respect to the future: she shows him the way. Surumi is "un símbolo, un camino y un precepto" [a symbol, a pathway, and a precept] (192).

Nevertheless, there are some indications that Lara was unable fully to impose on his own text this singular chronology, differentiating and aligning past, present, and future. Only *this* historical alignment offers the possibility of the populist double refusal, for the double refusal pre-supposes a stable present conforming "bolivianidad" from which to repudiate the false consciousness of the past. Lara's "present of nar-ration" in *Surumi*'s part 2, however, is not stable, as if his writing were motivated by a disordering force competing against biographical order, and rendering the time-space of Bolivianness uncertain, a question mark rather than an affirmation. Lara inadvertently produced the kind of historical narrative denounced by Montenegro as "anti-national": "nonsense creations, abrupt, arbitrary and truncated."

From a purely rhetorical perspective, the disordering force that blurs the "now," and thus its "before" and "after" as well, can be identified as what Butler terms the "prehistory of the subject," a time-space that Lara cannot map onto the filial timeline. The story of the emergence of the subject is aporetic, without foundation:

> The narrative that seeks to account for how the subject comes into being presumes the grammatical "subject" prior to the account of its genesis. Yet the founding submission that has not yet re-solved into the subject would be precisely the non-narrativizable prehistory of the subject, a paradox which calls the very narrative of subject formation into question. If there is no subject except as a consequence of this subjection, the narrative that would explain this requires that the temporality not be true, for the grammar of that narrative presupposes that there is no subjection without a subject who undergoes it. (*Psychic* 111–12)

If subjectivity is the result of self-narration, as the opening pages of part 2 suggest, then "who" initiates the narrative? This initiation becomes effec-tively impossible to narrate; it "exceeds the narrativizability of events" (*Psychic* 106). As Lara presents him, Wáskar is, from the very first, a creature of the page, an autobiographical voice: the first time "I" ap-pears, it is in the school composition. The author has been structurally prevented from narrating the birth of "I" except in and through the "I" already made present.

This disordering "prehistory" is significant for other reasons as well. Might it not be the sign of a populist history still in the making, one whose *ultimate* significance still remains shrouded to the author? The plurality of remembering stances — one more immediate, the other more distant — might perhaps be a signal of Lara's confusion about how to signify the time-space of self-encounter that is writing. In the more imme-diate remembering arc, self-narration is redemptive (lifting the mountain of shame); it is politically denunciatory and intimately pleasurable. It is a "gift" from the state, the means by which he becomes a subject of the state. In the more distant remembering arc, it becomes imbued instead with filial sentimentality: he writes with tears of loss for his mother, which are also tears of guilty self-recrimination; the gift of writing has turned into a debt he owes to his mother.

Lara was unable to clarify which of these responses ultimately determines the moral significance of Wáskar's narrative. Is writing a liberation from slavery, an emancipation from the past? Or is it a new form of subjection, this time to his own sentiments, such as his feeling of indebtedness to the past embodied in his mother? Certainly mestizo nationalism, and populism more broadly, play on the moral ambiguity of individuals' social advancement. The image of the populist leader exalted by the MNR is of a man whose political commitments are motivated by his consciousness of what he owes the people. Augusto Céspedes, with Montenegro a principal intellectual architect of the MNR, offers a portrait of the populist leader instrumentalized by the people; he acts on their behalf as if owing them something, rather than instrumentalizing the people for his own political gain. Writing in 1953, barely a year after his party's rise to power, he explains that its success was due largely to the ability of intellectuals like himself and his compadre Carlos Montenegro to identify completely with the people:

> la virtud esencial del grupo fundador [del MNR] — que debe ser siempre virtud de todos sus dirigentes — consistió en que insertábamos en las masas, con el ejemplo, nuestro propio sentido de los derechos del nativo. Nunca las empleamos en medio demagógico sino que . . . nos sumergimos en la masa. (Céspedes, "Carlos Montenegro" 61)

> the essential virtue of the founding group of the MNR — which must always be the virtue of all its leaders — consisted in the fact that we inserted in the masses, by our own example, our own sense of the native's rights. We never used the masses demogogically, but rather . . . submerged ourselves in the mass.

Lara, too, constructed an authorial "I" by exploiting the ambiguity between the subject who advances socially for his own self-interest, and the subject who advances socially in order better to serve those whom he has left behind. In an interview recorded in 1977, late in the author's life, he reflects on his debt to "the Indian":

> Aunque no he olvidado que soy mestizo, toda la vida he tratado de identificarme con el indio. Desde mi más tierna infancia he vivido junto a él, he dormido en su choza, he comido su lawa y compartido sus piojos. He visto su miseria, sus frustaciones, su desventura. Siempre me he sentido en deuda con él y por tanto he tratado

de trasladar su vida a mis novelas como una denuncia, como una
protesta. (Lara and Antezana 189–90)

Although I haven't forgotten that I'm a mestizo, all my life I've tried
to identify with the Indian. From the tenderest years of childhood
I've lived with him, I've slept in his hut, I've eaten his soup and
shared his fleas. I've seen his poverty, his frustrations, his unhappi-
ness. I've always felt indebted to him and thus I've tried to transfer
his life to my novels as a denunciation, as a protest.

Lara's relationship to Indians, as he posits it here, is thus similar to
Wáskar's relationship to his mother: both respond to the sacrifice of the
Indian by assuming that sacrifice as a debt that they must repay through
political action. The novel *Surumi,* then, can be understood as Lara's
attempt to compensate for the distance between past and present, between enslaved Indian and assimilated Indian or mestizo, by turning to
the ambiguous language of subjection — subjection to a master, subjection to one's sense of debt and sentimental attachment, flowing across
and linking together disparate social spheres.

In the end, it is the sentimental arc of remembrance that will hold
sway in *Surumi.* The figure of Surumi is placed at the origin point of the
story of "I," like a beacon in an otherwise confounding landscape of self-
transformation. By the novel's end, she will indeed have become affixed
to this point of the journey, its origin point, when the narrator refers to
her as the "precept" for his revolutionary struggle: "El panorama de la
lucha se extiende inmenso y arduo como el suelo boliviano. Pero Vin-
vela [his lover] es un auspicio y Surumi un precepto" [The panorama of
struggle extends immense and arduous like the Bolivian soil. But Vin-
vela is a sign of promise and Surumi a precept] (250). In these words,
the family frame — the wife of the future, the mother of the past — effectively lends temporal stability, a *timeline,* to the passage to freedom.
Here, Lara finally meets Montenegro's demand for the interior coherence
and temporal continuity of the national subject.

Stephenson writes about the "ambivalent mother" at the heart of
nationalist discourse of the 1940s, showing how good mothers were distinguished from bad on the basis of their suitability for mestizaje: those
who make possible the new social order, nationalism as cultural hegemony, are always educated mestizas; the rest disorder or fragment it,
part of what Montenegro termed "anti-nation": Indians, urban cholas,
elite women (Stephenson 38–39). In the texts Stephenson analyzes, the

ideal mother is a function of male sexual desire: a model wife for mestizaje. In a different twist, *Surumi* writes the mother from the perspective of the son. Indigenismo is generally built around a paternalist, pastoral civilizing mission: Indians as child-like innocents guided toward emancipation by a benevolent father/law. Lara's novel presents rather a civilizing mission undertaken in the name of the mestizo son. It turns filial remembrance into a central feature of its populist origin story. Put another way, it enacts the double refusal Rivera describes: refusing to repudiate his mother, the son claims authenticity as a national subject.

"We knew no other tongue": The Bilingual Stigma

What is the decolonizing potential of mestizo double refusals such as this one? As is characteristic of mestizo nationalisms in general, it is only partially fulfilled. A paternalist civilizing mission is still at its core, and to that extent, as Rivera points out, the mestizo nation is still an exclusionary one: "tanto partido de gobierno como partidos de oposición, acabaron construyendo concertadamente un sistema en el cual la inclusión excluía, pues sólo valía para aquellos que aceptasen — autonegándose — las normas de comportamiento 'racional' y ciudadano, que las élites consideraban como las únicas propiamente humanas, relegando a todas las otras formas de convivencia y comportamiento al ámbito amorfo de la naturaleza o lo presocial" [both the governing party and the opposition parties ended up working together to build a system in which inclusion was exclusionary, because it only worked for those who would accept — through self-denial — the norms of 'rational' citizen conduct, which the elites considered to be the only properly human norms, relegating all other forms of social life and conduct to the amorphous realm of nature or the presocial] ("La raíz" 85). Lara's anti-telluric progressive nationalism denaturalizes some aspects of the oligarchic disciplining of indigeneity — its association with telluric essence or with pastoral innocence — only to institute a new disciplinary regime that has in turn become naturalized. The true subject of the nation is the "I," his exemplary experience recounted biographically and structured chronologically, and providing the authentic phenomenology of the national "life." Zavaleta Mercado says it directly: the very possibility of an autonomous "yo" can only be realized in and through a national "yo" (Zavaleta 51). The idea that indigenous people might have "other forms of social life and conduct" that do not rely on the concept of "national history" for their authorization, forms that they might want to preserve, remains alien to Lara's indigenismo.

In effect, for Lara, mestizo and Indian experiences of self-negation were essentially the same. He made this quite clear when he revealed, in his autobiography, that his depiction of Wáskar's life at school drew heavily from his own experiences of material want and humiliation at the Colegio Sucre in Cochabamba (Lara, *Sasañan* 151). His decision to break up *Surumi* by inserting a first-person narration at its center seems to have stemmed from his sense that his own "I" and the "I" of his protagonist Wáskar were closely related. Lara used the first-person narrative in order to make his own political struggles in the prerevolutionary period, his own experiences of violence and marginalization, continuous with the experiences of Cochabamba's indigenous peasantry.

Lara's sense that the two experiences — of an Indian at school, of a mestizo at school — were comparable, if not identical, is in part a product of the instrumentalization of indigenous experience for mestizo political advantage. This is indeed one very persuasive account of the triangulated politics of Andean indigenismo: that one marginalized yet rising social group adopted the cause of another, far more oppressed group, on the grounds that both faced a common enemy (liberal oligarchy), and in order to strengthen its own claims to be the exemplary agent of reform or revolution (Salmón 58). Brooke Larson also refers, meanwhile, to the process of displacement that occurred when indigenista intellectuals proclaimed themselves the best mediators between the downtrodden and the powerful. Regarding Franz Tamayo and Alcides Arguedas, for instance, Larson has argued that there is an underlying continuity in their project to replace intermediary sectors with themselves as the privileged and "enlightened" conduits of interethnic relations ("Indios redimidos" 41). Through *Surumi*, we see how the rural boy turned urban student turned war veteran turned peasant organizer — each readable as a figure for Lara himself — displaces already existing mediators of Cochabamba's social geography, such as his parents, whose strong bodies and economic survival skills provide them with a limited measure of freedom; or such as the corrupt cholos who thwart their ascension, including the plantation's mayordomo and its cook. Lara displaces the Indian parents while endowing them with enormous symbolic value as an origin point, as a memory to be recuperated rather than repudiated. Fausto Reinaga found this a particularly objectionable element of Lara's work, accusing him of becoming "a venal dealer" in folkloristic indigenista literature, of selling out his indigenous heritage (Reinaga 106).

Yet the process of political displacement and symbolic recovery reflected in Lara's indigenista labor only partially reflects the historic tendency of nationalist elites. Unlike other indigenistas, or his contemporaries in the MNR and RADEPA, Lara did not participate in this symbolic division of the national space, did not assert the natural, rural space as the only authentically indigenous one, in a *disciplinary* form of modern pastoral. Furthermore, Lara's confusion about the difference between Indian and mestizo experience of self-negation, a confusion at the core of national populism, was itself the product of the liberal-oligarchic conflation of the two as threats to civilized modernity. In effect, at school Lara was taught from an early age to loathe his mother tongue, Quechua. He constructed his own sense of political marginality through references to a scene of public shame: the Quechua speaker at school humiliated for speaking a "rude and primitive" language. This scene can be found in his autobiography, as well as in his essay-anthology *La poesía quechua*, published only three years after his novel *Surumi*.

La poesía quechua consisted of a long essay about Quechua literature that was accompanied by a small anthology of poetry presented in both Spanish and Quechua.[29] A very scholarly text involving the excavation, classification, and interpretation of Quechua poetic forms according to the norms of the Western literary canon, this essay-anthology was also quite clearly a polemical intervention into political debates about the future of Bolivia and particularly about the role that Bolivia's indigenous people should play in that national future. Put briefly, Lara used this anthology to demonstrate the existence of a Quechua civilization stretching from the present back to the Incas, and thereby legitimate Indian participation in the construction of the modern nation. He was intent on refuting the claims of those liberal thinkers who, drawing from colonial sources, continued to view the Indian as "sin historia" [without history] (15); "un ser abyecto y reacio a todo impulso de progreso" [an abject being resistant to all drives toward progress] (14); and possessed, furthermore, of an extremely ugly dialect ["feísimo dialecto"] (15).[30]

Lara's attempt to bring that which had been excluded from "the lettered city" into its hallowed walls necessitated the careful construction of a scholarly persona who both hides and reveals his own ambiguous positioning across the lettered city's very perimeter. Unlike other indigenista writers, and unlike the majority of those who at that time had produced anthologies of Quechua works of one form or another and whom Lara used as sources for his own, Lara was himself a native speaker of Quechua.[31] This fact is one to which Lara will refer only obliquely in his essay, in a passage where the impersonal "we" of the scholarly voice merges, briefly, with a truly collective "we" representative of a buried community:

> El lenguaje indígena manchaba igual que un delito a quienes lo empleaban. Se lo abominaba en la tertulia y se lo prohibía en la escuela. Aquella prohibición todavía existía a principios del siglo actual. No olvidamos que en la escuela, allá en una provincia de los valles de Cochabamba, el maestro nos castigaba toda vez que éramos acusados de haber utilizado el quechua. Y la verdad era que no conocíamos otro idioma. (151)

> The indigenous language stained those who used it, the same as would a crime. It was abominated at gatherings and prohibited in school. That prohibition still existed at the beginning of the present century. Let's not forget that in school, there in a province of the Cochabamba valleys, the teacher would punish us every time we were accused of using Quechua. And the truth was that we knew no other tongue.

Using the language of "stain" and hence of sin, Lara returns once again to oppression experienced as stigmatization.

It is important to note that a scene like this one interpellated Lara as an Indian — a primitive — at a moment in his life when he would never have self-identified as such, nor would he have been so perceived in his home community.[32] Nor was it limited to Lara himself; there is much to suggest that he was voicing the sentiments of a significant social sector across the Andes. Bolivian scholar Guillermo Francovich wrote to Lara of the emotion Quechua poetry caused among "gente de la más elevada clase social" [people of the highest social class] in Sucre, pointing out that "No solamente el indio, sino el pueblo todo vive la emoción de esa poesía [en quechua]" [Not only the Indian, but the entire country feels the emotion of that poetry in Quechua] (Francovich). An admiring reader in Cuzco, Peru, called *La poesía quechua* "el mejor clamor rebelde contra esta humillación en que nos tienen y nos tenemos, respecto a los valores espirituales de nuestra madre raza" [the best clamor of rebellion against this humiliation in which they hold us and we hold ourselves with respect to the spiritual values of our mother race] (Latorre). A response to Lara's subsequent *Yanakuna* expressed similar views: "Como yo soy de la región quechua del sur del Perú, su libro me ha dejado como un mensaje de mi propia niñez. Ha despertado en mí no sé qué viejos sentimientos hasta ahora no revelados. Me ha vuelto a conectar con ese gran pueblo quechua" [Since I am from the Quechua zone of southern Peru, your book has been like a message from my own childhood. It has awakened in me old feelings hitherto unrevealed. I've connected again with the great Quechua people] (More).

Lara's words, as well as some of the responses his work elicited, reveal the disjunction between competing spheres of social distinction resulting from the expansion of education. This historical disjunction, I would argue, is largely responsible for Lara's confusion between mestizo and Indian experiences of liberalism, a confusion of which *Surumi* is symptomatic. The scene of public shame in *La poesía quechua* — so reminiscent of the scenes Lara crafted for his Indian protagonist in *Surumi* — is fundamental to the programmatic aims underlying his text, because it establishes his populist authenticity. It reveals that the liberal state provided people like Lara — small-town mestizos, cholos, provincial Quechua speakers — a horizon of identification-disidentification exclusively along the axis of Indianness. If the mestizo is, as Olivia Harris suggests, primarily a placeholder for "not Indian" (367), then it becomes available for a straightforward reversal of value. And this reversal — the double refusal with which I began this chapter — is an extremely potent instrument authorizing the subject of populism. Much like José María Arguedas would in the second half of his life, Lara could indeed authorize himself as a particular kind of mediator on the basis of native knowledge of Quechua: a bilingual mediator. He formulated his argument in such a way as to clear a space for the entry of an intellectual subject whose authority is positioned ambiguously between the authority of the native speaker and the authority of the intellectual and scholar.

In this sense, indigenismo can be said to have operated as a forum for a new class of socially ascending, educated, urban or newly urban provincials to enunciate and validate their Quechua–Spanish bilingualism, thus legitimating themselves as authentic spokesmen for Indians in a broader conflict of power with regional oligarchies. Lara, like others of his generation to whom he would refer as "lettered mestizos," used this consciously asserted bilingualism in order to gain intellectual authority and respect across otherwise antagonistic spheres of city and country, province and capital, in order to become a privileged mediator of an emergent national identity. Indigenista approaches to bilingualism like Lara's were thus part of a drive to center national identity on or in mestizos. And the first step in such a process is to confront the stigma attached to Quechua:

> El idioma de la raza madre es un estigma para la clase dirigente de Bolivia. El mestizo letrado imita al español de la colonia, ocultando además su origen bajo imaginarios blasones de nobleza y el indio enriquecido — también él — no vacila en seguir el ejemplo del mestizo. Nadie que se precia de civilizado, nadie que se siente capaz de hacerse entender en castellano se resigna a emplear el lenguaje materno, cada vez más desdeñado y relegado. Triste destino el de este idioma, única obra maestra que sobrevivió a sus creadores. (48)

> The language of the mother race is a stigma for Bolivia's ruling class. The lettered mestizo imitates the Spaniard of the colony, hiding his origin, furthermore, behind imaginary noble coats of arms, and the Indian who's gotten rich — he too — doesn't hesitate to follow the mestizo's example. No one who prides himself on being civilized, no one who feels capable of making himself understood in Spanish resigns himself to using the maternal language, increasingly disdained and abandoned. Sad destiny, that of this language, the only master work that survived its creators.

La poesía quechua, dedicated to stitching together as seamlessly as possible the history of the Quechua civilization with Bolivia's national history and with the history of the civilized "lettered city," attempts to establish that the mestizo's ability to move between Quechua and Spanish is a quality worth promoting rather than a source of shame. Combating the particular pressures of assimilation felt by lettered mestizos, and instilling in them the pride of their Indian heritage and language, becomes a significant, if veiled, message of the text. In both Bolivia and Peru, the mestizo's ability to move between Quechua and Spanish became, for the first time, a quality worth promoting rather than a source of shame. It was central to the idea that the mestizo is a dynamic agent of change, in fact the most dynamic national agent, and so of all the national subjects, the one most truly modern.

Antonio Cornejo Polar has written of indigenista texts that they operate a particular displacement away from the object of their discourse —

the Indian — and onto the subject enunciating the complaint against the oligarchic regime. This subject, the letrado author of the text, comes to occupy the center of the national stage, even if this subject is nowhere named in the text itself, and even if the figure of the Indian is ostensibly placed in this position as the text's protagonist (*Escribir* 189). Such would appear to be the case for the poetry anthology Lara produced. Although the figure of the "lettered mestizo" merits no more than a passing reference in Lara's text, its presence helps shift the focus of the essay, as Cornejo explains, away from the figure of the victimized Indian and onto the figure of the mestizo as victim; the mestizo defined here as the native speaker who has assimilated to the dominant culture and renounced his mother tongue.

By way of comparison, consider West Indian writer Derek Walcott's response to a recently published anthology of English literature from the eighteenth-century Caribbean. This anthology is made up of early texts and engravings by the English about their colonized island territories. These texts, Walcott writes, emit a "frowsty fragrance." He says,

> reading these texts that are hallowed by age requires an adjustment of mood. One must read like the historian, without moral judgements, to translate oneself into the tone of their time, which means for most West Indians, certainly the African and Indian and Chinese, a return to illiteracy. This is why the idea of a West Indian history wobbles on its pivot and ultimately collapses. (57)

Walcott's statement makes manifest the difficulty of establishing a line of literary descent stretching from this "frowsty" written tradition to the present production of letters in the Caribbean. Caribbean literary history is discontinuous, Walcott shows, because it is fractured by another history, the history of forced labor.

Both the novel *Surumi* and the anthology of Quechua literature that Lara produced likewise acknowledge the fracture implied by the history of Indian forced labor, a fracture that is registered at the level of national history and individual subjectivity. However, Lara's essay-anthology is designed in such a way as to bridge this gulf, by toppling this discontinuous national history and its subjects and erecting continuity in their place. The idea of a Bolivian history is rescued from collapse, because Lara maps his Quechua literary canon onto the already established timeline of Bolivian national history. It extends this timeline back to an anterior point not previously recognized as belonging to national history, but this does not decenter the primacy of the nation as the canon's structuring principle. It is not, in other words, a canon meant to ground the emergence of a separate and alternative Quechua national identity existing within the body of the Bolivian nation. Rarely, if ever, does Lara speak of the distinctive nature of Quechua identity as against Bolivian identity in order to prove "[its] essential right to a separate national destiny," as David Lloyd has shown was the case with Irish canon formations (*Nationalism* 3). Rather, as I have argued, Lara recenters Bolivian national identity *around* Quechua, and around its new speakers. The historical fracture of the conquest is thus sutured by Quechua, the Inca empire's only remaining trace of majesty, and through which he imagines a more modern majesty may yet be constructed.

Although mestizo nationalism was — and is — exclusionary, it nevertheless mobilizes and renders significant an experience of self-negation that was — and is — more or less widely shared, and puts forward a narrative of authentic self-realization that, as Rivera's comments suggest, continues to inform the oppositional politics of socially mobile sectors in the Andes. Rivera's "passage through the looking glass" was taken up by thinkers like Lara because it linked the unfinished work of decolonization — the incomplete nation — to an individual phenomenology of oppression. This is how Zavaleta describes the phenomenology of incomplete decolonization, in words that echo Lara's words from 1927:

> La incursión del extranjero en la vida propia nos impone un desarraigo, una enajenación que nos quiere mansos y sin astucia en una cueva hecha de miedo, materia prima incapaz de sí misma, extraños a nuestra propia naturaleza, a nuestra historia, a nuestros intereses, a nosostros mismos, babiecas sumisos a las formas ajenas. (42)

> The incursion of the foreigner in our own life imposes on us an uprooting, an alienation that wants us docile and dumb in a cave made of fear, raw material that is intrinsically incapable, strangers to our own nature, our history, our interests, ourselves, idiots submitting to alien forms.

The turn toward the disempowered, when couched as a turn to authentic self, was thus understood as also personally redemptive.

But this common ground of shame is the result of a significant elision between indigenous and cholo or mestizo experiences of exclusion.

Surumi and *La poesía quechua* establish a continuity between Indian suffering on the plantation and Indian suffering at school, but this continuity is superficial. Both involve enslavement and liberation, yet this metaphorical analogy is built across very different experiences of unfreedom. This elision reflects prerevolutionary alliance politics in Cochabamba, which married distinct experiences of oppression, of "enslavement," into one. In *Surumi* and *La poesía quechua,* one of these experiences refers to enslavement as a social system: it is represented by the pongo and the hacienda labor regime. The other refers to enslavement as a more ambiguous figure for subjectivity itself, for feeling and desire. It is represented on the one hand by the student's new-found love of writing, which "subjugates" him, and on the other by the feelings of inferiority he has internalized as a result of the racial stigma attached to him.

These latter forms of enslavement are proper to someone who has entered a sphere of formal equality — the school — but who finds himself living in the gap between ideal or abstract equality before the law and "the moral particulars of civil society," as Wendy Brown writes. Both Lara's Wáskar Puma and his autobiographical self-projection in *La poesía quechua* are examples of the liberal subject who has been "ideally emancipated" yet remains "practically resubordinated" (Brown 106). He longs to be destigmatized, to become unmarked, a desire that will be consistently thwarted until it becomes, resentfully, its opposite: the double refusal, the overt proclamation of filial loyalty to the race. Undertaken by "lettered mestizos" or "hijos de la cholada" — both names with which Lara had occasion to refer to himself — this rhetoric of refusal would resonate among large sectors of the population, becoming a key element of the hegemony of Bolivia's populist nationalism.

Chapter Three

José María Arguedas
and the Mediating Voice

El desgarramiento, más que de los quechuismos, de las palabras
quechuas, es otra hazaña lenta y difícil. ¡Se trata de no perder el
alma, de no transformarse por entero en esta larga y lenta empresa!
Yo sé que algo se pierde a cambio de lo que se gana. Pero el cuidado,
la vigilia, el trabajo, es por guardar la esencia.

Excising the Quechua words is an even longer and more arduous
feat than taking out the Quechua turns of phrase. It is a question of
not losing one's soul, of not being completely transformed by this
long, slow undertaking! But care must be taken and one must be
vigilant and work to retain the essence.

— José María Arguedas, "La novela y el problema
de la expresión literaria en el Perú"

This passage by José María Arguedas, taken from his seminal essay "La
novela y el problema de la expresión literaria en el Perú" [The Novel
and the Problem of Literary Expression in Peru], refers concretely to the
central dilemma of his process of literary construction: how to eliminate
Quechua words and "quechua-isms" from his writing without losing the
essence of what he wished to communicate.[1] It was also a formulation
that Arguedas used to describe the dilemma for the Quechua speaker
learning Spanish, i.e., for those gaining a new degree of social mobility
in a diglossic society. This linguistic process of acquisition and loss was
a central aspect of the cultural transformation taking place in the Andes;
Arguedas described it in all his work. Extrapolated to another level, it
can be taken as the description of an intellectual, abstracting stance on
Latin American modernization, at a time when modernization seemed
to imply global cultural homogenization: how modernizing nations integrate themselves into a developmentalist global order without giving up

something essential. This is a stance Arguedas adopted, notably in the last decade of his life, making the connection between this dilemma and his more intimate life and labors as novelist.

One of the most influential scholarly works on Arguedas since his death, Angel Rama's *Transculturación narrativa en América Latina* (Narrative Transculturation in Latin America) (1982), follows the author through the steps of this metaphorical concatenation built around the theme of change and permanence.[2] Arguedas's dilemma tapped into and expressed a desire that had become generalized among certain literary intellectuals by the mid-1970s: a desire that literature preserve something threatened with extinction. This became a desire for the mestizo, understood as the conduit for, and the living manifestation of, primordial indigenous spirit in the modern world.

Such a desire already circulated in 1950s Peru, though affixed to the role of the mestizo ethnographer rather than the novelist. In 1955, at a symposium in honor of "the illustrious mestizo" Inca Garcilaso de la Vega, Peruvian indigenista ethnologist Luis E. Valcárcel praised the Inca's ability to move "de adentro para afuera" [from the inside out]: from inside indigenous culture to the outside world. Valcárcel was at the time the Head of the Comité Interamericano de Folklore (Arguedas was the secretary). His words describe the importance and singularity of Garcilaso's *Comentarios reales* (Royal Commentaries) in terms that are highly significant for understanding the posthumous critical reception of Arguedas's novel *Los ríos profundos* (The Deep Rivers) (1958). Valcárcel accorded the Inca, an Indian who was also a mestizo — a confusing superimposition of identities characteristic of Arguedas (as well as Lara) — a founding and exemplary role in the creation of an authentically national ethnographic practice. Garcilaso "understood" Indian culture "from within" and transmitted this understanding "outward" (Valcárcel, "Garcilaso" 146). His capacity to cross boundaries by virtue of his dual belonging was framed by Valcárcel in terms of "unification" and "integration," words that became the centerpiece of Valcárcel's textual interpretation of the *Comentarios* and which led him to proclaim the Inca "creator of the Peruvian patria" (147).

"From the inside out" and "creator of the Peruvian patria" are catchphrases, recurring tropes in the celebration of the Indian-as-mestizo. Several more tropes found in Valcárcel's piece, and in the discussion that followed it during the symposium, round out this complex portrait.

Valcárcel drew attention to Garcilaso's special "empathy," so necessary for ethnography, Valcárcel argued, because through it Garcilaso
establishes "an intimate communication" (Valcárcel 140). He affirmed
Garcilaso's originality, in the sense of "the first," textually creating and
personally embodying "a new being" and "a new consciousness" (160).
On a slightly darker note, all the symposium participants reflected on
Garcilaso's psychological instability, marked by an internal "oscillation"
between Indian and Spaniard (150), and they spoke of the "tragedy"
of his bilingualism and biculturalism, which a Cuzqueño participant at
the symposium claimed proper to all Cuzqueños (152). Finally, turning to his textual practices, they celebrated his aesthetic achievement.
Valcárcel noted that Garcilaso's poetry represents the transferral to art
of magic and religion, and that Garcilaso infuses his poetic creation with
"a profound cosmic feeling" (154). It is precisely this feeling, another
participant will imply, that contemporary European culture has traded
in for materialism (161).

Empathetic and intimate boundary crossing; originality, integration,
and cosmic infusion; instability and tragedy: this description of Garcilaso
offers a remarkably useful template for interpreting Arguedas's life. These
tropes can all be found, in one way or another, in much of Arguedas's
literary and para-literary work, in his writings on Andean life, and also
in the greater part of the critical literature on Arguedas and *Los ríos
profundos*. The possibility of penetration without violence and of intimate knowledge without power, in short, of ethnography without its
colonizing function; the possibility of political-economic integration —
modernization — without its soul-destroying component, and of its aesthetic corollary, the interiorization of tragic social divisions heroically
sublimated by an integrating textual practice: these elements coalesce in
the lasting portrait of Arguedas. This is especially true of Angel Rama's
image of him, though he was not the only one to take up these terms.
Before Rama published *Transculturación narrativa,* posthumous critical
reception already focused on the presence of an indigenous worldview
in the novel, as a way to mark the novel's rupture with previous indigenista works and to identify the powerful coherence and consistency
of its vision.[3] Rama, however, systematized this approach, inserting it
within a narrative of grander proportions: the struggle of premodern
lifeways to survive modernity. This involved adopting key concepts from
structural anthropology, such as "pensar mítico" [mythic thought] and
"pensée sauvage" [the savage mind]. But it also involved the deployment

of a developmentalist literary history that was global in scope, in which Andean indigenous aesthetic expression was made equivalent to European popular culture of the late Middle Ages: both were oral-based and threatened with the Book. *Los ríos profundos* is transculturating, Rama argued, because "mythic thought" and "orality" have been structurally integrated with their opposites: modern historicism and lettered culture, respectively. And Arguedas achieved this synthesis because he knew indigenous culture from the inside and could bring it out: "Él [Arguedas], como las montañas andinas, buscó resguardar una tradición, aquella que conformó para él su universo infantil más pleno, y reinsertarla dentro de las culturas modernas de la dominación" [Arguedas, like the mountains of the Andes, sought to save a tradition that shaped his fullest childhood universe, and to insert it into the modern cultures of domination] (*Transculturación* 172). Thus *Los ríos profundos,* like other transculturated novels, achieved what Rama called "fidelidad al espíritu" [faithfulness to spirit] (*Transculturación* 123).

The image of the mestizo-as-Indian that Arguedas became for himself and for others relied on two self-projections that require extensive re-examining. The first revolves around the matter of Arguedas's cultural authenticity. Like Garcilaso, he was a mestizo who often self-identified as a nonacculturated Indian. Arguedas based this on formative childhood experiences: he was raised by Indians, first in the hacienda kitchen, later in an ayllu community; and he spoke only Quechua until adolescence.[4] Recent scholarship has now debunked nearly all aspects of this view and shown it to be a myth. Roland Forgues shows that Arguedas was fully bilingual as a young child ("El mito" 49). Alberto Flores Galindo points out that his earliest published work clearly thematized his own sense of nonbelonging to Indian communities (*Buscando* 328), while Amy Fass Emery, in her analysis of both his fiction and his essays on folklore, argues that Arguedas's narrative gaze had a marked tendency to project itself from above, desirous of the control and mastery such a perspective afforded, in colonialist style (Emery 50–54). John Landreau, finally, argues that it was not until the 1950s that Arguedas began publicly to establish a relationship between his childhood experiences and his fiction, creating an "autobiographical legend" based on his identification as an Indian that would become the basis for future interpretations of his work (Landreau 212–14). His self-identification as Indian, notes Landreau, so crucial to this legend, was noticeably absent in earlier work. In 1938 in his *Canto kechwa,* for example, Arguedas had clearly distinguished himself from "authentic" Indians (*Canto kechwa* 18).

Unlike the aggressive attempt by Vargas Llosa to consign Arguedas to the dustbin of history by unveiling the illusions at the heart of his self-construction, revisions like these actually help to better illuminate not only the particular contradictions of Arguedas's life and work, but of a whole generation of influential Latin American literary analysis constructed specifically on the critical appreciation of his fiction. Both Angel Rama's theory of narrative transculturation and Antonio Cornejo Polar's theory of literary heterogeneity were built on a foundation of Arguedian analysis, itself built on biographical "facts" that constructed Arguedas as privileged insider.

The second projection instrumental in promoting this redemptive view, and the one to which this chapter is dedicated to examining, is the idea that the mestizo's social function is primarily to serve as a mediating agent, moving within a society that has been modeled in dual terms, composed of two distinct, antagonistic worlds: the unchanging, integral, and interior world where indigeneity resides, and the rapidly transforming, fragmented, and exterior world of the modernizing nation. Rama has argued that Arguedas, like other transculturators, is a mediator between the "regional-interior" and "external-universal" dialectic that constitutes the limits of Latin America. The mestizo is, in this celebration of *Los ríos profundos,* a conduit for the Indian voice and spirit, operating in the service of an ideal social body often referred to as the Arguedian utopia: an interconnected world freed from conflictive inner divisions. By the end of his life, Arguedas had effectively become this person in his public self-projection, as his comments on receiving the Inca Garcilaso de la Vega Prize in 1968 demonstrate: "intenté convertir en lenguaje escrito lo que era como individuo: un vínculo vivo, fuerte, capaz de universalizarse, de la gran nación cercada y la parte generosa, humana de los opresores" ("No soy" 257) [I attempted to transform into written language what I was as an individual: a strong living link, capable of being universalized, between the great, besieged nation and the generous, human side of the oppressors ("I Am Not" 269)].[5]

This chapter questions the construction of the mestizo as "living link," as mediator between Indian culture and the most "human" aspect of the dominant Hispanic culture, and as preserver of essence, specifically of indigenous "soul." How did he bring these qualities into his written language, and how and why did his technique for doing so change over the course of his career? What is the relation between these concepts and Arguedas's changing concepts of Peru as a mestizo nation? What is the nature of the intimate connection between Indian and non-Indian spheres that Arguedas was trying to communicate in his literary prose?

Like most critics of Arguedas, I have developed my arguments by keeping his writing about his own life and fiction in the foreground of my analysis, especially his writings from the late 1930s and early 1940s, a very productive period of his life. This attention to his own writings, in my case, is not because "Arguedas on Arguedas" is the ultimate authority for my interpretations, but rather because I seek to offer a more nuanced account of Arguedas's changing concept of the mestizo: to develop an account of how the mestizo imagination develops in a diglossic society across the "interlocutory void" that constitutes "the predicament of the Spanish-American autobiographer," as Sylvia Molloy writes (4). Equally important, the return to key writings is undertaken in order to emphasize how he framed his conflicts as a writer in a quasi-religious idiom that has since fallen out of the critical vocabulary, using terms such as essence, soul, innocence, limpidity, spiritual intimacy, and spiritual conflict. Critics such as Cornejo Polar, Alberto Moreiras, John Beverley, and others have shown the extent to which transculturation becomes a code word for hegemonic mestizaje, i.e., for a program of indigenous cultural valorization and integration through political and economic subordination to the state.[6] Arguedas endowed these social transformations with the language of spiritual redemption, and this language requires reexamination if one is to understand what the mestizo signified for him in general, and for *Los ríos profundos* in particular; if one is to understand how this novel performs its integrating, mediating, communicative work; and if one is to understand the position that Quechua indigeneity is made to occupy at mid-twentieth-century and after.

Finally, Arguedas's descriptions of what he hoped his fiction would achieve and of the struggles he experienced in the process of creation bring out a component of his authorial enunciation that has been seriously downplayed in the critical literature. I refer concretely to his Quechua–Spanish bilingualism. The primary reason for this tendency to forego analysis of the bilingual inscription derives from the polemically personalized nature of much Arguedas criticism. Much like Arguedas himself, his posthumous interpreters have reacted as if stung by those who imputed political and aesthetic naïveté to Arguedas. As a consequence their criticism is very often couched as a defense of the author, a defense that rests on establishing that Arguedas's art was artifice rather than unmediated self-expression. Judging from how the first generation of his critics, many of them his friends or colleagues, framed their approach to his work, biographical readings of his prose are positively dangerous, for they seem to lend credence to the idea that Arguedas was not a technically accomplished artist. Thus Alberto Escobar insists that Arguedas's literary language has nothing whatsoever to do with his bilingual condition. In approaching an author's style and language, writes Escobar, one must address it as "artifice," and as such, one makes no distinction between a monolingual, bilingual, or multilingual writer (Escobar, *Arguedas* 66). My own critical readings of Arguedas, however, presuppose exactly the opposite, namely, that an author's linguistic situation can have a profound effect on his literary language, and that in Arguedas's case, in fact it does. I suspect that, were it not for the peculiar circumstances surrounding the reception of Arguedas's work in 1960s Peru, such an approach would constitute obvious common ground.

However, there is also another reason that explains why the bilingual inscription of Arguedas's prose has been subject to relatively little analysis. Many critics have addressed the cultural divides between the indigenous and the nonindigenous world that Arguedas attempted to cross in his prose fiction by showing how these divides are integrated into the work of art as a problem of literary form. As it appears in the work of many critics, this problem can be summarized as follows: Indian literary expression is oral, either song or story, whereas Western literary expression is written. Sara Castro-Klaren sums up the distinction like so: "Por un lado está el lenguaje, la educación sentimental del Quechua como sistema y ámbito lingüístico *oral* y por el otro está el lenguaje y sistema de *literatura* en español" [On one side is the language and the sentimental education of Quechua as an *oral* linguistic system and field, and on the other is the language and system of *literatura* in Spanish] (100, original emphasis). Confronted with oral culture, Martin Lienhard explains, "el texto escrito tiende a estallar, a fragmentarse" [the written text tends to shatter, to become fragmented] (129). Thus Arguedas, like other writers who drew from popular culture, had to figure out how to express in writing something that would naturally have occurred in song or story (Cornejo, "Indigenismo" 18; Rama, *Transculturación,* 43–48).

Critics have consequently searched for the traces of this conflict between writing and orality, occidental and nonoccidental cultures, in the fiction itself, where the conflict either has been harmoniously resolved or tragically laid bare, or simply persists as an underlying duality, as the case may be. And they have tended to transform orality from an attribute into an identifying, if not essential, feature of indigenous culture. The question of cultural conflict has been posed, then, as one of fidelity or betrayal: how can Arguedas be true to the Indian world when he has taken up the tools of its oppressors to express it?

Yet Arguedas's obsession with fidelity was not posed in such protonationalist terms. He framed the problem rather differently: how can he be true to his aural memory of the world he grew up in if that world knew Quechua but the world in which he writes does not? That aural memory is a challenge to capture and communicate, not because it is oral (for most childhood memories of the verbal environment are of things heard, not read or written), but because it took place in Quechua yet must be communicated to a non-Quechua-speaking audience. This chapter thus addresses *Los ríos profundos* as a meditation on the bilingual condition, and dwells on Arguedas's art of translation as well as, in one case, his art of mistranslation.[7] Arguedas's language can be understood as the result of what Martinican writer Edouard Glissant would term "une poétique forcée," a forced poetics. Adopting a distinction between "language as a collective practice" and *langue* as a system of signs (in the sense meant by Saussure), Glissant writes:

> A forced poetic arises there where the need to express confronts something impossible to express. This confrontation can become tied up in the opposition between expressible content and the suggested or imposed language [Saussure's "langue" or the system of signs].... One has to clear a space through the sign system toward a language [i.e., collective practice] which may not exist within the internal logic of that system. A forced poetic emerges from the awareness of this opposition between the sign system one uses and the language one needs. (Glissant 236–37, my translation)

Arguedas, in other words, was forced to develop a way to use Spanish to express a content belonging to Quechua. That content consisted in part of his own memory of Quechua speech and song, and thus remained intimately connected to his own personal experience: how to express his own memory? But the content belonging to Quechua also consisted, for him, of particular kinds of verbal experiences, most especially onomatopoeia, that he believed could occur only in Quechua as a consequence of its particular linguistic nature.

In *Los ríos profundos,* the narrative persona Arguedas created to speak in a redeeming language and voice is figured as a messenger for Quechua as soul or spirit, moving between a profound indigenous interior and a violently divided exterior, the fragmented world of the liberal nation-state. As many critics have shown, that interior is a natural world, whole and internally interconnected; its spirit is made of song, and it is song that keeps it interconnected. This view of the novel will remain more or less intact in my arguments. But the question of the symbolic form to which this vision has been attached will be reconfigured in light of Arguedas's bilingualism. My aim is to reconsider the redemptive aspects of *Los ríos profundos,* Arguedas's most widely celebrated novel, on the level of its personal inscription, that is, in the voice and language of its first-person narrator, focusing specifically on the figure of the bilingual mediator or messenger as emblematic of the mestizo. Thus in what follows I begin with an extensive reexamination of the first-person narrative voice of *Los ríos profundos* and the peculiar "I" that Arguedas subtly constructed. I then argue that the link between spirit and orality cannot be understood without a third term, the Quechua language. The spatial enframing of "interior culture" and "exterior culture" was primarily a question of language for Arguedas, of being "inside" or "outside" Quechua. Quechua was, in other words, the heart of his conception of indigeneity. The mediating voice in *Los ríos profundos* is thus first and foremost the projection of a bilingual voice, but this bilingual voice, as I will show, contrasts sharply, in both form and symbolic significance, to the other bilingual voices that he projected over the course of his career. Translation, self-translation, and mistranslation will be the terms that structure my arguments: that Arguedas managed to communicate a particular quality of Quechua, its iconicity (onomatopoeia), in Spanish, a language with far fewer sound-symbolic resources, through a translating practice composed of elaborate metaphor; that this kind of translation came to replace Arguedas's earlier literary technique, named "mistura," which he had described as mestizo self-translation, i.e., communication of the inner self; and finally, that he modeled the novel's narrator on a common literary trope found in Quechua songs, the figure of the bird as messenger to the absent beloved, partially as the result of his mistranslation of a key Quechua intertext.

The Innocent Voice

Literary analyses of narrative voice in *Los ríos profundos* from the 1970s and 1980s tend to be enmeshed in the cultural politics that developed in the wake of the Boom around the universality (read: commercial viability) or not of given authors. Critical work by Angel Rama and Julio Ortega on this novel is overtly interested in celebrating the technical complexity of its construction in order to reclaim Arguedas as a master narrator who belongs in the same "universal" category as Rulfo, García Márquez, Cortázar, etc. (Rama, *Transculturación* 229). The main thrust of these analyses has been to downplay or reject autobiographical readings of the novel—that its "I" is an autobiographical projection of Arguedas—because they do not want to provide any more fuel for what Ortega terms the "obscurantist idea" that Arguedas was a naif with the same Rousseau-ian view of nature as his narrator, an idea promoted most notably by Mario Vargas Llosa in his *La utopía arcaica*. "La verdad es más compleja" [The truth is more complicated], insists Ortega (18).

Arguedas himself makes this critical recapture difficult. In the years immediately before his death, Arguedas tendentiously asserted a view of himself as different from his peers on the matter of literary technique, as made manifest in his comments on various Latin American writers in a "Diary" that he knew would be read by others ("Primer Diario" in *El zorro* 10–12) and his interventions at the 1965 Primer Encuentro de Narradores Peruanos in Arequipa. On this latter, particularly notorious occasion, Arguedas promoted the idea that he started as an "innocent" writer, who used personal feeling and raw experience rather than technical mastery to craft his writing. He spoke of how he approached the writing of what would become his first published story, "Warma kuyay":

> La realidad es que cuando empecé a escribir yo no tenía la menor idea de que hubieran técnicas para escribir. Yo comencé a escribir porque tenía una necesidad irrestible de enunciar, de describir el mundo que yo había vivido en la infancia.... Lo escribí ("Warma kuyay") en un estado total de inocencia en cuanto a la técnica y ha resultado siendo el mejor de los que he escrito. (*Primer Encuentro* 171)

> The truth is that when I started to write I hadn't the least idea that there were techniques of writing. I began to write because I felt an

> irresistible need to speak, to describe the world in which I'd lived
> as a child.... I wrote [the story "Warma Kuyay"] in an utter state
> of innocence with respect to technique, and it has turned out to be
> the best story I've written.

Many of those present immediately seized this affirmation and twisted
it against him, essentially accusing him of naïveté for thinking he was
naïve. "There is no state of innocence," Salazar Bondy corrected him
(*Primer Encuentro* 180).

There is much to suggest, if one reads the full transcript from this
conference, that Arguedas's claims of technical innocence were reactive,
self-promoting interventions; like any number of writers, he constructed
a public persona around controversial or eccentric attitudes. Yet certainly
in the past and in private he had bristled when accused of technical
naiveté.[8] A decade after his death, however, this attitude, combined with
the obviously complex construction of *Los ríos profundos,* became for
Rama a further instance of the redemptive possibility of transculturation:
Arguedas had managed to preserve an unwordly, local identity, obtaining
"faithfulness to spirit" within a highly integrated and complex modern novel, i.e., in and through its modernizing technology. Thus, Rama
writes, "nuestro propósito es registrar los exitosos esfuerzos de componer
un discurso literario a partir de fuertes tradiciones propias mediante
plásticas transculturaciones que no se rinden a la modernización sino
que la utilizan para fines propios" [Our aim is to register the successful
efforts to compose a literary discourse on the basis of strong traditions by
means of flexible transculturations that do not submit to modernization
but rather use it for their own ends] (*Transculturación* 75).

My reading of the novel will refocus these issues in two ways. First,
though the category of innocence is highly significant for understanding
narrative voice in *Los ríos profundos,* Arguedas's language is closer to a
moral and theological idiom than to the Weberian framework implicit in
Rama's analysis. For the narrator, innocence is not threatened by modernization and technological disenchantment, but rather by original sin
and worldliness, i.e., corrupting knowledge. The protagonist's story unfolds in "the world of men," a world of boundaries and conflict, but
the narrator, in a passage I will discuss below, tells us that he originally
comes from "the region" of bird song, a diffuse immaterial realm from
which he was torn. The narrative as a whole takes place between these
two places, one corrupt, the other innocent.

Second, the fear and confusion about the autobiographical nature of this novel misses an obvious point: there is in fact an autobiographical inscription here, since the novel is composed of a narrating "I" who recounts past events from his life. The challenge in dealing with this inscription is not to identify this persona's relation to Arguedas — is he or is he not Arguedas? — but rather his relation to the novel's protagonist-hero, a fourteen-year old boy to whom it is difficult to affix a proper name and who is often confused with the narrator. My reading emerges from the fact that these two personae are recognizably different, that they have distinct "personalities," for lack of a better word. One provides an intensely subjective, emotionally intimate point of view, while the other is disembodied, unobtrusive, and anonymous. This disjunction, furthermore, cannot be accounted for in terms of the combination of "magic" plus "realism," or "spirit" plus "science."

Los ríos profundos is narrated primarily from a first-person perspective, in an autobiographical mode: recounting past events, the narrating "I" is presumably an older version of the novel's fourteen-year-old hero (*Transculturación* 272). The novel often appears to have been narrated from the perspective of this child — a point to which I will return in a moment — but technically speaking, this cannot be the case. On purely temporal grounds, a distinction between narrator and protagonist must be recognized. The first sentence of the novel, which describes "el Viejo" [The Old Man] — "Infundía respeto, a pesar de su anticuada y sucia apariencia" (21) [He inspired respect, in spite of his old-fashioned and dirty appearance (3)] — reveals the temporal distance between narrator and protagonist, for it presents this portrait of the protagonist's uncle several sentences "before" the protagonist actually meets him. As it is set up at the novel's opening, this temporal distance means that the narrator knows more than his protagonist about the situations and events of that protagonist's life. The difference between narrator and protagonist in Arguedas's novel corresponds to Genette's narratological distinction between "point of view" and "voice" (Genette 186). To the question "who sees?" i.e., from whose perspective is the story focused, the answer in *Los ríos profundos* is, "usually the boy hero." To the question "who speaks?" i.e., who narrates? the answer is, "usually the boy become an adult."

There is nevertheless enough slippage in the narration to render insufficient this basic identification of the narrator as the child-become-adult. The narrator does not just recount the life of the hero, but rather dwells extensively on matters that are tangential to the events of his life; matters that are in fact not organized narratively in terms of events, but rather through elaborate present-tense description. Faced with the complexity of the narrative voice in *Los ríos profundos,* many critics have proposed that the novel contains separate, multiple narrators. In addition to the autobiographical narrator, whom Rama calls the "Principal Narrator," is another who has been identified as a cultural mediator. Rama goes so far as to name him "the Ethnologist" (*Transculturación* 270). Ortega has argued that they are not separate entities, but rather separate manifestations of a plural Narrator, singular yet possessing several identifiable voices that often blend together while also establishing themselves as distinct (Ortega 17). As in Rama's analysis, one of these manifestations is a kind of cultural translator, communicating to the author's intended audience, namely, cultural outsiders.

These interpretations highlight the communicative and intercultural aspects of the work, stressing (and rightly so) the extent to which Arguedas embedded a consciousness of the narrative's implied audience — non-Andean, non-Quechua-speaking readers of Spanish — into the novel. But these critics' investment in the novel's pluri-vocality is also determined by a desire to make of this novel a model for the ideal of the modern nation-state: a Peru whose cultural plurality is nevertheless governed by unity and integration. The novel's indigenous voice or perspective, by this reading, has been framed and organized by a non-indigenous voice, whose task it is to help "us" understand the more obscure elements of the indigenous worldview, yet without disrupting the overall unity of the novel.

In fact it is impossible to separate these narrators out from one another in terms of their respective cultural identities, to determine when we are in the presence of an indigenous narrator (or an Indian-identified narrator), and when we are in the presence of a nonindigenous, highly knowledgeable ethnologist. To do so involves artificially breaking down linguistically and thematically unified passages, even sentences. For example, a segment taken from one of the novel's most famous passages illustrates how separating out "the Ethnologist" from the "principal narrator" requires one to break down the sentences into separate clauses, as if these were so many component parts of a complexly assembled machine:

> Era estático el muro, pero hervía por todas sus líneas y la superficie era cambiante, como la de los ríos en el verano, que tienen una

cima así, hacia el centro del caudal, que es la zona temible, la más poderosa. Los indios llaman "yawar mayu" a esos ríos turbios, porque muestran con el sol un brillo en movimiento, semejante al de la sangre. (26)

The wall was stationary, but all its lines were seething and its surface was as changeable as that of the flooding summer rivers that have similar crests near the center, where the current flows the swiftest and is the most terrifying. The Indians call these muddy rivers *yawar mayu* because when the sun shines on them they seem to glisten like blood. (7)

We might say that the second sentence of the two just quoted is the work of the "ethnological" narrator, since it uses the explanatory "eternal present" mode of ethnographic description, a description centered on what "they" — "Indians" — say or do. Regarding the first sentence, however, a clear identification is impossible; one has to say that it is mixed between the two narrators: it starts with the primary narrator, then shifts to the ethnological narrator with the present-tense clause "that have...."

This ethnological narrator is imagined to be situated both inside and outside of the Andes, or somewhere in between. But "ethnologist" does not really explain all that this narrator "does," that is, he is not limited to displays of learned analysis, of objective knowledge, of cultural information; he is also a vehicle for the transmission of intimate subjective knowledge. His "information" tends often to slide into intimation, intuition, or just plain longing. Consider the following two sentences:

El arrayán, los lambras, el sauce, el eucalipto, el capulí, la tara, son árboles de madera limpia, cuyas ramas y hojas se recortan libremente. El hombre los contempla desde lejos; y quien busca sombra se acerca a ellos y reposa bajo un árbol que canta solo, con una voz profunda, en que los cielos, el agua y la tierra se confunden. (47)

The myrtle, the *lambras,* the weeping willow, the eucalyptus, the *capulí,* and the *tara* are all clean-wooded trees whose branches and leaves may be trimmed frequently. Contemplating them from afar, whoever seeks shade approaches them and rests under a tree that sings alone in a deep voice in which water, earth, and sky mingle. (24)

The ethnological view starts with a statement of what appears to be natural fact and then moves to a description of human experience that, given how most people have read this novel, has been inferred to be the experience of "Andean man," though in the sentence itself, the word "man" is culturally or geographically unmarked (hence the translation into English as "whoever"). Then, in the subtle shift so characteristic of Arguedas's sentences, the initial reporting of what such men do is transformed into a different kind of utterance, not ethnological, but rather the direct expression of such a man's experience of the natural world: "rests under a tree *that sings alone in a deep voice*" (emphasis mine). This narrator, that is, tends to forget where he is or to whom he is speaking, ceases to translate culturally, and blurs the line between himself and the scene he describes: he becomes one with it.

Furthermore, he tends implicitly to affirm the particular experience of the protagonist, thus subtly situating the omniscient perspective in a subjective location. When he describes in detail the flight of birds in a particular town and then notes that only travelers notice these details — "La gente del lugar no observa estos detalles, pero los viajeros, la gente que ha de irse, no los olvida" (48–49) [The people who live there do not observe these details, but travelers, people who must leave, never forget them (25)] — we know that he has made the singular experience of the protagonist (the central traveler of the tale) the source of this general statement. The effect is to authorize the protagonist's experience, memory, and knowledge to lend it the weight of an eternal, impersonal truth. Yet it is far from being, for all that, the "objective source of information on the Peruvian ethnological reality" that Rama claimed (*Transculturación* 277).

It is impossible to determine whether the narrator is experiencing Andean culture from the inside or the outside. The attempt to restore clearly marked boundaries by naming distinct narrative positions, by identifying what is proper to each voice, thus runs counter to the narrator's apparent ignorance of, or disregard for, such a system of cultural enframing. I would argue, then, that past critics have insisted on marking primal differences the better to celebrate the integrating function of the mestizo mediator. It is as if, in the absence of this distinction, the revolutionary action of the novel, its rupture with tradition and its originality, could not be appreciated. It is this action that allowed Arguedas to break from the limits of regionalism and indigenismo, as Rama argues of all "narrative transculturators," and to step down from the superior and distant position of the folklorist, as Silvia Spitta argues (145).

And yet the novel is simultaneously omniscient and subjective. The impulse to classify the novel's narrative voice by breaking it down according to discrete categories is understandable: it responds to the difficulty of properly identifying this voice, which goes beyond the autobiographical inscription. There is a particular quality to this narrator that defies his categorization as just the older or adult version of the hero. I mean the remarkably self-effacing nature of the narrator, his tendency to be present without making himself known, except *as* the hero. Almost no information about the narrator — the storyteller, presumably in the present — is provided. We know he is different from the hero, because older and more knowledgeable. We do not know, however, *how much* older or wiser. There is no explicit framing of the story of the past from the perspective of the present, as one might expect in a more classic fictional autobiography or memoir.[9] In *Los ríos profundos*, although a few signs are present to indicate that time has elapsed between the events and their telling — the use of the past tense, the difference between what narrator and hero know — none is temporally precise; the reader does not know whether the narrator is five or fifty years older than the protagonist.[10]

As a result of this lack of information about the narrator, the relationship between himself and the child remains undefined. Though he knows more than his hero, he demonstrates no condescension toward the protagonist, no ironic superiority. The distance between them is not expressed in terms of a repudiation or even a qualification of the younger self's views. Nor does this narrator communicate nostalgia or a longing for the period he recounts from the perspective of the present. Arguedas thus places the reader in the presence of an extremely circumspect persona, who says nothing about where he is as he narrates, when he narrates, what effects the narrated events have on him as he narrates, or how they determined the course of his life. The narrator of *Los ríos profundos* is in this regard completely anonymous. Distanced, unobtrusive, and disembodied, he accords the child protagonist an enormous degree of autonomy. So great is this autonomy that it often misleads one to think that it is the child who is narrating. The narrator in effect allows his younger self's point of view, dominated by the intensity of his adolescent emotions and the fervor of his beliefs, to guide the narrative. As Cornejo has argued, the distance between them is covered over by the use of the first person, providing the effect of a singular identity (*Universos* 103).

Only a few exceedingly brief self-referential moments offset, albeit obliquely, the narrator's anonymity and bring us closer to the matter of his identity. These are moments when the narrator refers to himself in the present tense, as in the following sentence, when he describes the ayllu community in which he lived as a child: "Los jefes de familia y las señoras, mamakunas de la comunidad, me protegieron y me infundieron la impagable ternura en que *vivo*" (70, emphasis added) [The family chiefs and the older women, the *mamakunas* of the community protected me and instilled in me that kindness in which I *live* (42, emphasis added)]. And later, speaking of a bird as the protagonist waits with his friend on the street in Abancay: "Su canto transmite los secretos de los valles profundos.... ¡Tuya, tuya! Mientras oía su canto, que es, seguramente, la materia de que *estoy hecho*, la difusa región de donde me arrancaron para lanzarme entre los hombres, vimos aparecer en la alameda a las dos niñas" (209, emphasis added) [Its song transmits the secrets of the deep valleys.... *Tuya, tuya!* As I listened to its song, which is surely the stuff of which I *am made*, that nebulous region from which I was torn to be cast in among men, we saw the two girls appear in the poplar grove (149)]. In these surprising moments, the speaker interposes himself into the story of the seer and momentarily speaks for himself, not just as or for the protagonist. There is thus a brief conjoining of voice and point of view in what could be termed a collective "location": speaker and seer come from the same two unbounded places, the "diffuse region" of bird song and the motherly tenderness of the ayllu, also a region of song. It is only because of this shared origin in the immaterial region of song that the narrator and the protagonist can be said to be one and the same, and that the narrator can be said to be recounting a story about himself.

Yet because these origins are unbounded and immaterial, they suggest a place and a time where/when there is presence yet not identity, in the sense of a bounded self-sameness. These particular origin stories thus tip us off to the fact that we are not reading a secular autobiography and that the novel will be implicitly organized around the distinction between these diffuse, immaterial regions of sound and bounded, material regions; between the eternal region where something like the soul resides — the sky, the heavens, the inner self — and the temporal earth. The novel would then become not just a truncated autobiography, the story of a youth on his way to manhood, a story that does not get very far in *Los ríos profundos;* it would also be a spiritual autobiography, detailing a very different kind of journey. In fact the novel is not a coming-of-age story, that is, the protagonist does not change and grow over the course of the months. On the contrary, he resists all change, understood as maturation; and the narrative is structured by a series of what Rama terms "illuminations," which he likens to moments of divine inspiration (*Transculturación* 225). Over the course of the novel the protagonist's view of the world is not broadened or reformulated but rather reaffirmed and strengthened. The hero's development or growth is thus secondary to the effort of recognizing and retaining an inner truth.

The tendency to confuse him with the narrator, meanwhile, should be considered the result of a conscious illusion on the part of Arguedas, namely, the construction of a self-effacing mediator. The narrator is thus not primarily a mediator between occidental and nonoccidental cultures, a conduit for their mutual intercommunication and transformation, but rather, more modestly, a mediator or conduit for the self-expression of the protagonist, his instrument and dependent. Translated into the language of film, we might say that the narrator offers a voice-over, speaking from "off," but does so in such a subtle way that we don't notice his distance from the events he recounts. His function is to make us believe that he is present in the hero. The temporal gap between narrator and protagonist is downplayed, and we forget that the narrator exists in one time and the protagonist in another. Such a narrative construction is not particularly noteworthy in itself, except insofar as it allows one to pose the question of the mediator's identity in a new way: the successful mediator is *not only* the boy caught between two cultural worlds, non-Indian and Indian, but also an older yet ageless voice situated between "the world of men" and the diffuse, eternal region of song.

Thus the novel refuses a feature that, given the autobiographical inscription, we might have taken for granted, namely, Bildung. The novel does not tell a story of growth or development. More to the point, since this is a story about a mestizo, it does not chart his progress along the path of social integration and ascension. Quite the opposite: the novel ends when the protagonist is prevented from following through on his education, banished from school by the advent of a typhus plague. *Los ríos profundos* thus offers a story of *interrupted* mestizaje; interrupted, furthermore, by a cataclysmic event of biblical proportions. Divine intervention, in the form of a malediction, liberates the protagonist from his fate as a letrado and cleanses him. It is this innocent voice that narrates *Los ríos profundos,* as if passion were merely a stage he had passed through before returning to "the matter of which he is made," which is not matter at all.

Quechua's "Internal Community of Meaning"

That voice is marked orally, subtly figured as speech or song. Rama has argued that the novel "is singing" whenever a Quechua song appears amid its pages (*Transculturación* 248). This observation is meant in part to underscore the idea of an underlying oral-based culture, ethnically indigenous, serving as a kind of source material for the novel: it is the "worldview" of this culture, argues Rama, that Arguedas was attempting to transmit in the written form of the novel and of whose presence Arguedas wanted the reader to become aware, in part by making us "hear" his text. Arguedas, writes Rama, "quiere que el lector oiga, como él, la canción " [wanted the reader, like him, to hear the song] (248). While this singing occurs primarily in those passages where Arguedas transcribed the lyrics of Quechua songs directly into the text, Rama qualifies the narrative overall within the oral register, as spoken or sung, rather than written, in a voice that extends through the majority of the text. This voice "es la del narrador que está diciendo, más que escribiendo la historia" [is the narrator's, who is speaking rather than writing the story] (254). Cornejo, too, has pointed to Quechua song as the narrator's ultimate and impossible reference point (*Escribir* 195).

My argument here builds on these observations, but with one substantial revision: orality in this novel is not opposed to writing. It is rather a function of a specific quality of Quechua, its highly developed sound-symbolic resources, specifically onomatopoeia, a quality that is noticeably underdeveloped in Spanish and other European languages (Nuckolls 239–40). Arguedas confronted this difference between Spanish and Quechua constantly as he wrote, and it is this difference in particular, rather than a broader cultural distinction between orality and literacy, that Arguedas's narrator mediates in the novel and that conditions the kind of translations one encounters throughout it. Thus, rather than speaking of "oral culture," I will focus specifically on "Quechua." And Quechua, furthermore, will come to configure a whole socio-geographic sphere and become a way of framing indigeneity more broadly, as a field of natural belonging that is constructed by language and is organically linked to the Andean landscape. Not surprisingly, there is a telluric consciousness that infuses Arguedas's early para-literary writings, as it did so many provincial Andean intellectuals. Though "race" is rejected in favor of "culture" or "spirit," the language of primordial belonging, telluric origin, and historical destiny remain. His thoughts on Quechua as conveyor of essence, a spirit rooted in the Andean land, in large part derive from this consciousness. And yet this was perhaps the only idiom available to express the implications of Quechua's "fondness for iconicity" and the "special importance" that sound imagery assumes in that language (Mannheim 184) for orienting Quechua speakers in particular ways toward their environment.

An article published June 6, 1948, in *La Prensa*, a Buenos Aires newspaper, titled "Acerca del intenso significado de dos voces quechuas" [Concerning the Intense Meaning of Two Quechua Words], is key for unpacking the elaborate ideological construction behind the literary language of *Los ríos profundos*.[11] It is an attempt to communicate a particular kind of Andean experience, not the one of hate and conflict described in his first two books, *Agua* (1935) and *Yawar fiesta* (1941), but a more sublime, integrated, and transcendent experience based on relationships to trees, music, stars, and birds. As it emerges in this article, such an experience takes place in an Andean community constructed linguistically through Quechua. The language community he describes in this piece configures a sphere of authentic indigeneity, although its authenticity is not to be construed in strictly racial or ethnic terms: it is an ethnically inclusive community, the only qualification for membership being native knowledge of Quechua. As with Jesús Lara, the lack of distinction between "native" and "native speaker" is crucial here: all those who speak Quechua natively constitute a single community, whether or not they are Indian; this notion allows intellectuals of provincial background, like Lara and Arguedas, the ability to claim themselves one with Indians.

The article concerned the complex of meanings associated with two Quechua word-sounds. One of them is a word, "illa," which refers to the propagation of certain kinds of light. The other is a noun ending, "-yllu," which refers to the propagation of certain kinds of music. Arguedas claimed that these word sounds relate to one another to form a kind of community, "una interna comunidad de sentido" [an internal community of meaning] (147). Within this internal community, the propagation of light and sound are closely related because both have "disturbing effects" (149).

One argument that Arguedas was making implicitly in this piece is that in Quechua the sound of words is linked to the meaning of words: sound can be an indicator of meaning. "-Yllu" is actually onomatopoetic, claims Arguedas in the first sentence of the article (147). And "illa," though it is not onomatopoetic, takes on this quality through its sinesthetic association with "-yllu": by the end of the piece, Arguedas has identified "illa" as *the sound form of a visual experience:* the experience of certain kinds of light has the sound "illa." The internal community of meaning created by these two sounds is not a matter of association, in which the listener of a certain word sound is reminded of another similar sound, proceeding then to create a meaningful link — through memory — between otherwise disparate words. -Yllu does not just "sound like" "illa"; it does not just remind the listener of illa. Rather, for Arguedas their common meaning is embedded in the word sounds themselves: sound itself has meaning, both denotative and connotative. Sound and meaning are one in the linguistic community he describes. Thus, as William Rowe has argued, for Arguedas onomatopoeia is a quality to be found in all of Quechua, in the language as a whole, and not just in certain specific words (*Mito* 103).

This idea that in Quechua meaning is embedded in sound had a special importance for *Los ríos profundos:* Arguedas copied this article into the beginning of the novel's chapter 6, entitled "Zumbayllu," a word composed of a Spanish verb root ("zumbar," to buzz, hum, whir) and the Quechua suffix -yllu, and referring to a whirling top. As per the copied article, Arguedas implied that this suffix carries a meaning particular to Quechua culture, a meaning it carried over into its new "location" at the termination of a Spanish root. And this idea, not coincidentally, corresponds to a whole theory of mestizo artistic forms that Arguedas developed in part through his research on mestizo artists in Huamanga (Ayacucho), in a study published in 1958, the same year as the novel. In this study, he argued that mestizo religious artists, and *only* they, were able to integrate harmoniously prehispanic religious iconography into the Catholic saint's retablo ("El arte" 156). Arguedas was intent to show that, through the intervention of mestizo artists, Quechua *meanings* survive even when uprooted and displaced to social contexts outside of the indigenous community; that these meanings are embedded in the verbal forms themselves, rather than in the community that creates or interprets them.

Furthermore, Arguedas believed that Quechua functioned within a wholly different system of reference than Spanish. The article's penultimate paragraph, entirely omitted from the transcription in *Los ríos profundos,* provides an argument about how referentiality functions for Quechua signs. He writes:

> Como la música que nombra *yllu, illa* denomina la luz que causa efectos trastornadores en los seres. Ambas palabras son vastas, de una vastedad que sólo es posible en idiomas como el quechua: en realidad estas voces tienen un contenido ilimitado. Nombran y explican. *Pinkuyllu* no sólo nombra el instrumento: define los efectos que causa y el origen de su poder.... Y *killa* no sólo nombra a la luna, contiene toda la esencia del astro, su relación con el mundo y con el ser humano, su hermosa, su cambiante aparición en el cielo. ("Acerca" 149)

> Like the music that *yllu* names, *illa* denotes the light that causes disturbing effects on people. Both words are vast, of a vastness that is only possible in languages like Quechua: in reality, the content of these words is limitless. They name and explain. *Pinkuyllu* not only names an instrument; it defines the effects caused by the instrument and the origin of its power.... And *killa* not only names the moon; it contains the complete essence of that star, its relation to the world and human beings, its beautiful, changing appearance in the sky.

In this view of Quechua, words and word sounds acquire a communicative life of their own, as if independent of the people who utter them; language constitutes community. Those who live "in" this community, meanwhile, can experience apparently limitless communication with one another, for it is a place where words "name *and* explain," as he says (my emphasis). Every word is a concept and encapsulates a history, familiar to every native speaker of Quechua. One has the impression, from reading this description, that for the members of this community, grammar has no significance; words — or sounds, more precisely — carry meaning, and these sounds configure social life.[12]

This understanding of Quechua language as a community reveals why, for Arguedas, *explaining* Quechua culture to outsiders became essentially a matter of *translating* Quechua words (outsiders are thus essentially defined as non-Quechua speakers), and translating them, furthermore, as groups of sound. And because these words name and explain, a well-translated Quechua word involves not just an equivalent name in Spanish, but also an explanation. This is so, not because Spanish lacks the proper equivalents for words like "pinkuyllu," an instrument local to the

Andes. The necessity for cultural interpretation in moving from Quechua to Spanish is rather for Arguedas a function of the specific properties of Quechua and not the result of historically inscribed cultural differences.

The celebrated technical achievements of *Los ríos profundos* lie primarily in Arguedas's ability metaphorically to enter into this community and bring the reader along with him. The literary language Arguedas developed in *Los ríos profundos* created the effect of entry into a special community in large part through explanation-as-translation. This technique gives shape to some of the most famous prose in the novel. The passage describing the protagonist's first encounter with the Inca walls in Cuzco, in the novel's first chapter, is one such example, for it is developed through an elaborate meditation on the meanings of the Quechua words "yawar mayu." Or consider the passage describing the protagonist's arrival in the town of Abancay with his father. The passage begins with a quasi-etymological explanation — similar to the yllu/illa passage, though much briefer — about the associations that the word "Abancay" brings to the narrator's mind. The passage begins with the following lines:

> Se llama *amank'ay* a una flor silvestre, de corola amarilla, y *awankay* al balanceo de las grandes aves. *Awankay* es volar planeando, mirando la profundidad. ¡Abancay! (58).

> *Amank'ay* is the name of a wildflower, a yellow lily, and *awankay* the term used for the soaring flight of the large birds. *Awankay* means to glide, gazing down into profundity. Abancay! (32)

For Rowe, this passage exemplifies how Quechua words allow the narrator to feel the essence of things (*Mito* 108); the purpose of the Quechua words in the novel, Rowe shows, revolves around this ability to lead to deeper awareness of the essential connections among otherwise disparate experiences or objects — in this case, a flower, the act of flying, a town. Arguedas, in this instance as in others throughout the novel, and much as he did in the yllu/illa article, leads the reader through an associative interlinking, moving from word to word to trace an underlying holistic framework that the juxtaposition of related Quechua word-sounds reveals. This prose thus uncovers and communicates the "internal community of meaning" that Quechua speakers perceive.

In this passage, Arguedas reveals the internal community of meaning through a poetic reconstruction in Spanish. The two initial words —

amank'ay and *awankay* — along with their definitions, build on one another as intensifiers, collecting energy that is finally released with the utterance of the city's name: "¡Abancay!" This intensifying sequence sets up linkages between the words through a complex set of hidden metaphors; through these metaphoric relations, the narrator expects to arrive at a final image distilling the essence of the town: "Debió de ser [the passage continues] un pueblo perdido entre bosques de pisonayes y de árboles desconocidos, en un valle de maizales inmensos que llegaban hasta el río" (58) [It must have once been a town lost amid groves of *pisonayes* and unfamiliar trees, in a valley of immense cornfields that stretched down to the river (32–33)]. This final image subtly works on the previous lines, transforming juxtaposed words that are phonetically similar yet without any apparent semantic connection, into a coherent metaphor that weaves together the disparate meanings identified in the first lines. This interweaving is made possible by an operation that the author hides from the reader, namely, the transferral of one referent's attributes to another. The attributes of "awank'ay" (wildness, flower, yellowness) along with those associated with "amankay" (immensity, bird, gliding) are transferred to "¡Abancay!" But they are not transferred intact: they are brought together and reconstituted in a somewhat different form. The flower's wildness, in "awank'ay," becomes connected to a forest in "¡Abancay!" (perhaps through the underlying Latin *silvanus*). The flower's yellowness, meanwhile, is implied in the image of a cornfield, which, because it is immense, is also associated now to the bird's great size. The image of "¡Abancay¡" that emerges from this process of increasingly complex metaphorization — a valley town rich in cornfields and lost in a wild forest — is therefore semantically related to the original two words. "¡Abancay!" itself, meanwhile, comes to be metaphorically enriched by this underlying connection, for one can now imagine that Abancay looks as small as a yellow flower would to the eyes of a large planing bird.

Contrast the metaphoric construction of Arguedas around the word "amank'ay" with Jesús Lara's, in a novel written five years earlier: "En las caras terrosas reventaba la alegría como la flor del amanqay en las grietas de la montaña" [Happiness bloomed in the muddy faces like the amanqay flower in mountain crevices] (*Yanakuna* 292). Lara, too, brings us "into" an Andean world with this metaphor, but he does not present it as a world created by word sounds. Arguedas, in contrast, is intent on showing the existence of an underlying "internal community of meaning" in Quechua.

The Quechua words (amank'ay, awankay, Abancay) are initially connected only through sound, through a rhythmic consonance. The single phonetic change that distinguishes each from the others — "m," "w," and "b" to the Spanish-trained ear (keeping in mind that a Quechua speaker would also notice the different kinds of aspirations that distinguish the various /k/ sounds from one another) — intimate that these words are really all slight variations on a single experience or idea, as if their disparate meanings were in fact one at the root. Yet for a Spanish speaker this semantic connection must be explained, "translated," as Arguedas does, through a narrative in Spanish that describes the meaning of each word. We imagine now that we are able to understand what the word "Abancay" might connote to a poetically minded Quechua speaker. The combination of these two operations, one elaborated through the juxta-position of sounds, the other elaborated through a translation in poetic prose involving the construction of several interlinked metaphors, allows a Quechua meaning to infuse a Spanish text.

Understood within the immediate context of the narrative, however, this passage brings the reader "into" a Quechua community at the very moment it reveals the absence of such a community in Abancay. The description of the town does not stop with the harmonious figurative convergence. The key phrase "it must once have been" sets us up for the subsequent divergence:

> Hoy los techos de calamina brillan estruendosamente; huertas de mora separan los pequeños barrios, y los campos de cañaverales se extienden desde el pueblo hasta el Pachachaca. Es un pueblo cautivo, levantado en la tierra ajena de una hacienda. (58–59)

> Today its tin roofs shine with a horrible glare, blackberry patches separate one neighborhood from another, and the sugar cane extends from the town to the Pachachaca. The town is a prisoner of the hacienda, on whose alien land it was built. (33)

The town is bathed in a harsh brilliance, not a soft glow; its extension has been interrupted by foreign, domesticated plants, not the natural fauna of the Andes; its fields are of cane, not corn; and it is not its own master, but belongs to the plantation. "¡Abancay!" as sound/idea, reveals the absence of the natural community of meaning, its fragmentation: plantation society has captured and divided what was once free and whole. This is the essence of the "hell" of Abancay, as the narrator will come to term it.

Genette offers the following definition of narrating: "a shifting but sacred frontier between two worlds, the world in which one tells, the world of which one tells" (236). The distinction between these two worlds corresponds to the distinction between this novel's innocent, distanced narrator and its passionate mestizo protagonist; they are in separate worlds. The world "in which" narration occurs is not the conflicted social world of Abancay "of which" the bulk of the story is composed. The protagonist's world is fragmented; the narrator's is integrated.[13] The narrator reveals this difference repeatedly, especially in the novel's first chapters. Rama, in defining the features of "transculturated narrative," argues that the distance between these two worlds is shortened: "se acorta la distancia entre la lengua del narrador-escritor y la de los personajes, por estimar que el uso de esa dualidad lingüística rompe el criterio de unidad artística de la obra" [the distance between the narrator-author's language and the characters' language is shortened because it is felt that this linguistic duality breaks with the criterion that the work be artistically unified] (*Transculturación* 41). Such is not exactly the case in *Los ríos profundos*. The integrating language of the narrator intimates the existence of an integrated world, but this is not the characters' world. As Cornejo has noted, at the heart of the novel lies a conflict between the universe understood as "totalidad coherente, compacta, absolutamente integrada" [a coherent, compact, absolutely integrated totality] and "la realidad de un mundo desintegrado y conflictivo" [the reality of a disintegrated and conflictive world] (*Universos* 100).

Evidently the plantation explains the existence of this conflictive and disintegrated world. An alternative, integrated world is, however, often referred to, as in the excursus on yllu/illa; or in the protagonist's description of the ayllu in which he lived as a child, located in "la más pequeña y alegre quebrada que jamás he conocido" (70) [the smallest, happiest valley I have ever known (41–42)]. But it is the cohesiveness of the translating voice that creates the internal community largely absent from the events of the story. It is as if the language of the narrator provided a primary restitution of a loss of community, a loss that is recounted over and over again across the novel. Eve-Marie Fell claimed as much for the writing of Arguedas's last novel, *El zorro de arriba y el zorro de abajo*

(The Fox from Up Above and the Fox from Down Below) (1971), a novel marked by an attempt to "integrate, through language, a series of ruptures and antagonisms" (xxvii). As in Arguedas's last novel, in *Los ríos profundos* the lost community is also restored in the enunciation of the narrative, but now as an aesthetic experience. The narrator as mediator thus both translates and redeems the Quechua community. He makes whole what is dispersed or fragmented, re-creating it in his own voice. Quechua's internal community of meaning, such as it is manifested in *Los ríos profundos*, exists at a remove from the world of terrestrial human relations, in a spatially undefined relationship to it: somewhere under, above, beyond, within. But certain voices from that community, such as the narrator's, can make it manifest itself in this world. The narrator is thus a prophet of sorts, engaging in acts of revelation: he reveals an underlying unity of meaning amid a world of conflicting signs. But this unity is not composed of a single Word but is rather a hidden system of interrelations.

Though his writings on Quechua may perhaps seem to us impressionistic or subjective, in fact Arguedas had effectively identified and described one of the linguistic aspects of Quechua that has since been more thoroughly explored, namely, the prevalence of iconicity, or sound symbolism.[14] This aspect of Arguedas's insight has not always been recognized. For example, Rama, in an effort to downplay Arguedas's specific attachments to Quechua, argued that everything Arguedas said about the qualities of Quechua words could equally well have been said by a Spanish poet about Spanish words (*Transculturación* 241), as if it were only a question of poetic investment. This corresponds to Rama's generalized discomfort with the idea that Arguedas himself might have held magical beliefs in the power of language. Thus Rama repeatedly attempts to distance Arguedas from the magical beliefs he depicted in his fiction, whether by making "mythic thought" the common substratum underlying all art, modern or primitive, or by insisting that Arguedas's "reverence" for the word derives from his filiation to late nineteenth-century aesthetic movements rather than from his experience of Quechua (*Transculturación* 241). Rowe offers a more judicious assessment of Arguedas's theory of onomatopoeia, arguing that Arguedas's theory may be untenable on the basis of Saussurean linguistics but is still "valid in a cultural sense." Because it reflects an important element of Andean lifeways, namely, "the mutual relationship of shared being between man and nature," human sounds in Quechua are intrinsically linked to the object world ("Introduction" xxvii). Thus, although Arguedas's theory may be incorrect from a stictly linguistic point of view, it does describe an existing quality of Quechua: phonemes accrue a symbolic meaning in Quechua (Rowe, *Mito* 104–5)

Rama shifted the terms of the problematic underlying Arguedas's literary construction. Arguedas himself always insisted that the problem derived from his Quechua–Spanish bilingualism: how to express in Spanish words and scenes that he "heard," internally, in Quechua. But Rama translated this problematic, so to speak, into a conflict of greater transcendence for an intellectual troubled by the course of Latin America's modernization, namely, how to harmonize the conflict between modern-lettered and traditional-oral societies; or speaking in specifically literary terms, between the bourgeois, individualizing realist form of the European novel and the communal, cosmological lyricism of Quechua folk songs.

The Dirty Voice:
Mistura and the Quechua "Conquest" of Spanish

We can better appreciate the importance of the "innocent" voice in *Los ríos profundos* if we situate it with respect to Arguedas's earlier fictions and if we understand how far Arguedas had by then distanced himself from an earlier concept of mestizo language and identity. The literary operations in *Los ríos profundos,* which rely heavily on translation and of which the "Abancay" passage is but one example, are widely recognized as an Arguedian invention that dates to around 1950. Arguedas at that time published an essay recounting his own trajectory as a writer, "La novela y el problema de la expresión literaria en el Perú" [The Novel and the Problem of Literary Expression in Peru]. In it he declared that translation had replaced his earlier technique for representing indigeneity in narrative fiction, a technique developed in *Agua* (1935) and *Yawar fiesta* (1941), which he referred to as "mistura" (mixture). Originally deployed by a disapproving critic, mistura referred to the linguistic confusion of Arguedas's prose, which was "neither Spanish nor Quechua" ("Entre" 26). In 1939 Arguedas appropriated the term for himself, turning the negative connotation on its head in order to claim mistura as politically and aesthetically avant-garde: mistura, he declared, represents the death of "pure" Spanish, heralding a new age in which Quechua is no longer to be despised and mestizos have fully come into their own as a bilingual national majority. In 1950, however, Arguedas decided to abandon mistura in favor of translation: "Yo, ahora, tras dieciocho años de esfuerzos, estoy intentando una traducción castellana de los diálogos de los indios" ("La novela" 173) [I am just now, after eighteen years of effort, attempting a Spanish translation of the Indians' dialogues (xx)]. That is, he transitioned from a literary language achieved through Quechua–Spanish *mixing,* to one achieved through *translating* from Quechua into Spanish. The importance of this transition cannot be overestimated. It is essentially this move, of which *Los ríos profundos* remains the paradigmatic example, that garnered him an international reputation. In order to assess its importance, it is necessary to understand more clearly how the previous language, mistura, was technically constructed and what it signified for Arguedas in terms of his understanding of mestizo positionality and, more specifically, mestizo artistry.

Arguedas talked about mistura at several key moments in his career, notably in the essays "Entre el kechwa y el castellano, la angustia del mestizo" [Between Quechua and Spanish, the Mestizo's Anguish] (1939) and "La novela y el problema de la expresión literaria del Perú" (1950), and in the speech given at the Primer Encuentro de Narradores Peruanos (1965). In these three instances, there is remarkable consistency in how Arguedas characterized mistura: it is a written Spanish that has been syntactically changed under the influence of Quechua. In "Entre el kechwa y el castellano," Arguedas saw it in the writing of his mestizo high school students in Sicuani, in the "sintaxis destrozada" [destroyed syntax] of their Spanish (27). In "La novela," he referred to it as "sutiles desordenamientos" [subtle disorderings] of Spanish (171). And as Arguedas would later recollect, in the 1965 speech, mistura was produced "mezclando un poco la sintaxis quechua dentro del castellano, en una pelea verdaderamente infernal con la lengua" [by mixing Quechua syntax a bit with Spanish, in a truly hellish battle with the language] (*Primer Encuentro* 41). This idea of a syntactic effect on Spanish by Quechua — a Spanish syntax "destroyed," "disordered," or "mixed a bit" with Quechua — remains a constant across the twenty-six years of his reflections on the subject, although one notices, in the vocabulary Arguedas employed to describe mistura, that as time passed he would attribute to Quechua less and less of an impact on Spanish.

However, although the idea of linguistic mixture remained a constant whenever Arguedas talked about mistura, there is very little else that is consistent in his description or deployment of it over the years. It seems to have been above all a concept that Arguedas relied on when he was on the defensive, to communicate the particular nature of his aesthetic struggles and thereby authorize his linguistic innovations against the critical attacks his novels often provoked. At times he used the term "mistura" to refer to the literary language of his Quechua-speaking characters, a Spanish heavily marked by Quechua. The following dialogue from the first edition of *Yawar fiesta* serves as an example:

> — ¡Carago! ¡Pichk'achuri va parar juirme! Sempre, año tras año Pichk'achuri ganando enjualma, dejando viuda en plaza grande.
> — K'ayau dice va traer Misitu de K'oñani pampa. Se han palabrao, dice, tawantin varayok', para Misitu.
> — ¡Cojodices! Con diablo es Misitu. ¿Cuándo carago trayendo Misitu? Nu'hay k'ari para Misitu de K'oñani. (25)

> "Damn! Pichk'achuri gonna stand its ground. Pichk'achuri winning saddlecloth, leaving widow in bullring." [. . .]
> "K'ayau community says they're gonna bring the bull they call Misitu down from K'oñani plain. They say staffbearers have sworn to bring Misitu."
> "Nonsense! Misitu's with the devil. When the hell they ever bringing Misitu? No man's brave enough to stand up to Misitu from K'oñani." (19)[15]

Is this language mimetic? Arguedas's comments are confusing on this matter. On the one hand, this speech certainly appears to imitate spoken language, at least partially so. The alteration to Spanish vowel-sounds in the words "sempre" and "cojodices" are clear instances of such an imitation, mimicking a Quechua "accent" in Spanish; the repetition of the word "dice" is also a marked characteristic of "Andean Spanish." Yet on the other hand, Arguedas roundly denied that this speech was naturalist. He wrote, "¡Pero los indios no hablan en ese castellano ni con los de lengua española, ni mucho menos entre ellos! Es una ficción. Los indios hablan en quechua" ("La novela" 172) [But the Indians do not speak that Spanish, not with Spanish speakers, and much less among themselves. It is a fiction. The Indians speak in Quechua (xix)]. Thus one infers that most of the linguistic constructions in the above-cited passage are expressions of this "fiction" that Arguedas created to represent Quechua speech. He noted that this fictional language was later horribly exaggerated by other authors, and to his dismay was generally mistaken for the Indians' true form of speech in Spanish.

Mistura makes more sense if it is understood as a solution to the problem of the "interlocutory void" that Arguedas encountered in Lima. As part of his repudiation of mistura in 1950, Arguedas offered a justification that insisted on the importance of his experience as a Quechua speaker: in the scenes from the Andes that he wanted to represent, the Indian characters would have been speaking Quechua; this was as he heard them, and this was how he wanted to put them to paper. To translate their speech into Spanish would have constituted a negation of his own hearing, would have meant displacing himself from the center of the writing process. He asked, "¿En qué idioma se debía hacer hablar a los indios en la literatura? Para el bilingüe, para quien aprendió a hablar en quechua, resulta imposible, de pronto, hacerlos hablar en castellano" ("La novela" 172) [What language should the Indians be made to speak in literature? For the bilingual person, for one who first learned to talk in Quechua, it seems impossible to have them suddenly speak Spanish (xix)]. Yet Arguedas was equally conscious of the fact that his readers were monolingual Spanish speakers. We might say, then, that this use of mistura offered an imperfect solution to the problem of bilingual authorship. He "heard" those voices in Quechua, but could not write them in Quechua. Barred from actually using Quechua in a literature to be consumed by an overwhelmingly monolingual metropolitan audience, Arguedas nevertheless insisted on marking the speech of certain characters as not-Spanish, and on doing so linguistically.

But there are yet more ways to understand Arguedas's use of this language. He noted that he used mistura to communicate the "epic" nature of the struggles for control of agrarian resources that were taking place in the highlands between indigenous communities and gamonales (hacienda owners) ("La novela" 171). In *Yawar fiesta* the Indian voices are most often expressing anger at the injustices to which they are submitted by the "trinity" of judge, priest, and landowner. The "incorrect" Spanish in which they speak, the language that Arguedas invented for them, can be read as a kind of violence on the dominant language, a violence to the language of the state that is consonant with the violent emotions expressed by speakers resisting the institutions of the state. The following line from *Yawar fiesta*, of an Indian comunero responding to the threat of his land being dispossessed, suggests a Spanish altered by rage: " — ¡Mi ojo premero sacará! ¡Como killincho ladrón, mi ojo premero comerá!

¡Comun yaku jajayllas!" (*Yawar fiesta* 14) ["My eye first he'll take out! Like thieving sparrowhawk my eye first he'll eat! *Comun yaku jajayllas* !" (8)]. Although language is not an obvious element of the social conflict that the novel represents, it becomes through mistura a site of antagonism and violence, as if the conflict over land and water rights had migrated to realms otherwise distant from it. Mistura, by this reading, operates as a kind of displaced violence. Arguedas himself had implied as much in the early reference to mistura's "destruction" of Spanish syntax. Seen in this light, mistura looks very similar to the avant-garde strategies of Jorge Icaza in his indigenista novel *Huasipungo*. In that novel, the language of the principal male characters — Indian and non-Indian — has a ruptural quality, intensified by the great quantity of insults and interjections. The fragmented nature of their speech performs a *rhetorical* violence that the social impotence each character experiences with respect to more powerful institutions prohibits him from carrying out.

Mariátegui, in an analysis of avant-garde poet Martín Adán, referred to such a poetic phenomenon as "el disparate puro" [pure nonsense], whose disorderly irruption in the text has a revolutionary function, breaking with traditional forms that are "dry and dead" (*Peruanicemos el Perú* 155). Arguedas's usage of mistura in the first edition of *Yawar fiesta* verges on the "pure excess" or "pure absurdity" Mariátegui had described. It confirms that in those years Arguedas valued this altered Spanish as the sign of the social-political awakening taking place in the Peruvian Andes. Indeed, in a 1940 letter to his friend the poet Manuel Moreno Jiménez, he explained that the language of *Yawar fiesta,* which he was then in the process of composing, was inspired by the Indian peasant mobilizations he witnessed. In October of that year, he heard an indigenous leader address a large political assembly in Quechua. He told Moreno that the language of *Yawar fiesta* was made "con la misma voz que escuché ayer de ese indio de San Pablo, con sus mismas palabras, con idéntica emoción" [in the same voice I heard yesterday from that Indian in San Pablo, with the same words, the same emotion] (Forgues, *La letra* 92). Written in mistura, the novel transmitted the emotional essence of a fighting Quechua.

Perhaps echoing Mariátegui's dictum, Arguedas wrote that he considered mistura to represent the death of "pure Spanish" and to announce a new era in which Spanish will become infused with the "genius" of Quechua. This Spanish would reflect the mestizo nationality that he saw being born in the Andes. In another letter to Moreno, written in the same period, he reflected again on his novel *Yawar fiesta:*

> La obra ha nacido de la raíz misma del pueblo cuya vida palpita en la novela; y sale a luz empapado en la sangre del mestizo y del indio, que hablan y se realizan todavía en kechwa. Claro que este hecho puede dificultar su traducción, acaso también su absoluta comprensión por parte de muchas gentes; pero no importa eso. Tengo la idea de que quien pueda escribir en castellano bien cernido, y dominado, desde buena altura del panorama y la vida de nuestro pueblo serrano, no podría, en cambio, describir con la fuerza y la palpitación suficiente, este mundo en germen, que se debate en una lucha tan violenta y grandiosa. (Forgues, *La letra* 90)

> The work is born from the very root of the people, whose life throbs in the novel; and it comes into the world drenched in the blood of the mestizo and the Indian, who still speak and fulfill themselves in Quechua. Of course this fact can make translation of the book difficult, perhaps, too, its full comprehension by many people. But that doesn't matter. I have this idea that whoever can write in well-polished, well-mastered Spanish, from high above the panorama and the life of our mountain people, would not, on the other hand, be able to describe with enough strength and feeling this germinating world, caught in such a violent and grandiose struggle.

Here Arguedas expresses a completely different relation to literary language than he does in 1950, in the passage from "La novela y el problema de la expresión literaria en el Perú" cited at the opening of this chapter. In 1950, Arguedas was seeking to tear Quechua out of his language. In 1940, in diametrical opposition to his words in 1950, Arguedas was confident that only a Spanish "birthed" by Quechua could express the living reality of the Andes; the more untranslatable this language, the more authentically it would represent the "violent and grandiose" nature of Andean society.

In his words to Moreno, Arguedas appropriated the prophetic and organicist tone that marked the indigenista militancy of *Amauta* and, most especially, the indigenismo espoused by Cuzco intellectuals in the 1930s. Arguedas's ideas about mestizo language and creativity reflect the influence of Uriel García's *El nuevo indio* (The New Indian) (1930). In that book, García essentially recoded terms like "Indian" and "mestizo," inventing a new taxonomy reflecting the "spiritual" rather than "racial" nature of identity. The "new Indian" is "today's Indian," who is not really Indian at all in the ethnic sense, says García, but rather "a moral entity." Thus, he proclaims, "Today's Indian...is every man who lives in America, with the same spiritual or emotional roots as he who farmed and made use of it in ancient times" (8). The "new Indian" is thus "el mestizo espiritual" (107). The spiritual mestizo, in García's formulation, is vigorous and passionate, forged of ancient drives, the loves and hatreds of the conquest, the colony, and the republic (107). Much like Arguedas's *Yawar fiesta*, covered in the blood of birth, García's new Indian (the spiritual mestizo) is a fertile, dirty being best exemplified in the "chola chichera"; "her chichería" (chicha saloon) is "the cave of nationality" (174–75).

The idea that mistura might be the language of new social actors is lent further evidence by the fact that Arguedas associated it with the writing produced by his Indian and mestizo high school students. In the very earliest appropriation of the term, mistura referred to the *written* language that Quechua speakers produced as they were learning Spanish in school. This language bore the traces of a conflict particular to mestizos and Indians learning to be more fully bilingual. In his 1939 essay, "Entre el kechwa y el castellano, la angustia del mestizo," he referred to a conflict between the language of the mestizo's inner soul or spirit, whose fullest expression has always occurred in Quechua, and the language — Spanish — required of those who have entered the institutions of the liberal, modernizing nation-state. He wrote,

> El hombre del Ande no ha logrado el equilibrio entre su necesidad de expresión integral y el castellano como su idioma obligado. Y hay ahora, un ansia, una especie de desesperación en el mestizo por dominar este idioma.... El castellano aprendido a viva fuerza, escuela, colegio o universidad [sic] no le sirve bien para decir en forma plena y profunda su alma o el paisaje del mundo donde creció. ("Entre" 26)

> The man of the Andes has not achieved a balance between his need for full expression and Spanish as his required language. And there is an eagerness now, a kind of desperation in the mestizo to master this language.... Spanish learned by force, primary school, secondary school, university [sic], does not serve him well to express,

fully and deeply, his soul or the landscape of the world where he grew up.

In 1940 Arguedas organized the publication of a small sample of his students' writings from the school. The collection was titled "Pumaccahua," after the school's name, and in his prologue to it Arguedas affirmed the importance of the works therein collected toward resisting the style and content of a national pedagogy utterly uninterested in local knowledges. Thus Arguedas's intent to further the students' knowledge of "la realidad espiritual de los pueblos de las distintas regiones del país" [the spiritual reality of peoples from different regions of the country] (*Pumaccahua* 1), starting in fact from their own knowledge of how and where they lived. The following fragment of a student composition was written by an Indian student named Quispe Alanoca, to whom Arguedas developed a personal attachment (Forgues, *La letra* 117, 121–22). It demonstrates what might be considered a "naturally occurring" form of mistura, as Arguedas understood it:

> El rendidor indio la cumbre libró de su hogar; y en el ya aislado campamento que de amoratada luz la tarde inundaba, del negro Chhuko, colega triste del indio, resuenan los aullidos por los ecos de la sima repetidos. Llora sobre la tumba del indio, y bajo aquella cruz de ichu, toca suavemente la hierva menuda aún manchado con sangre, y espera el fin de tan intenso sueño. Después de la muerte del indio, todavía rondaban los condores y el pitpit; la sima campo de la brega, un día la cruz del entierro, ya por tierra, ni una memoria, ni una fama ¡ho no! sobre la tumba del indio serrano, cesaron la voz triste del negro Chhuco; más del ilustre animal allí han quedado los huesos esparcidos, sobre la tumba del valiente indio. (*Pumaccahua* 13)

The high peak freed the hard-working Indian from his home; and in the already isolated encampment which the evening inundated with purplish light, black Chhuko's, sad companion of the Indian, howls resound across the echoes of the chasm, repeated. He cries over the Indian's grave, and beneath that cross of mountain grass, softly touches the small grass still stained with blood, and waits for the end of so intense a dream. After the death of the Indian, the condors and the *pitpit* still hovered around. The chasm, field of toil, one day the cross of the burial, already underground, neither memory nor renown, alas! on the mountain Indian's grave, ceased the sad voice of black Chhuco. There lie the scattered bones of more than the illustrious animal, on the tomb of the brave Indian.[16]

Mistura is thus marked by its position in a process of language acquisition, emerging out of the mestizo's desire to express himself fully and the imposition of another language. It referred to a condition of social interstitiality, one of whose primary markers was language. Thus, in 1950, Arguedas referred to *Yawar fiesta*'s mistura as "language in the leap": "Haber pretendido expresarse con sentido de universalidad a través de los pasos que nos conducen al dominio de un idioma distinto, haberlo pretendido en *el transcurso del salto;* ésta fue la razón de la incesante lucha ("La novela" 173, my emphasis) [To have attempted to express oneself with a sense of universality through the steps that lead one to master another language, to have attempted this *in midleap,* that was the reason for the never-ending struggle (xx, my emphasis)]. Arguedas was referring to the problem of forging a voice that testifies to its own social transformation. More than anything else, mistura attempted to express the bilingual's struggle to communicate.

Whether referring to the invented language meant to signal Quechua dialogue in a Spanish-language text, or to the language of the Quechua speaker trying to express himself in Spanish writing, mistura embedded the problems of the bilingual author squarely in the text. However, neither of these intended effects appears ever to have been appreciated by Arguedas's readers. Arguedas himself admitted that the misrecognition of his invented Indian language for a real language rendered mistura pointless as a literary strategy. And concerning the idea of mistura as the expression of the mestizo's social interstitiality, Arguedas was unable to get this view of mistura across in his fiction. There is nothing in the narration of either *Agua* or *Yawar fiesta* that marks it as a stylized version of the *written* language of the recently "castilianized" Indian, and no critics that I am aware of ever recognized this aspect of it. Part of the problem lies in the fact that the Spanish syntax of *Yawar fiesta*'s language is not nearly as "disordered" or even "mixed a bit" by Quechua as Arguedas claimed (Rowe, *Mito* 49–60). A telling contrast can be appreciated when Arguedas's literary language is read alongside the language of his students at Pumaccahua, as can be found in the composition by Quispe Alanoca I cited above. Nothing in the prose of *Yawar fiesta* comes even close to this language. If this example from Quispe's essay is an example of mistura, then mistura was terribly attenuated in Arguedas's novel. Its intertextuality and performativity — simultaneously citing the mestizo's writing and reenacting its production — went unperceived. As an attempt to express the particular drama of the new bilingual — the mestizo struggling to express his inner soul in Spanish — by finding an authentic language to testify to the experience of diglossia, mistura fell on uniformly deaf ears.

Mistura was criticized repeatedly by readers, and although it involved a Spanish that was not nearly as transformed as the Spanish found among Arguedas's students, it was nevertheless almost universally considered to be incomprehensible and crude. Arguedas reported to Moreno that Luis E. Valcárcel, sitting on a jury panel for a literary prize that Arguedas lost, told him by way of explanation, "para quien no haya 'vivido con los indios,' mi libro es *ininteligible*" [for someone who has not 'lived with the Indians,' my book is *unintelligible*] (Forgues, *La letra* 128, original emphasis). A good friend from university days also criticized the novel's language in the strongest terms, citing Soviet literary critics to show that Arguedas's use of a Quechua-inflected Spanish was "excessive," and that it detracted from the main purpose of the literary form, namely, that the author and his reading public become as one (Forgues, *La letra* 126).

Arguedas's words to Moreno suggest that he was fully aware that the language of *Yawar fiesta* was difficult. In 1940 he had written, "Of course this fact can make translation of the book difficult, perhaps, too, its full comprehension by many people. But that doesn't matter" (Forgues, *La letra* 90). Yet despite this apparently carefree attitude toward his readers' comprehension, there is evidence to suggest that Arguedas nevertheless considered that mistura *was* communicative, despite its difficulty. In an earlier letter to Moreno, he had written of *Yawar fiesta*:

> Nuestro triunfo estará, en que la obra cumpla su destino. Y ese fin, esa vida, no la puede lograr sino con el lenguaje en que está escrita; no hay otro, hermano; es el lenguaje de esa tierra, el único que puede decir fuerte y limpio el dolor, la tragedia de la gente que sufre en ella. (Forgues, *La letra* 92)

> Our triumph will be in the work's fulfillment of its destiny. And it cannot attain that goal, that life, except with the language in which it is written. Brother, there is no other, it is the language of this land, the only one that, strongly and cleanly, can tell of the pain, the tragedy of the people who suffer here.

Arguedas here defends his language, as if perhaps anticipating the future rejection. He refers to the ability of this language to speak "strongly and cleanly" of what he wants it to speak. Strength and cleanliness refer to communicative qualities, to the work's clarity, its ability to transmit a message. Though its Spanish is "dirty," soaked in the blood of the Andes, as he had also written, it nevertheless communicates "cleanly." Cleanliness does not refer to the transparency of Arguedas's words per se, but rather to the direct correlation he saw between form and referent: the altered language is true to the altered reality it depicts. Arguedas considered this work to be, above all, expressive of the social environment in which it was produced.

These contradictory statements about the work, both clean and dirty, communicative and difficult to understand, suggest that Arguedas himself did not fully know what he was searching for with mistura. But the disjunction is heightened even further when these concepts of cleanliness and dirtiness, which he used to describe the communicative capacity of his work, are understood not just as descriptions of standard vs. nonstandard language, but also as signs of a changing moral economy underlying Arguedas's work. He had written in 1940 that *Yawar fiesta* expressed his own passionate involvement in the world around him: "Claro que la obra no tiene la limpidez estética y castellana impecable; se siente que el autor es atropellado por el ambiente y la vida del mundo que describe; y el kechwa resume en su lenguaje, casi por todas partes" [Of course the work does not have an impeccable aesthetic and Spanish limpidity; one senses that the author is battered by the environment and the life of the world he describes; and Quechua oozes in his language almost everywhere] (Forgues, *La letra* 90).[17] Its language, that is, expresses *him*. Yet ten years later, Arguedas would revise this vision and construct a radically divergent account of *Yawar fiesta*, insisting that it was the product of his search for greater emotional distance from the world he was depicting.

He claimed that *Yawar Fiesta* was narrated as objectively as possible, and contrasted it to his previous fiction, the stories of *Agua*. *Agua* was written "with hatred," he wrote, whereas *Yawar fiesta* was narrated "con pureza de conciencia, con el corazón limpio, hasta donde es posible que esté limpio el corazón humano" ("La novela" 168) [with a clear conscience, with a clean heart, insofar as it is possible for a human heart to be clean (xv)]. We can take this emotional impartiality to be a form of narrative omniscience, given that *Yawar fiesta*'s narrator is all-seeing, whereas *Agua*'s is always limited to the first person. Arguedian "cleanliness" in this instance is quite different from the cleanliness of his earlier comments. Here cleanliness is next to godliness, as it were, pointing us to an underlying moral framework that prizes limpid emotionality, and that seeks to rise up out of worldly passions toward a state of moral purity. Arguedas had noted, in effect, that in *Yawar fiesta* he had discovered a certain kind of omniscience, an impartiality, that allowed him to represent as faithfully as possible even those characters representative of social types for whom he felt little sympathy. *Agua*, in contrast, was narrated with the singular intensity of someone who hates, and this is because Arguedas wrote it, as he tells it, as a member, rather than outsider or omniscient surveyor, of the community he described: a small town clearly divided into two groups, "irreductibles, implacables y esencialmente distintos" (168) [irreducible, implacable, and essentially different worlds (xvi)], namely, oligarchs and Indians. He writes of *Agua*, "¿Qué otra literatura podía hacer entonces, y aún ahora, un hombre nacido y formado en las aldeas del interior?" (169) [What other literature could a man born and brought up in the interior villages write then, and even now? (xvi)]. It is as if the Arguedian narrator, in this instance, were thoroughly consumed by the partisan violence of this social system. But in 1950 he would repudiate this passionate consumption, and the resulting partial narrative perspective, for being spiritually unclean. Notice, by the way, that in this description the partiality of the narrator is not marked in the language of modern particularity; his identity is not determined by culture, ethnicity, race, class, or gender. He is simply on the side that hates.

Clearly this repudiation of *Agua*'s moral dirtiness and the subsequent elevation of *Yawar fiesta*'s moral cleanliness was a retroactively imposed trajectory. In 1940 Arguedas had stressed that the obscurity of the novel's language was the result of violence done to it by an author consumed by the political fervor of the moment. He had exalted the messiness that resulted. In 1950, he stressed the opposite, that the novel sprang from his own emotional remove, and that this remove was a sign that he had been morally cleansed. Chronologically speaking, this reversal appears to correspond exactly to his decision to relinquish mistura. By 1950 he declared himself to be abandoning mistura in favor of "correct" Spanish. He wrote that, in *Los ríos profundos*, the struggle for universality "through the steps which lead us to master another language" has come to a conclusion, and this conclusion is Spanish, "medio de expresión legítimo del mundo peruano de los Andes" ("La novela" 174) [the legitimate means of expressing the Peruvian world of the Andes (xx)]. In fact, he had already begun revising *Yawar fiesta* in the 1940s, with the aim of bringing its language more into line with standard Spanish.[18]

The values he'd assigned to "cleanliness" thus underwent a significant change in that ten-year period. Cleanliness now referred to universality rather than the transmission of an individual engagement, as it had with the "decir limpio" [clean expression] on which he'd prided himself in his letter to Moreno. Cleanliness was best embodied in standard Spanish rather than the difficult language expressive of the bilingual condition and the political unrest of the countryside. Gustavo Gutiérrez, the liberation theologian who became an important figure for Arguedas at the end of his life, analyzed how Arguedas used the term "limpidez" [limpidity] to refer to "identidad . . . como opuesto a alienación [identity . . . as opposed to alienation] (37). "Dirtiness" refers to alienation and sin, to a lack of identity and soul (41).

Yet it is also possible to argue the opposite. The dirty Spanish of *Yawar fiesta,* whatever one thinks of its aesthetic merits, expressed Arguedas's struggles and his particular social location. It reflected his decision to be true to what he heard, however difficult the result might have been for his audience to understand. It was "true" in its own particular way. Whereas the Spanish of *Los ríos profundos,* for the most part cleaned up and standardized though difficult and at times obscure, reflects Arguedas's decision to subordinate his own aural awareness to his readers'. Though this Spanish might have been morally limpid, it was not as "true" to his bilingual condition.

Bilingual Figures

The difference between the poetics of *Yawar fiesta,* valorizing linguistic rupture and authorial expression, and the poetics of *Los ríos profundos,* valorizing metaphoric linkage and authorial displacement, reflect in turn a fundamental difference in Arguedian accounts of the bilingual site of enunciation. The bilingual voice of mistura was modeled on the mestizo, as Rowe has argued (*Mito* 46). But who is the mestizo? The portrait of the mestizo that begins to circulate in Arguedas's articles in the late 1930s depicts someone searching to express an interior experience, an "Indian soul," but who is unable to make use of his native tongue, Quechua, for that expression. It is fair to say that in these years, the struggling bilingual is the figure par excellence of the Arguedian mestizo.

Arguedas claimed that the mestizo's soul and root is Indian, and then offered his high school students in Sicuani as examples: they are "estudiantes mestizos en cuya alma lo indio es dominio" [mestizo students whose soul is dominated by Indianness] ("Entre" 27). Writing of Guaman Poma de Ayala, in the same year (1939), he noted, "en mil páginas que escribió se siente la tremenda lucha de este indio con el idioma en que se ve obligado a expresarse" [in the thousand pages that he wrote one senses this Indian's tremendous struggle with the language in which he felt required to express himself] ("Doce meses" 30). A year later he reiterated the force of this "tremendous struggle," now as a contemporary socio-linguistic experience in the Andes, in his reflections on his experience as a schoolteacher in Sicuani, a town near Cuzco. Regarding the written work of his students, and of his friend Quispe Alanoca in particular, he wrote:

> En algunas de estas composiciones se reconoce en forma clarísima el problema espiritual más penoso del mestizo: el problema del idioma. Estando presente este conflicto en todas las composiciones de los alumnos y en su hablar y escribir de todos los días. Pero en la composición de Quispe Alanoca el conflicto se siente más angustioso. Quispe es un alumno indio, sus padres son indios de Sicuani. Quispe se expresa bien y limpio en kechwa, es un idioma genuino y legítimo; y cuando se ve obligado a traducir sus inquietudes y todo su mundo interior en castellano, se confunde. De ahí lo oscuro de su idioma. En el fondo de ese estilo oscuro se siente una doble ansiedad: la del indio que se duele de la miseria de su vida y la del indio que sufre por traducir ese dolor en un idioma todavía extraño. (*Pumaccahua* 10)

> In some of these compositions one can clearly recognize the mestizo's most painful spiritual problem: the problem of language. This conflict is present in all of the students' compositions and in their daily speaking and writing. But in Quispe Alanoca's composition, the conflict feels more anguished. Quispe is an Indian student. His parents are Indians from Sicuani. Quispe expresses himself well and cleanly in Quechua; it is a genuine and legitimate language, and when he feels required to translate his preoccupations and his

interior world into Spanish, he gets confused. That explains the obscurity of his language. One senses a double anxiety at the heart of
this dark style: the anxiety of the Indian who feels the pain of the
poverty of his life, and the anxiety of the Indian who suffers from
having to translate this pain into a language that is still foreign
to him.

Ten years later, in 1950, he again referred to this inner conflict as an
ongoing struggle ("La novela" 170). The experience of the mestizo as
Arguedas understood him, in whose soul the Indian is dominant, and
whose social position is marked linguistically, is at the heart of what
Arguedas was trying to express with mistura.

It is clear that Arguedas understood his own voice as a writer to have
emerged through this same conflict, caused by trying to express an inner
reality in a foreign language: "Realizarse, traducirse, convertir en torrente
diáfono y legítimo el idioma que parece ajeno; comunicar a la lengua
casi extranjera la materia de nuestro espíritu. Esa es la dura, la difícil
cuestión" ("La novela" 170) [To realize oneself, to translate oneself, to
transform a seemingly alien language into a legitimate and diaphanous
torrent, to communicate to the almost foreign language the stuff of which
our spirit is made: that is the hard, the difficult question (xviii)]. Arguedas
turned repeatedly to the language of driven emotion, emphasizing conflict, struggle, desperation, and anxiety. Through this physical intensity,
a portrait of an embodied mestizo begins to emerge in these writings: the
mestizo who is somewhere (at school), doing something (writing in Spanish), feeling something (anxiety and desperation). And this concept of the
embodied mestizo is worth holding on to, for it provides a rare insight
into the mestizo's locus of enunciation. Arguedas saw the mestizo's anxiety and desperation to master Spanish as the result of an intense drive to
communicate, a desire to express oneself fully: "[el mestizo] nunca cesará
de adaptar el castellano a su profunda necesidad de expresarse en forma
absoluta, es decir, de traducir hasta la última exigencia de su alma, en la
que lo indio es mando y raíz" [the mestizo will never cease to adapt Spanish to his profound need to express himself in an absolute manner, that
is, to translate even the most urgent need of his soul, where Indianness is
the driving command and the root] ("Entre" 27). This need was always
personal, when Arguedas described it. Yet it arose in public institutions:
primary school, secondary school, university, as part of a process of public self-affirmation that was about making a personally held experience

and knowledge, understood as Indian and rooted in the geography of the Andes, *non*-disjunctive with the non-Indian, non-Andean social location, namely, the institutions of the liberal nation-state. Although this self-affirmation might mark the speaker as different or alien with respect to the institution, that does not seem to have been its main purpose, for Arguedas; nor was it simply a pedagogical issue (teaching others about the indigenous Andean world). It was essentially a process of making the self known to others, and it was internally driven by a desire to communicate. Notice that the mestizo is not internally divided or conflicted, in the sense of being ambivalent, in this portrayal. The anguish he feels does not stem from a conflict within the self's desire, but rather from a conflict between the self's desire to be expressed and the language at hand to do so.

He endowed the linguistic experience with a spiritual and subjective intensity, amply and repeatedly described, as if to mask the institutional, impersonal reality of the social situations in which this experience took place. Of his students in Pumaccahua, he wrote: "La conquista del idioma es la mayor *lucha espiritual* del mestizo actual en todo el Perú" [The conquest of language is the present-day mestizo's greatest *spiritual battle* throughout Peru] (*Pumaccahua* 10, emphasis mine). Yet he was essentially dramatizing the experience of provincial education. This process likely involved physical displacement away from home communities and was certainly an important access point to gain social status, in other words, a key to upward social mobility and cultural assimilation. The most common source of desperation and anxiety to master Spanish that one can imagine for this mestizo would have resulted from the widespread racist prohibitions against speaking Quechua in public institutions; and shame would have been the driving force urging him to speak Spanish — a racism of which Arguedas was manifestly aware, it should be noted. In 1940 he referred to "la necesidad imprescindible de hablar castellano para 'ser algo,'" noting, "todo indio que desea y pugna por ingresar a la vida activa del país, todo hombre de la sierra que pretende superarse y progresar, debe antes aprender el castellano, porque el gobierno, los negocios, la cultura, la enseñanza, todo se da y se hace en castellano" [the unavoidable necessity of speaking Spanish in order to "be something" . . . any Indian who wants and fights to enter the active life of the country, any man from the mountain region who seeks to improve himself and progress, must first learn Spanish, because government, business, culture, teaching — everything happens in Spanish] ("El wayno" 35). In 1945, meanwhile, he laid the problem out in stronger terms, condemning the treatment Indian students received: "todo el proceso del aprendizaje escolar es una viacrucis de golpes, de humillación y sobre todo de un íntimo, peligroso, falso y progresivo sentimiento de inferioridad" [the entire process of learning in school is a terrible ordeal of blows, humiliations, and most of all, of an intimate, dangerous, false and progressive feeling of inferiority] ("Un método" 42). But most of the time Arguedas veiled these realities, couching the experience in terms of a spiritual struggle for self-expression. Nevertheless, mistura attempted to mark this experience of passage. It was meant to signal the dynamism of a growing class.

Mistura was built around a notion of the mestizo as someone who has Quechua *within* him; it is the language of his soul or spirit. Translation and self-translation thus become confused. "To realize oneself, to translate oneself": these are the words Arguedas used in 1950 to describe the effort behind mistura. The same formulation can be found in an earlier essay as well, in 1939, when he wrote of the mestizo "translating" the urgent needs of his soul ("Entre" 27). In Arguedas's words it is the soul that is given authority, as if the entire process were being realized in the service of a being outside the material time and space of the state institution. The injunction to communicate in Spanish thus comes to be attributed to a force that is both within and beyond the mestizo student. This is perhaps an apt allegory for the process of interpellation to the state. Much like Jesús Lara, in his description of Wáskar Puma's experience of writing a school composition, Arguedas thought of school as an instrument that would enable him to communicate with his own interior rather than as an institution with its own authoritative ends.

Meanwhile, the fact that the Quechua speaker had no interlocutor whatsoever in the institutional settings where this spiritual struggle takes place remains practically unsaid. Arguedas rarely touched on what Molloy calls the "interlocutory void" conditioning autobiographical expression in Spanish America, meaning in this case, the fact that expressing oneself in Quechua was out of the question. We might go so far as to say that the experience of "anguish" that Arguedas described was nothing but a complex compensating move for the (self) violence of assimilation, a way to deal with the fact that, for the Quechua speaker yearning to speak the language of his soul in school, only Spanish will do.

There is much of this image of the mestizo, actively expressing his profoundly Indian soul, that corresponds to a concept of the mestizo circulating in the Cuzco of the 1930s and 1940s. This "neoindianismo," Marisol de la Cadena argues, was calculated to endow the mestizo with cultural authenticity, part of ongoing regional struggles with Lima for political control and cultural self-definition (131–76). But in addition to the ideological component of this construction of mestizo identity, its use to gain new political legitimacy for regional mestizos, it is worth underscoring the extent to which it reflects a notion of regional Andean social identifications as fluid in ways for which contemporary race-class taxonomies cannot account. In other words, it does not mark a clear ethno-racial line distinguishing mestizos from Indians.

In effect, Arguedas never invested much intellectual energy in defining and distinguishing these two groups from one another. Fernando Mires attributes to Arguedas the first serious attempt to understand the "ambiguity" of Indian identity. As Mires describes it, for Arguedas, "the Indian [or Indianness] extends like a shadow over social and national reality. The mestizo would be, in this sense, a prolongation of the Indian under new forms that coexist with the Indians' other forms of being" (142). This ambiguity explains why, in a 1939 essay, Arguedas did not notice the apparent contradiction of stating in one paragraph that mestizos are the majority sector in Peru and in another that the Indian constitutes 60 percent of the nation ("Entre" 26). For Arguedas in these early essays, mestizos are *in essence* Indians. Both of them remain "within" the linguistic community that Quechua creates, which is a vast, inclusive community.

Arguedas's vision of the mestizo in the late 1930s and early 1940s, then, foregrounds the problem of the bilingual author. Both share the same site of enunciation. If students like Quispe Alanoca provide a model of the mestizo who enunciated *Yawar fiesta*, who serves as the exemplary figure for the bilingual voice of *Los ríos profundos*?

Arguedas's 1958 study of mestizo artists in Huamanga (Ayacucho) provides a striking possibility. The image Arguedas offered of the master sculptor Don Joaquín López, the most accomplished of the retablo artists Arguedas examined, shows a very different kind of mestizo figure. The Huamanga artist is not the interstitial figure engaged in a process of social mobility that the earlier essays portray. Rather he is a member of an established ethno-class whose origins date back to the colony. The primary function of the mestizo, Arguedas argued in this piece, was to be an intermediary between Spanish and Indian ("El arte" 146). In fulfilling this duty into the twentieth century, the mestizo artisan Don

Joaquín López lives a life without apparent contradiction: "Se trata del caso de un artista en quien se muestra, por el mismo hecho de su calidad personal, las virtudes características de los hombres de su cultura. Decimos 'virtudes' por denominar normas de conducta, ajuste armonioso de tales normas, adecuación plena interior y práctica, a las tradiciones que rigen la comunidad a la cual pertenece" [We're talking about the case of an artist who demonstrates, due to his personal qualities, the virtues characteristic of the people of his culture. We say "virtues" to denote norms of conduct, harmonious adjustment of such norms, a full, inner and practical adaptation to the traditions that govern the community to which he belongs] ("El arte" 147). Gone is the drama of self-expression that characterized the mestizo in earlier writings, a drama embedded in the title of the 1939 essay: "Between Quechua and Spanish, the Anguish of the Mestizo." The earlier concept of the mestizo invoked an almost existential crisis, an anxious need to affirm the self in a situation of intense contradiction caused by the disjunction between "inner" and "outer" languages.

Los ríos profundos is essentially the story of this dynamic, disjunctive process, Arguedas's first extended fictional account of it. Yet it is not narrated with mistura. Rather, the narrative voice, at the level of the linguistic inscription, is integrating rather than disjunctive. And, as I have already suggested, it is disembodied and anonymous. This change corresponds to Arguedas's new vision of mestizaje. The mestizo artist Don Joaquín López that Arguedas portrayed in 1958 enables cultural transformation at a national level by serving as a bridge between otherwise antagonistic social groups. He is a double participant in native and occidental culture ("El arte" 157), able to link to Peru's growing urban culture in a way that Indians cannot; he mediates the relation between Indians and Lima ("El arte" 151). But as Arguedas describes him, Don López himself is not engaged in a process of self-transformation. He remains the same, even as the world around him changes. There is thus a strong similarity between this man and the narrator of *Los ríos profundos*. Both are mediators lacking self-interest, conduits for creative cultural transformation who remain themselves unchanged by the process. They are mestizos, but not of the kind Arguedas had described two decades before, that is, they are not searching to express and establish their own independent "cultural personality."

In Uriel García's model the mestizo or "new Indian" effectively supersedes and replaces the "old Indian," whom he referred to as a thing of the past, a "dead soul" (109). But in Arguedas's evolving portrait the mestizo never fully claims his privileged space as the sole creative force impelling the national destiny forward. By the writing of *Los ríos profundos* the mestizo rarely, if ever, operates in his own name, out of his own ambitions, drives and desires. When he takes center stage in Arguedas's writing, as in *Los ríos profundos;* or in the figure of Rendón Willka, in *Todas las sangres;* or in the figure of Don Joaquín López, the retablo sculptor from Ayacucho, it is in a self-effacing manner, as if he were reduced to his essential function of interconnector — "vínculo vivo" [living link], as Arguedas would say of himself in 1968 — with no identity or interests of his own that are not determined by this function. The Arguedian mestizo in its ideal form, as he manifested it from 1950 on, is thus a profoundly relational being, rather than an identity for itself.[19] Not until the mid-1960s and his interest in the urban cholo culture of the coast would Arguedas return to the idea of the mestizo as a cultural personality in his own right. It is little wonder that Arguedas's struggle to be the "vínculo vivo," couched in moral terms, intersected so neatly with the increasingly hegemonic view placing the mestizo at the heart of Latin American nationality. Arguedas's limpid mestizo provides a metaphor for an ideal political state, so ideal that it becomes a nonstate: an entity seeming to have a purely objective integrating existence, rather than expressing the particular interests of one social sector at the expense of others. Profoundly indigenous or, rather, indigenous in the way Arguedas came to understand indigeneity, this state appears innocent of power.

The Mediating Voice

In his writings during the 1930s and the 1940s, Arguedas described nascent bilingualism as a highly emotive and conflictive process of self-transformation, a spiritual conflict involving the soul. This portrait of the self-translating mestizo corresponds, clearly, to the protagonist-hero of *Los ríos profundos,* the one through whom the narrative is focalized. Yet unlike this protagonist, the narrator of *Los ríos profundos* is not a self-translator, for he does not place himself subjectively at the center of the narration. Like the retablo artist Don López, this narrator, the one who enunciates the narrative, is self-effacing and unobtrusive, a go-between.

The figure of the go-between is of course of paramount importance to the novel, providing Arguedas with ample occasions to meditate on the nature of the mediator figure. We can take these as meta-fictional moments, for they offer a reflection on Arguedas's art itself and on how he conceived the artist's role. Perhaps the most famous such reflection is Arguedas's depiction of the "zumbayllu," a whirling top. The protagonist-hero hopes that its song will link him again to his distant father. Occurring in the same chapter and equally as significant, though subject to somewhat less critical analysis, is the scene where the protagonist-hero adopts the role of a go-between himself. Like Cyrano de Bergerac, he has been called on by his schoolmate Antero, who would like to woo the object of his affections, a young woman of Abancay's gentry named Salvinia, by sending her a letter. Antero asks the protagonist to write the letter, because his way with words has gained him a certain renown. Antero says, "Oye Ernesto, me han dicho que escribes como poeta. Quiero que me hagas una carta" (110) [Hey, Ernesto, they tell me you write like a poet. I'd like you to write a letter for me (71)]. As far as I can tell, this is the first time that our protagonist has been given a proper name. He is nameless until the moment when he is called on to display his linguistic virtuosity in written, literary Spanish. Ernesto is not named here as a bilingual, but as a speaker and writer of Spanish and as person of letters. In the social economy of Abancay, this has conferred on him the status of the proper. This newfound proper status, which brings him onto the margins of a new sphere of belonging that includes proud plantation heirs like Antero, makes of him an exultant, almost aggressive go-between who confuses his own desires with Antero's. Yet he quickly rejects this role because it causes him to feel shame. Abandoning the Spanish letter he is writing for Antero, he writes a love letter in Quechua to his own object of desire — and shame becomes pride. Yet as will become clear, the Quechua letter also involves a paradoxical kind of self-effacement that is key to understanding the predominant narrative voice of the novel as a whole. In this passage centered on the role of the go-between, the novel offers a reflection on the tension between different styles of being an intermediary. Keeping the image of the retablo sculptor Don Joaquín López in mind, this involves a meditation on different styles of being mestizo.[20]

The Quechua letter that Ernesto writes demonstrates that the hero's desires are independent of the landowner's, and that there are moral differences between them. Ernesto decides to write it only after experiencing "una aguda vergüenza" (114) [an intense feeling of shame (74)] while writing for Antero, a shame that causes him to switch course. This passage in the text underscores the distance between Ernesto and the narrator. In this moment, the translating narrator becomes clearly differentiated from the self-translating hero. The first words of the letter Ernesto produces are given to us in Quechua; then the Quechua stops. Then it is translated into Spanish along with the rest of the letter. All that we see of the Quechua is a fragment of a line.

> Y escribí:
> "Uyariy chay k'atik'niki siwar k'entita"...
> "Escucha al picaflor esmeralda que te sigue; te ha de hablar de mí; no seas cruel, escúchale. Lleva fatigadas las pequeñas alas, no podrá volar más; deténte ya. Está cerca la piedra blanca donde descansan los viajeros, espera allí y escúchale; oye su llanto, es sólo el mensajero de mi joven corazón, te ha de hablar de mí. ¡Oye, hermosa, tus ojos como estrellas grandes, bella flor, no huyas más, detente! Una orden de los cielos te traigo: ¡te mandan ser mi tierna amante...!" (114, original ellipses)

> And I wrote:
> *Uyariy chay k'atik'niki siwar k'entita...*
> "Listen to the emerald hummingbird who follows you; he shall speak to you of me; do not be cruel, hear him. His little wings are tired, he can fly no farther, pause a moment. The white stone where the travelers rest is nearby; wait there and listen to him; hear his sobs; he is only the messenger of my young heart; he shall speak to you of me. Listen, my lovely one, your eyes are like large stars; beautiful flower, do not flee anymore, halt! An order from the heavens I bring you; they command you to be my tender lover...!" (74–75)

The first line is Ernesto's work, but the subsequent translation is purely the narrator's.

Rowe has argued with great insight that the narrative of *Los ríos profundos*, the story it recounts of the adolescent hero's life, is in reality the prehistory of the one who recounts it ("El lugar" 131). How did the hero become the narrator? Rowe emphasizes the novel's end, when the hero turns to face the land of the dead and chooses to journey toward it, passing through the plague zone. Death, thus, lies in the prehistory of the narrator. The scene of the two letters, I would argue, foreshadows that dissolution and conversion. It is an important moment on the path to that becoming. It can be imagined as a fork in the road, in which first one path is chosen before being rejected in favor of the other — not exactly Quechua chosen over Spanish, but one form of being in the world over another. The presence of this fork in the road reminds us that Ernesto is not the narrator, or at least not yet, while at the same time offering a glimpse into what he will have to do to arrive at that destination: renounce the body and diminish the self in order to become pure voice.

Cornejo points out that the Quechua letter refers its reader immediately to the realm of song (*Escribir* 195). With the command "Listen," it points to a figure for a frail, modest voice: the bird. Its wings are tired; it does not speak for itself, but rather for the writer: "he shall speak to you of me." The bird is the deputy of the self. As an innocent messenger, the bird referred to here becomes a figure for the narrator: bird song, we remember, is the narrator's diffuse place of origin and the matter of which he is made. Like the artistry of Arguedas's favorite mestizo artist, this rhetorical gesture is a self-effacing one. The author of the letter does not proclaim himself in his own voice, but rather through the voice of another. And yet despite this, it is a voice to be found everywhere, because it is in the song of birds. The letter thus performs a rejection of the proper naming to which its author has just been subjected, by purposefully confusing the voice of the author with a ubiquitous natural voice which emerges from a "region" and a "matter" without boundaries.

The figure of the bird in this letter, either as a messenger of love or as figure of the absent beloved, is clearly a biblical trope. But it is also a rearticulation of a trope found in many of the Quechua songs interspersed throughout the novel, especially those sung in the chicherías, and it can be found in countless other Quechua songs from the Andes as well.[21] But according to Arguedas it is not just a trope from the oral-folk tradition but also from the classical Inca tradition. Shortly before the appearance of *Los ríos profundos*, Arguedas published his translation of three hymns ascribed to the Inca Manco Capac, transcribed by Joan de Santacruz Pachacuti Yamqui Salcamaygua, one of the so-called "Indian chroniclers," in his *Relación de antiguedades deste reyno del Piru* (An Account of This Ancient Kingdom of Peru) (1613). Regina Harrison has shown that these translations had a tremendous effect on Arguedas's own poetic creation, and that he incorporated aspects of these hymns' structure, especially the element of invocation and apostrophe, into the Quechua poetry he wrote subsequently (Harrison 122).

The third of these hymns in Pachacuti's text consists of Manco Capac's instructions to the priests (Itier 143). Arguedas's translation of this hymn was first published in 1955 as part of an extensive article on Quechua hymns and was then included in his anthology of Quechua poetry in 1965. In Arguedas's translation, the bird appears in a metaphor explaining what kind of voice the supplicant must adopt in his address to God: he must sing in the voice of a lark. In that way, the renunciating self — fasting — attains a joyous expression that communicates with an other who has no earthly form. Arguedas's full translation of this third hymn reads as follows:

> Con regocijada boca,
> con regocijada lengua,
> de día
> y esta noche
> llamarás.
> Ayunando
> *cantarás con voz de calandria*
> y quizá
> en nuestra alegría,
> en nuestra dicha,
> desde cualquier lugar del mundo,
> el creador del hombre,
> el Señor Todopoderoso,
> te escuchará.
> "¡Jay!" te dirá,
> y tú
> donde quiera que estés,
> y así para la eternidad,
> sin otro señor que él
> vivirás, serás.
>
> (*Poesía quechua* 13;
> "Himnos" 126–28;
> emphasis mine)

> With your mouth rejoicing,
> Your tongue rejoicing,
> By day
> And tonight,
> You will call.

Fasting,
You will sing in the voice of the lark
And perhaps
In our happiness,
In our joy,
From everywhere in the world,
Man's creator,
All-powerful Lord,
Will listen to you.
"Jay!" he'll say to you,
And you
Wherever you may be,
And forever so,
With no other lord but him
You will live, you will be.

The proper language of divinity, this hymn suggests, is the language of birds; singing "with the voice of the lark," one makes oneself heard by God.

As Harrison shows, Arguedas would later call on the power of the bird's voice in his poem "A nuestro padre creador Tupac Amaru/Tupac Amaru Camaj Taytanchisman" [To Our Father Creator Tupac Amaru] (Harrison 123–24). The text of this prayer is thus an intertext for that poem, as Harrison demonstrates. The hymn is also, I would argue, an intertext for *Los ríos profundos*. However, what makes this prayer significant for the novel is, perversely, the fact that it contains a serious mistranslation. Arguedas's translation is the only one of the many published translations to have mentioned the voice of a bird. Arguedas himself, when he first published this translation, explained its essentially poetic nature: it was not to be considered a literal translation. Yet precisely because it was rendered poetically rather than literally, he considered it to be especially faithful to the spirit of the original ("Himnos" 122–23). Underlying these assertions, clearly, is a notion of poetry as a language of the spirit. Arguedas understood the piece to reflect one of the highest and most sacred expressions of Inca religiosity; thus he resorted to the modern-day language of spirit — poetry — in order to get at its essence.

This piece has had many translators and has been anthologized often.[22] Yet only Arguedas's translation contains a reference to a bird. It appears, in fact, to have been his exclusive poetic invention. Lara, for example, who translated and published the poem earlier, in the 1940s, renders the bird lines like so: "Esperarás limpio de todo" [You will wait cleansed of everything] (*La poesía quechua* 158). Arguedas's translation, like all others before 1985, derived from the transcriptions of the original text made by Clements Markham (1873) and Marcos Jiménez de Espada (1879); its first translator was M. A. Mossi, who worked from these transcriptions (1892), though apparently without a rigorous knowledge of Quechua (Itier 135). These transcriptions and all the resulting translations are now considered defective. The original transcriptions were made by scholars unable to read the original properly; they could not determine where one word ended and another began. Most Quechua-speaking translators, such as Lara and Arguedas, were thus faced with a Quechua transcription with pockets of nonsense, for which they compensated in their translations by attempting to reconstruct the original Quechua words. However, César Itier, a scholar of colonial Quechua and recent translator of this text, points out that they did so with little knowledge of the difference between colonial and contemporary Quechua and secure in the belief that the text was of Inca origin. They were thus unable to perceive that the text displayed the influence of Christian evangelization and was as a result composed in a Quechua whose religious idiom had already been seriously affected by missionaries (Itier 139). Itier declares his own recent translation definitive, based on rigorous analysis of colonial Quechua, and renders the lines in question like so: "Ayunando, lo esperarás" [Fasting, you will await him] (Itier 143).

All of this gives one license to think that Arguedas's translation, his rendering of this line as "you will sing in the voice of a lark," might in fact have been a radical mistranslation, based on a faulty transcription of the original text and a dose of wishful thinking.[23] More than anything else, it reflects his own poetic interpretation about the form and language of Inca spirituality.[24] In his anthology of Quechua poetry, Arguedas compared the Quechua hymns of what he thought to be Incan origin, such as the one quoted above, with Catholic Quechua hymns. He wrote, "Los [himnos religiosos incaicos] revelan que la relación del hombre con Dios fue más de gratitud y regocijo que de temor; los [himnos católicos] trataron de fundar en la conciencia de la grey india el espanto, la humildad sumisa, el desprecio a la vida" [The Incan religious hymns reveal that man's relation to God was more a matter of gratitude and joy than of fear; the Catholic hymns tried to instill horror, submissive humility, and contempt for life in the consciousness of the Indian flock] (Arguedas, *Poesía quechua* 6). Yet in the light of recent scholarship, this distinction between pre-Western "gratitude and joy" for life and Western "fearful, submissive contempt" for life cannot be sustained.

Nevertheless, this distinction is central to the construction of *Los ríos profundos,* for which this hymn-poem becomes an intertext through the trope of the bird as divine messenger. The poem triangulates two scenes in the novel: the scene of the Quechua letter, and the scene, several chapters later, when the narrator declares himself to be originally from and of the realm of bird song, "the stuff of which I am made." Bird song is his origin, that diffuse realm in which he lived before becoming a man, which one can take to be doubly significant, referring both to "humanity" as well as to adulthood. It is the place where he lived before he became a person, or before he became an adult. Thus Ernesto, in imagining himself in the figure of the singing bird, symbolically projects himself back to his origin. That realm is not the mortal matrix or womb, but rather the sky or the air. But it is also, as the hymn and the Quechua letter suggest, not a place at all, but rather a medium, a means to communicate with an absent beloved, such as the divine, or an ideal lover. Bird song is both an origin place and a conduit; a "region" and a kind of language. It is, therefore, a figure for Quechua itself as Arguedas understood it: a sound that creates a sphere of intimate belonging, a "community of meaning," and hence a kind of shared location.

The narrator, intimating this voice as his place of origin, also intimates his own entirely mediatory nature: a messenger between the divine and the earthly, between past and present. Speaking this language, he makes his origin present as a kind of ephemeral return, and he also reasserts himself as a mediator between the soul and earthly bodies. If we perceive this as the predominant narrative voice of the novel and as an ideal authorial self-projection, then the novel itself comes to be invested with the same joyous yearning to be recognized by a higher order, a yearning to cease perhaps to be "I." It must be expressed according to divine instructions: voiced by a human cleansed by fasting and singing like a bird.

In *Los ríos profundos,* the narrative voice that emerges as the expression of this position testifies to a process of conflict and change while remaining free of it. The projection of this narrative voice, purified of its material entanglements in the dirty sphere of lived social relations, i.e., worldly power, unfolds on two literary levels in the novel: at the level of a search for a language cleansed of the signs of its bilingual enmeshments, a language in which Quechua has been excised from its home in the Spanish of a bilingual; and at the level of narrative voice, of an "I" cleansed of self-interest and seeming to exist only as the medium for the passions of another. The narrator thus figured is distanced from, non-identical to, the mestizo protagonist whose story this novel tells. Yet they are the same in essence and in origin: creatures of Indian song, Quechua creations.

In 1940 Arguedas had already predicted that Spanish would be the mestizo's "definitive" language, though "he" had not yet conquered it. But it would not be pure Spanish. He wrote,

> De esta pugna del mestizo por adaptar el castellano a la versión de su alma, en que lo indio es lo fundamental, el castellano saldrá íntimamente influenciado por el kechwa, que es el idioma de los hombres que ha criado esta tierra. Pero el castellano ha de ser, sin duda alguna, el idioma definitivo del mestizo. Hoy mismo lo es ya; pero no se ha logrado todavía el pleno equilibrio entre el castellano y la necesidad de expresión absoluta del mestizo. La conquista del idioma es la mayor lucha espiritual del mestizo actual en todo el Perú. (*Pumaccahua* 10)

> Out of the mestizo's struggle to adapt Spanish to the expression of his soul, where Indianness is fundamental, Spanish will emerge intimately influenced by Quechua, which is the language of those whom this land has reared. But Spanish will undoubtedly be the mestizo's definitive language. It is already so today; but the right balance between Spanish and the mestizo's need for absolute expression has yet to be achieved. The conquest of language is the most important spiritual struggle of the present-day mestizo throughout Peru.

Published nearly twenty years after these lines, *Los ríos profundos* provides an interesting historical perspective from which to assess these views. Judging by this novel, Spanish has indeed become the mestizo's definitive language. Is it a Spanish "intimately influenced" by Quechua, as Arguedas predicted? Yes and no, depending on how one interprets Arguedas's words. It is, to the extent that the narrative enunciation is the fruit of extensive poetic mediation on the part of a bilingual. Thus speaker and listener, writer and reader, find themselves to have been intimately influenced by Quechua, though in ways of which they themselves perhaps remain unaware. Yet it is not, to the extent that Spanish itself, symbol for Arguedas of a status quo being transformed from within by agents of its own creation, remains grammatically unchanged.

Arguedas's words were uttered in 1940 in a redemptive tone. What is it that he wished himself and other mestizos to be redeemed from? One imagines, in light of this novel, that he was searching for redemption from the interlocutory void, one that he confronted and that he imagined every Indian or mestizo to be confronting, with every enunciation uttered in Spanish. *Los ríos profundos* inscribes that search in its enunciation, in the creation of an "I" modeled on the one who sings to God in the Inca hymn and who seems to have, briefly, transcended the interlocutory void. But it also inscribes the failure of that search in its use of a Spanish that everywhere bears the traces of that void and of the need to communicate across it.

The novel thus performs a kind of symbolic labor on the signs "Quechua" and "Spanish." Spanish comes to be the sign of a fall from grace into the world and into the body, rather than, as in the first edition of *Yawar fiesta,* the sign of a new nationality in the making, one drenched in the bodily fluids of animal birth. Quechua, meanwhile, stabilizes that Spanish sign by appearing as its mirror opposite: emotive spirit reaching out across the void to envelop an absent or divine being.

What to make of the fact that this possibility stems in part from Arguedas's mistranslation of a Quechua text? Glissant understood that the forced poetics of the bilingual emerge out of an experience of need, of the writer's need for a particular language. Glissant called this need "l'insoupçonné tourment," the unsuspected torment (236). Given Arguedas's experiences as a writer and his need to write himself — a need that not all novelists share — one can understand why the possibility of compensating for or overcoming the interlocutory void might have been so important to him. What is interesting to note, however, is that the language he needed at the beginning of his writing career was not the same as the language of *Los ríos profundos;* and that it eventually ceased to be Quechua per se, but rather a language of spirit. From this perspective, one can see why the interlocutory void experienced by the "bilingual I" becomes, for Arguedas's readers, ultimately indistinguishable from an overall negative experience of embodied modernity in Peru. Anthropologist Beth Povinelli has argued that "*Indigenous* is nothing less than the name used to designate the state of Being prior to modernity and its concomitant identity formation, nationalism" (260). In effect, indigeneity, when cleanly transmitted, seems in this novel to signify redemption from the tragic divisions of the modern nation-state.

Chapter Four

Rosario Castellanos
at the Edge of Entanglement

Fue un ser concreto ante una tarea concreta: la escritura....

She was a specific person faced with a specific task: writing....
— Elena Poniatowska, *¡Ay Vida, no me mereces!*

What is essential to a given life? The indigenista threads of Rosario Castellanos's fictional autobiography *Balún Canán* (1957) did not start out
essential but became so, woven in as part of her developing aesthetic and
ideological vision and particularly as part of her feminist vision. Castellanos was in Europe when she first began to narrate her attachment to
Chiapas, Mexico, her home state, through indigenismo. In 1950, before
her departure abroad, she spoke with outright disdain and self-loathing
of Chiapas, evidenced repeatedly in her letters to Mexican philosopher
Ricardo Guerra, her lover at the time. She mocked "the man of the
tropics" while on a brief visit to Tuxtla Gutiérrez (*Cartas* 26), reserv-
ing even stronger derision for Comitán, her hometown, which she found
"completely improbable." She followed her declaration of disbelief with
an extensive list of all the local customs transgressing her cosmopolitan sensibilities. Her contempt for provincial backwardness extended to
indigenous Chiapanecos as well as to their more prosperous and assimilated compatriots, whose attempts to appreciate "the advances of
civilization," such as the cinema and the Ferris wheel, she found laughable. She ended her account with mock-existential despair: "Ya basta.
Como el absurdo es intolerable, he decidido irme de aquí" [Enough.
Since absurdity is intolerable, I've decided to leave] (*Cartas* 32). Back to
Mexico City, and from there to Madrid for a year. Yet once in Europe
she surprised herself with her own feelings of nostalgia for Chiapas and
"el rancho" (*Cartas* 85). The outpouring of emotion grew strongest on

encountering, at the Musée de l'Homme in Paris, ethnological artefacts from Chiapas:

> yo quería llorar toda feliz y triste porque en una de sus vitrinas de arte precolombino había lanzas y vestidos de los lacandones y chamulas y retratos de sus chozas. . . . Fíjese, ya no era siquiera México cuyo recuerdo me es más o menos soportable. Sino Chiapas, como quien dice la mera entraña de uno (*Cartas* 97).

> I wanted to cry, all sad and happy, because in one of the pre-Columbian display cases there were spears and clothing from the Lacandons and the Chamulas, and pictures of their huts. Can you imagine? . . . Can you imagine? It wasn't even Mexico City, the memory of which I can more or less tolerate. But Chiapas, one's very core, as they say.

Chiapas as "entraña," as her core or her heart — that this "core" spoke to her and that she listened to its voice, is made evident if one compares her autobiographies from before and after her year in Europe.

Castellanos grew up in a region whose ethnic majority was indigenous, in a house served by indigenous people in which indigenous languages were spoken, and during a time in which revolutionary nationalist indigenismo was an ideological mainstay of the Mexican political regime. Yet the narrative of her childhood did not *of necessity* involve indigenista depictions. On the contrary, her first autobiographical prose text, a story titled "Primera revelación" [First Revelation], written and published in 1950 and concerning the death of her brother, has no discernible indigenista theme whatsoever. Set in the house of the same Comitán oligarch in which *Balún Canán* would be set, and depicting similar events from her life, it nevertheless contains no mention of indigenous people nor of the racialized social conflicts dividing Chiapas. The history of the Cárdenas-era social reforms, so crucial to making *Balún Canán* a novel of the Mexican Revolution, is likewise utterly absent. Castellanos, in other words, in some sense *chose* to make her autobiographical fiction an indigenista work, and indeed to begin it with an indigenous voice, culled from a Spanish translation of the Maya Book of Council.

How did Castellanos arrive at this choice to begin the life story she constructed with an Indian voice and to place interethnic relations at its center? And what is the significance of this choice for understanding the experimental form she lent to her novel of female coming-of-age? Like other provincial indigenistas, her turn toward indigenismo was a turn toward childhood and the past, and was thus significant on a personal and biographical level. It occurred in the months following her return from Europe and her decision to go back to Chiapas and led eventually to her desire to join the Instituto Nacional Indigenista. It was part of her re-vision of her familial past, writes Marta Robles (152), of gaining a more distanced perspective on her family history in the very moment of returning to the site of its most dramatic unfolding. It allowed her to return to the place of her birth without assuming her birthright, that is, without assuming her position as a landowner and a rancher, a position which she portrayed through the iconic figure of Doña Bárbara and from which she consciously sought distance.

This chapter on Castellanos's novel *Balún Canán* examines how Castellanos's turn toward indigenismo and her regional origin were integral to her bid for a new kind of independence — intellectual, aesthetic, female — and traces the changing stances toward indigeneity that this entailed, indigeneity in the multiple senses of origin, land, and Maya Indian culture. This independence came to be embodied in the solitary self and to be expressed through what Spivak has called, with Charlotte Brontë's *Jane Eyre* in mind, "the unique creative imagination of the marginal individualist," which Spivak identifies as central to the development of female consciousness in the West ("Three Women's Texts" 151). This solitary self is the one who appears at the end of *Balún Canán*. The novel is organized in such a way as to underscore the emergence of a new individual, a process depicted as only tentatively redemptive, and then only on a personal rather than a collective level. The first-person narrator's individual voice emerges as the final point to a narrative of many-layered losses, not in celebration but in melancholic consolation, as if something precious had been born in the midst of tragedy. The narrator authors her first words, shakily, in a world in which she is now definitively on her own. Banished first from the unstable "we" created by shared words and silent affinities with her nana (her Mayan nanny), then again from the "we" created by the shared terrors and silent complicities she'd experienced with her brother, then finally from the "we" created by her role as her mother's silent shadow, the narrator has become by the end of the novel an utterly lonely figure, someone who knows "the taste of solitude," as she herself says (*Balún Canán* 289).

Castellanos plotted this story of loss and tentative consolation across the difficult years of 1930s Chiapas. Divided into three sections and organized chronologically, *Balún Canán* describes the impact of the Cárdenas presidency on the regional planter class as its most prominent families — including that of the seven-year-old narrator — contend with the growing strength of previously subaltern social sectors, including both Maya Indian laborers and the local middle class. These now have the support of the federal government, beneficiaries of its struggle to wrest a measure of political control from regional elites and consolidate the revolutionary nation-state. Castellanos writes this story of "pro-Indian" government policies, like rural education programs, primarily from the perspective of characters who occupy marginal positions with respect to the two competing centers of power: the federal government and the local planter elite. The novel's protagonists are children, servants, wives, bastards, spinsters, Indians. Especially in the second section of the novel, national events are interwoven into a narrative that brings the fortunes of these individuals into a relation of immediacy to the otherwise distant and impersonal workings of federal law and order. For almost all of the characters, this story of the government's intrusion into provincial life unfolds as the unveiling of old histories of resentment and insecurity, linking personal desires and grievances to the narrative of the state's formation.

The family the novel describes, the events recounted, the individual characters portrayed — all bear more than a passing ressemblance to Castellanos's family and its experience of the 1930s. The girl-narrator is clearly an approximate version of Castellanos herself. Yet as Debra Castillo says, *Balún Canán* is "no traditional autobiography" (229). *Balún Canán* is organized around an individual, that is, a human life, but for various reasons that individual cannot be said to be at the center of the narrative. Her hold on the narrator function is tenuous at best, and she is frequently displaced in the novel by other narrators. The most notorious and obvious displacement of "I" occurs in the transition between the novel's Part One and Part Two, when "I" simply stops narrating for close to one hundred and fifty pages, the entire length of Part Two. She goes to sleep, lulled into dreams by her nana: "Duerme ahora. Sueña que esta tierra dilatada es tuya" (74) [Sleep now. Dream that this wide land is yours (71)].[1] While she dreams, an impersonal narrator comes to the fore and takes over the narration to describe "what is remembered of those days" (75), days on the Argüello family's hacienda Chactajal. When the third and final part of the novel opens, the first-person narrator has returned, but it is not easy to determine whether the traumatic events that occurred while she lay dreaming have made an impact on her consciousness. Like Lara's *Surumi*, *Balún Canán* is divided among first- and third-person narrators, introducing a significant fracture in the voice of a novel that is otherwise thematically and temporally unified. Several years after its publication Castellanos went so far as to apologize publicly for her decision, responding to the implicit view that she had failed to live up to the aesthetic breakthroughs of the "new narrative" by writing a novel that was not internally unified:

> La estructura desconcierta a los lectores. Hay una ruptura en el estilo, en la manera de ver y de pensar. Esa es, supongo, la falla principal del libro. Lo confieso: no pude estructurar la novela de otra manera. (Carballo 419)

> The structure is disconcerting for the readers. There is a break in the style, in the way of seeing and thinking. I suppose that is the book's principal flaw. I confess: I could not structure the book any other way.

Though it may be the only one considered a flaw, the transition between first- and third-person narration is not the only displacement of "I" in *Balún Canán*. Part One is filled with such displacements, with other ways of "seeing and thinking." The most significant of these occur in the novel's first pages as a result of two indigenous speech acts. One is contained in the epigraph, an invocation to meditate on origins taken from the *Popol Vuh*. It begins with an injunction: "Musitaremos el origen" [We shall meditate on the origin]. Whose origin? The novel's opening lines, uttered by the girl's Maya nanny, compound the *Popol Vuh*'s decentering of the autobiographical narrative away from "I" and bring us into a world of confused and overlapping stories. The nana says: "Y entonces, coléricos, nos desposeyeron, nos arrebataron lo que habíamos atesorado, la palabra, que es el arca de la memoria" (9, original ellipsis) [And then in anger they dispossessed us, they robbed us of what we had amassed, the word, which is the ark of memory].[2] In its portentous, cryptic, collective utterance, the nana's narrative appears to us as a continuation of the epigraph from the *Popol Vuh* (Lienhard 214). At the start of the story of herself that "I" tells we thus find another story, another's story, which is in fact another *book*. This book is first put into play by the author herself, for it is she who has chosen the epigraph, and subsequently by one of her characters, the nana, who takes up the voice of the Mayan book. The nana is the first narrator to tell the story of "I"; and she tells this story from a completely different perspective than "I" will.

This enunciation is an important event, for it reenacts what Martinican novelist-philosopher Edouard Glissant refers to as the colonial "point of entanglement" where previously separate cultures join fates (36). It is a point of origin so fractured and unstable that it is impossible to narrate as *a* history. A truly decolonized history of the Americas, argues Glissant, can occur only by returning, figuratively, to the point of imbrication and the multiple stories it has generated.[3] The words spoken by the nana emerge from this point of entanglement and make it a feature of everyday life. They electrify the social field, polarizing it, setting people into patterns of collision, affinity, and separation. Narrating a history of stolen words, they bring us to the point where "mine," "ours," and "yours" have become violently and unjustly confused. It will become immediately clear that there is no single story that can possibly speak the truth of this event. The dilemma such a multiplicity of stories entails is enacted there and then on the novel's opening page, when two versions of the same history clash: the girl's response to her nana's words is to invoke Christopher Columbus, to contest and undermine the colonial history recounted in medias res by her nana. She tries, rather lamely, to counteract her nana's perspective with another version of events, asserting the point of entanglement as a discovery rather than a conquest.

What is at stake here is not just the power of narration, but the power to possess. The object of the verbs in the nana's sentence is "the word," yet "dispossess," "rob" and "amass" also bring to mind questions of property: Indian lands. The nana's story reveals the historical slippage between stolen land and stolen word-memory when it comes to narrating the Conquest. It thrusts us into a colonial history of naming, in which the word is also an act of material possession-dispossession. The hacienda Chactajal, jewel of the Argüello patrimony, will soon become known to the reader as the sign of this still-contested act of naming.[4] The distinction between entangled stories and entangled lands collapses when possession is understood — through the legal framework that legitimates it — as a question of naming and narrating local belongings. Land, writes Ileana Rodríguez, "makes a history which is not the history of one narrative but of several, the history of an uninterrupted continental narratology, the history of a map of disputed borders, limits, and frontiers in the ever-polemical discussion of nation and nationality" (4).

"I" thus first emerges as a character in someone else's story — the nana's story, codified indigenous history (both oral and written) — rather than as the narrator of her own. Her story of discovery, including *self-*discovery, must compete with that other story of conquest and indigenous dispossession. At *Balún Canán*'s beginning an indigenous voice has as much control over the narrative as "I" does. And as a consequence, "I" is shown to exist for someone else, as an object, prior to existing for herself. Before her nana, "I" is but an "anis seed," a mere speck.

This chapter offers an extended analysis of these various displacements of "I" over the course of the novel and, following from Jean Franco's seminal study *Plotting Women,* proposes to link these internal changes to Castellanos's elliptical path across the terrain of Mexican indigenista nationalism, "plotting" the construction of her life story. My primary interest will be to show how Castellanos integrates herself into a national narrative, a feat that Franco considered to be largely impossible for twentieth-century Mexican women. In her analysis of Castellanos's novel *Oficio de tinieblas,* like *Balún Canán* an ambitious and complex account of race, class, and gender relations in historical Chiapas, Franco examines the factors that impede the emergence of a female heroine; that make it difficult to "plot" a woman into the center of the novel without closing with a symbolic reinscription of her social subordination, such as her death or exile. The main reason for this impossibility, according to Franco, is that Castellanos chooses a third-person historical novel as her vehicle. Because this genre serves inevitably as a national allegory, Franco implies, it must encode a truth about "the problems of the nation as a whole" through its exemplary characters. And because Mexican nationalism is so resolutely masculine, there is no way to construct a positive female national figure in such a genre (*Plotting* 146). "What is at stake," writes Franco, "is whether a 'heroine' is possible at all within the terms of the epic or master narratives of the nation" (132).

However, the answer in the negative — no way for women to be Mexican heroes — is foretold in Franco's classic definition of hero narratives, in which women play the role of obstacle along the hero's path to self-transformation. In such a model, women are doomed everywhere, not just in Mexico, to a split and partial rather than full identification with the hero, since in positioning themselves with respect to the classic hero narrative they identify with both the hero (male) and the hero's obstacle (female).

The national(ist) stakes for women writers can also be understood in a different way, however, by foregrounding the intellectual era in which Castellanos came of age as a writer: the era of Octavio Paz's vision of the Mexican everyman trapped in a "labyrinth of solitude"; of Juan Rulfo's fracturing of Mexican biography into a mound of broken pieces; and the serious questioning if not cancellation, as critic Jorge Aguilar Mora writes, of any attempt to unify the personal with the mytho-historical (Aguilar 13). Might not the possibility of plotting a female heroine be affected by these influential reflections on whether any individual biography can be exemplary of the collective experience? To so many writers in this period, Mexico appears as a melancholy nation, a country of shadow dwellers, nobodies, and ghosts.[5] It may not have been possible to plot a heroine, yet among intellectuals in 1950s Mexico, it was not easy to plot a hero either.

What about an anti-heroine? In those portions of *Balún Canán*, comprising half of the total, in which the lyrical voice and childish perspective of the first-person narrator dominate, there emerges a new, potentially strong female voice, yet one that is by no means heroic nor straightforwardly national-allegorical. It is, rather, a marginal voice, affirming itself from a place of solitary wandering and mourning, and providing us with an absolutely partial account of national events. A heroine, in Franco's model, may not be possible, but *Balún Canán* demonstrates that a tremendously compelling anti-heroine is, through Castellanos's construction of a marginalized and lonely female voice. Emanating from a watchful position of near-invisibility, she is nevertheless poised to discover something of redeeming value — herself — in her solitude.

Castellanos's depiction of the marginalized individual can be seen as a response to a certain heroic narrative of nation, a response she shared with her intellectual contemporaries. Despite Castellanos's self-deprecating comments about *Balún Canán*'s lack of internal unification, its fractures might be considered to be largely consistent with aesthetic trends of the period (O'Connell 85; Messinger 6). Indeed, Walter Benjamin's comment about the European Bildungsroman reveals a certain logic to her choice. He writes, "By integrating the social process with the development of a person, [the Bildungsroman] bestows the most frangible justification on the order determining it" ("Storyteller" 80). The novel's flaw, seen in this light, may in fact be a sign of its author's very conscious hesitance to integrate the girl's story more fully into a narrative of national history. Her girl-narrator is insignificant, a mere "anis seed," as her nana calls her. To chart national history by means of her personal history would be to make the national narrative as "frangible," tentative, and incomplete as she is.

And yet, even as she sought to preserve a residue of what she called "nonsynchronicity," a consciousness of individual, aesthetic marginalization, Castellanos synchronized this autobiographical fiction to established national narratives of Mexican modernity. This chapter addresses the tension between the synchronous and nonsynchronous aspects of the life Castellanos plotted into the web of Mexican nationalism. It begins with an analysis of *Balún Canán*'s prehistory, examining the personal and poetic writings that preceded that novel. These bring out a new range of meanings surrounding Castellanos's approach to her life story and demonstrate that her turn to indigenismo was a response to the provincial modernity of Chiapas, with its own distinct shape and history, and to her own gendered position as the heir to a colonial legacy. The chapter then turns to *Balún Canán* to show how Castellanos extended her newly found indigenista voice unevenly across this autobiographical novel. An analysis of the novel's perspectival transitions and displacements — of its different ways of "seeing and thinking" — reveals the tensions in Castellanos project. Her attachment to a marginal and "small" perspective was offset by her desire to find an omniscient view. Her sense of the multiplicity of national histories and ways of thinking coexisted with her need for a singular narrative of modern progress that could make her own moral and intellectual development meaningful. The fractured composition of Castellanos's novel, I will argue, is the direct result of these unresolved tensions.

Finally, this chapter considers how these tensions underlying the novel's changing narrative perspective might be linked to the changing circumstances of the authorial enunciation, to the event of writing itself. Many years after the novel was written, Castellanos told an interviewer that her understanding of her relationship to Indians had changed while she was writing the novel and as a result of the writing, that it had awakened in her a consciousness of her debt to Indians (B. Miller 136). This chapter attempts to find the trace in the novel's craft of this awakening of indigenista consciousness as debt, to capture the time of writing in the author's journey toward authenticity and autonomy. The journey occurred across a changing social field, one that affected what it means to be a good woman and a virtuous person and that was initially marked by multiple and conflicting laws whose legitimacy remained a matter of contest. Yet by the end of *Balún Canán* these conflicts appear to have been suppressed, not at the level of the historical events the novel represented, but at the level of narrative perception. The multiplicity of perspectives cedes to a single perception more in tandem with mainstream indigenista nationalism and with the Mexican state's definition of normative social identities.[6] She arrived at a voice and perspective in line with official indigenismo. This perspective can be found in her image of indigenous culture as lawless, as outside the pale of civilization, and this image, which I will analyze below, serves to validate and empower the female narrator on her path of self-discovery. The development of this female anti-heroine of Mexico's modernity thus comes to be subtly dependent on revolutionary nationalism and its ideology of progress. Castellanos ended the novel in a very different place than she began it, invoking the ethno-racial distinction between Indians and other Mexicans along a primitive-modern divide. How and why does the path of female self-discovery merge with the civilizing mission of indigenismo?

Plotting Indigenista Women

Castellanos's letters to Guerra as well as her first indigenista writing, the poetry collection *El rescate del mundo* (The Rescue of the World), published in Chiapas in 1952, provide a context for her turn toward indigenismo that remains largely hidden if *Balún Canán* is read as an autonomous text. These writings help identify the conditions leading to the *mood* of Castellanos's indigenista narrative, mood in the sense discussed by Genette, that is, as the chief category defining the "regulation of narrative information" (162). What we know in a narrative is chiefly a question of what we see, Genette suggests, because mood is in large part a function of our "view" of what is narrated. As with a picture, it "depends for precision on the distance separating me from it, and for breadth on my position with respect to whatever partial obstruction is more or less blocking it" (162). Overall, the mood of *Balún Canán* is shifty: both inside and outside, obstructed yet insightful, sometimes fully distanced and sometimes fully within. It corresponds to a particular place of enunciation, one marked biographically at the site of a return home and dominated symbolically by two distinct icons of indigeneity: Rómulo Gallegos's Doña Bárbara and the Maya craftswomen celebrated in Castellanos's *El rescate del mundo*.

Returning to Chiapas after a year abroad in Spain, Castellanos reflected sardonically on her experiences back on her family's lands, in a letter to Ricardo Guerra:

> Yo era la mujer fuerte. Mi corazón, una roca incomovible. Mis convicciones, mis proyectos, claros y constantes. Y además yo era una amazona capaz de soportar ocho o diez horas a caballo sin mostrar el menor signo de fatiga, de asistir, sin pestañear, a las hierras (ese calor sofocante, esas nubes de polvo, esa cantidad de bichos picándolo a uno). Y además hábil para los negocios, capaz de sacar adelante el rancho. Cuando me pongo a ver esto, ahora, me da risa. ¿De dónde saqué una imagen tan estrafalaria? De Doña Bárbara de Rómulo Gallegos, lo menos. Pero era un papel que me quedaba grande y me exigía un enorme esfuerzo. (*Cartas* 175)

> I was the strong woman. My heart, an immovable rock. My convictions, my projects, clear and firm. And moreover I was an Amazon, capable of tolerating eight to ten hours on horseback without showing the least sign of fatigue, of helping out, without blinking, with branding the livestock (that suffocating heat, those clouds of dust, the multitude of biting insects). And furthermore, clever at business, able to make the ranch prosper. When I look back at that now, it makes me laugh. Where did I get such a weird image? From Doña Bárbara by Rómulo Gallegos, no less. But it was too big a role for me and required an enormous effort.

For anyone attentive to Castellanos's autobiographical legend, which she constructed over the years in countless interviews and essays, above and beyond the lengthy fictional exposition contained in the novel *Balún Canán*, there is an element of revelation to this statement. Two important elements of her autobiographical legend need to be revised in light of it. One, Castellanos frequently alluded to the ways in which her mother would state, more or less explicitly, that her daughter was worth less than her son. Castellanos implied that these maternal rejections were the direct expression of a patrimonial law excluding women from the right to own lands, as if her mother was voicing the patriarchal law in her own words. This dispossession of the daughter is central to the fiction in *Balún Canán,* but is not, apparently, a reflection of Castellanos's own circumstances. As the above quote makes clear, she did inherit at least part of her family's economic patrimony. Two, Castellanos also frequently implied that her family had lost its lands in Chiapas as a result of the Cárdenas-era land reforms of the 1930s, converting an important oligarchic family, a regional power force, into a member of the anonymous urban middle class. Who knew, then, that Castellanos's family still possessed ranch lands in Chiapas into the 1950s and that they were held in the name of the daughter?[7]

Less surprising, perhaps, is that Castellanos would have felt herself interpellated by this particular image of womanhood. María Félix had starred in the *Doña Bárbara* role not ten years earlier in the hugely successful Mexican film version of Gallegos's 1929 novel, a film directed by state-movie-industry favorite Fernando de Fuentes in 1943. Castellanos's indigenista turn had much to do with projecting a counter-image of herself, one that responded to, among other things, particular images of Mexican womanhood that her return to Chiapas called to mind. Gallegos's heroine had become by then a veritable icon, associated with a number of ideas that, at the time of *Doña Bárbara*'s publication, could be considered socially progressive. Chief among these is the idea that the primal forces of indigeneity impede the onward march of the modernizing nation-state. By indigeneity, I don't just mean "Indianness," but the whole symbolic complex erected by modernizing intellectuals who established that nationality is a form of nativism, of being native to the land, yet construed that land as a site of barbarity that exerts a negative force on its inhabitants. Both the land and the people who live on it must be tamed and civilized if they are to become properly national. Although in 1950s Mexico these notions must have been viewed by many intellectuals as quaint if not laughable, part of the ideological apparatus of an increasingly ossified revolutionary state, they seem to have resonated deeply for a woman who had only recently decided to abandon cosmopolitan Mexico City and Madrid for provincial Chiapas. Castellanos's embarrassed admission to Guerra may have been served up as proof to her friends back home in the capital that she had not lost her ironic edge. And in articulating the image in her self-deprecating way, she slyly robbed it of some of its harsher associations, including the one — female strength and independence — that may have played most unfavorably to her male lover, her intended reader: how could this physically weak and philosophically inclined woman be "la devoradora de hombres," "la domadora del llano" [the woman who devoured men and tamed the prairie], as Doña Bárbara was famously known?

The early twentieth-century elaboration of the "civilización vs. barbarie" trope that animated the Doña Bárbara image informed Mexican revolutionary nationalist policies in ways that would have profoundly affected Castellanos' self-understanding as a Mexican citizen. Hostility to provincial conservatism dominated revolutionary nationalist attitudes to the further-flung regions of the federation, especially Chiapas. Regional elites had been placed under national control by the Cárdenas government relatively recently, after a struggle whose main weapons, on the national side, were land reform, popular education, and indigenismo broadly speaking.[8] Not coincidentally, the first regional center of the Instituto Nacional Indigenista (INI) would be established in San Cristóbal de las Casas, the state's colonial urban center. Castellanos worked there in 1956 and 1957, and remained an employee of the INI until 1961. The official mission of the INI's San Cristóbal center targeted indigenous people exclusively: "El Centro Coordinador Indigenista tiene por función elevar los niveles de aculturación del grupo indígena en el que se halla establecido para promover su integración a la vida económica y social de la Nación" [The function of the Indigenist Coordinating Center is to raise the level of acculturation of the indigenous group wherever the Center is located, in order to promote their integration into the social and economic life of the Nation] (Caso, *¿Qué es el INI?* 40). However, it is clear that Castellanos understood her indigenista work there as part of a broader mission to challenge the everyday exercise of ladino cultural hegemony, which she likened to a system of slavery.[9] In a letter to a friend written while she worked at the Center, she recounted the story of an Indian servant woman who had been thrown out on the street when she became seriously ill; her employer feared she would die and did not want to pay for the funeral. The INI hospitalized this woman at its clinic, where she recovered. But then her former employer resurfaced. On finding out the Indian woman was better, the employer stormed the clinic, spouting "bad words and insults," demanding that her servant pay off the debt she had accrued or else resume her servitude. Castellanos ends the story about this unfortunate Indian woman on an uplifting note, as the Institute intercedes on her behalf against her employer: "Pero esta mujer ya tiene quien responda por ella. Se pagó la deuda y la muchachita es libre" [But this woman now has a defender. Her debt was paid and the girl is free] (cited in *Rosario Castellanos* n.p.). Every word in Castellanos's narration of these events reveals the INI's perspective regarding the need to civilize and modernize not just Indians, but an entire regional culture based on a quasi-feudal system of servitude.

Meanwhile, Mexican women as a category were still suffering politically from their association with the "barbarian" forces of militant religiosity, the legacy of the Cristero war. Female citizens were denied national suffrage until 1953 as a direct result of the Cristero war (particularly due to women's involvement in the assassination of president-elect Obregón in 1928). In the 1930s women came to be labeled superstitious and conservative by the government, and thus a "backward" influence on the modernizing nation. Mexican women were deemed inherently anti-revolutionary (Soto 113). These events and their afterlife are directly represented in *Balún Canán,* which includes several scenes depicting the alliance between provincial elite women and the church, an alliance that is repressed by the government. The closure of church-run institutions for girls and women, such as those Castellanos depicts in the novel, had been a crucial piece of anti-church action by the state since the liberal reforms, part of the state's efforts to shape female subjectivities to suit the needs of both the Republican and the revolutionary regimes. Secularism and "the need for an educated citizenry," as Ana Macías writes (17), features common to both regimes, advanced the creation of a constituency of middle- and upper-class women endowed with a special, though subordinate, role in the formation of national identity. In the postrevolutionary period, this role would be seriously questioned in light of women's participation in the Cristero uprising. When the closure of girls' schools is juxtaposed against the opening of rural Indian schools mandated by Cárdenas, as it is in Castellanos's novel, it becomes clear that the fabric of Mexico's "modern progress" was stamped with a markedly uneven pattern across race-gender lines.

Nevertheless, the revolutionary government's pejorative view of women's ability to participate in the growth of the modern nation made use of an ideological vocabulary similar to the one historically used to describe the role of Indians in Mexican national life. For both kinds of subjects, their capacity for rational participation in civic life is questioned and becomes the basis for denying them the rights of full citizens. Seen as victims of ideological apparatuses running parallel and counter to the state — whether the church or the caudillaje of regional patrones — both women and Indians require rescue and redemption by the state in order to be free.[10] In contrast to the racial theories of the nineteenth century, revolutionary nationalists viewed the weakness of these subjects as socially rather than biologically determined. Prominent indigenista anthropologist Ricardo Pozas would write in 1954, echoing Manuel Gamio's earlier pronouncements, "el indio es debil, pero no por su propia naturaleza, sino por circunstancias históricas; hay que hacerlo activo, destruir su apatía e irresponsabilidad, hay que despertar en él el amor a la tierra" [the Indian is weak, but as a result of historical circumstances, not as a result of his nature. He must be made to become active, his apathy and irresponsibility must be destroyed, his love of the land must be awakened] (Pozas 252). The parallels established in Castellanos's novel between the treatment of women and the treatment of Indians, both of them "voices from the silence," as Victorien Lavou argues in his study of the same name, have their origin in a nationalist modernizing ideology of which Castellanos was only half critical — only "half," because she too doubts the capacity of these citizens to dominate rationally their own wild natures.

In light of the historical circumstances surrounding the incorporation of women as full citizens, the doubts as to their capacity for reason, and the anxiety about the threat that indigeneity, broadly conceived, might pose to the rationalization of the revolutionary project, it seems that the Doña Bárbara figure signaled Castellanos's own ambivalence about where she would fit in the moral battle between civilized and barbaric femininity were she to exercise certain forms of economic power. In such a context, it is not surprising that Castellanos shed the Doña Bárbara role as soon as she could and domesticated herself. She was determined to cast off this mask as well as others and "be who she really was." Her "true self," it turns out, also conforms to feminine stereotypes, yet without any of the patriarchy-threatening attributes associated with Doña Bárbara. She wrote to Guerra about this "true self":

> Un ser débil, sin ninguna madurez en ningún sentido, voluble, inconstante porque no sabe lo que quiere ni lo que debe ni lo que puede hacer. Que en un rancho debe estarse muy sentada en su casa mientras los hombres hacen las tareas de los hombres. Y que tiene derecho a dormir si quiere dormir, a escribir si lo necesita y a no entender nada del campo.... Fíjate que felicidad.... Por eso me he decidido a ir yo personalmente y, por más trabajo que me cueste, por más humillante y doloroso que me parezca, por más que este gesto me acobarde, desenmascararme. (*Cartas* 175–76)

> A weak being, with no maturity in any sense, voluble, inconstant because she doesn't know what she wants nor what she should or can do. Who, on a ranch, must sit still at home while the men do the work of men.... And who has the right to sleep if she wants to sleep, to write if she needs to, and to understand nothing of country life.... Imagine what happiness! ... That's why I personally decided to leave here and — however much work this gesture might cost me, however humiliating and painful it might be, however much this gesture might scare me — strip off my mask.

What is left, when all of Doña Bárbara's formidable attributes have been subtracted, is the portrait of a house-centered woman with time on her hands to pursue her literary vocation and make herself a better person. In the process of stripping off her masks, she gratefully domesticated herself and embarked on the path of self-improvement. Castellanos did what Doña Bárbara had refused to do or had been unable to do because of her headstrong nature: she went back inside the house.

Castellanos's reflections on the image of Doña Bárbara make manifest a reactionary cultural politics underlying the progressivism of nationalist discourses. Yet Castellanos adopted this cultural symbol for her own purposes. It became a part of her attempt to carve out a new field of female virtue, one in which a personal search for authenticity was particularly meaningful. Strange as it may sound regarding the author of such ironic tales as "Lección de cocina" [Cooking Lesson], Castellanos made domesticity instrumental to that search. Not the domesticity of the consumer housewife immortalized in novels by Carlos Fuentes, or the domesticity Castellanos would depict with irony and ambivalence in later years, but a more anachronistic account of domestic labor and private space endowed with special moral virtues. Here it should be noted that the history of the ideology of domesticity in Mexico follows its own particular course. In the latter half of the nineteenth century, during the Porfiriato, moral authority was vested in the female domestic sphere in ways quite similar to the United States. To be a wife and mother was, rhetorically at least, a privileged form of contributing to nationhood. Minister of Education Justo Sierra, in a 1904 speech responding to women who struggled to achieve equality before the law, reinforced this domestic ideology: "let men fight over political questions, [let them] form laws; you ought to fight the good fight, that of feeling, and form souls, which is better than forming laws" (cited in Macías 15). "Women," writes Jean Franco, "were especially crucial to the imagined community as mothers of the new men and as guardians of private life, which from Independence onward was increasingly seen as a shelter from political turmoil." Gender is effectively "recodified" in this period, Franco argues, which resulted in "the carving out of a territory of domestic stability and decency," a new gendered separation of spheres (*Plotting* 81). But in the wake of the Revolution, and especially the Cristero wars of the 1920s and 1930s, secularizing strands of nationalist thought severely undermined this ideology of domesticity by associating women and women's spaces — such as the home or the girls' school — with the threatening power of the church. By the end of *Balún Canán*, decent women's homes have become a front in the war between church and state. No longer a haven from the political public sphere, the domestic sphere becomes politically charged and newly significant; its moral sanctity is denied by the state and its physical boundaries violated. The domestic woman is no longer innocent because isolated from the fractious terrain of political life; she must actively prove herself once again fit for civic life by cleansing herself of the stigma of fanaticism and superstition.

Castellanos's attempts to get out from the "farce" of the Doña Bárbara role, as she called it, go far toward explaining the indigenista nature of her subsequent writing, a collection of poems published in Chiapas in 1952. Titled *El rescate del mundo* and considered by its author to be the first poetry expressing "algo de acento propio" [something of my own voice] (García Flores 6), the collection reads like an attempt to save herself, her home state, and all the forces of indigeneity — human and nonhuman — from the imputations of barbarism. The poems in the collection operate a neat reversal, constructing a wise and benevolent image of indigenous people and tropical nature to counteract images of violence and ignorance. Respect and humility characterize the attitude assumed by the poems' "I," who addresses Indians and the Chiapan landscape with reverence. *Rescate* is filled with acts of submission, all of them couched in pedagogical terms: the poetic "I" is like a student or a supplicant, kneeling before the indigenous world and the regional landscape in search of enlightenment. In the poem "Una palmera," the title's palm tree is "señora de los vientos," the lady of the wind — the breath of sound, poetry itself. The poet arrives in her presence "Desde el país oscuro de los hombres" [From the dark country of men] and gazes on this lady on bended knee (*Obras* 77). Echoing Arguedas in her appeal to a sphere of relations beyond the "country of men," Castellanos links poetry and indigeneity together. Both belong to another country, an illuminated one, to which the author turns in her search for another mode of perception.

In "Cántaro de Amatenango" [Clay Pitcher from Amatenango], Castellanos invokes the indigenous clay jug as her teacher, using a reference to the biblical "good Samaritan" to mark the poet's turn to the indigenous object as a search for virtue (*Obras* 72). In "Lavanderas del Grijalva" [Washerwomen of the Grijalva], the poet exploits the metaphor of moral cleansing in the image of the washerwomen removing stains from garments, and asks to learn their craft so as to cleanse herself (*Obras* 75). In "Escogedoras de café en el Soconusco" [Women Coffee Pickers of Soconusco], the coffee pickers of the poem's title receive the same treatment, cast as diamonds in the rough. Their wisdom is wrapped in rags, their steps are righteous (*Obras* 75). In "Tejedoras de Zinacanta" [Weaverwomen of Zinacanta], she brings in the Ariadne theme, demanding of the Indian weaverwomen: "mostradme/mi destino" [show me/my destiny] (*Obras* 77).

In a 1965 interview, Castellanos criticized indigenista literature for its idealizations of Indians: "Uno de sus defectos principales reside en considerar el mundo indígena como un mundo exótico en el cual los personajes, por ser las víctimas, son poéticos y buenos. Esta simplicidad me causa risa" [One of its principal defects resides in considering the indigenous world as an exotic world, in which the characters, as victims, are poetic and good. That simplicity makes me laugh] (Carballo 422). Yet the poems from *El rescate del mundo* are indigenista in precisely this way. Indian women are good women, these poems say; they are righteous, generous, patient, and wise. Furthermore, because each poem contains within it a Chiapan placename — Zinacanta, Grijalva, Soconusco, Amatenango — the re-vision of Indian women as wise and good works on another level as well, for it involves a re-vision of the tropical land. The contempt Castellanos had felt for her home state, expressed in her letters to Guerra less than two years before, has now turned to reverence.

This poetry nurtured her growing regionalism, whose seed had already been planted in absentia, as so often happens. Castellanos was in Spain when she developed a narratable attachment to Chiapas, when she recognized her familial home as an Indian place within her: Chiapas as "la mera entraña de uno" [the very core or heart of oneself], recognizable as hers, indeed as the essential truth of herself, only when it is laid out before her in the display case of the museum. The examples of Castellanos's writings dating from the years just prior to *Balún*

Canán discussed here — letters to Ricardo Guerra, early poetry, her first published autobiographical prose — suggest that her attraction to indigenista literary conventions originated in part in her desire to find a home space that she could rightfully call "civilized." "Civilized" not so much in the sense meant by Gallegos, as a condition of bourgeois social values and European-style personal comportment threatened by savage indigeneity, but more importantly, in the sense consecrated by the Musée de l'Homme behind panes of glass: a culture preserved and untouched, both temporally and morally, from the alienation and emptiness of modern cosmopolitanism. Castellanos's return to Chiapas, after her year in Spain, was undertaken as part of a moral cleansing. It was a turn away from Mexico City, painted by her, in her letters from spring 1951 while still in Madrid, as a moral abyss:

> Yo ya no quiero seguir viviendo sola en México, entre puras gentes desequilibradas, en un ambiente falso y desempeñando un papel inauténtico y tonto. Ya no quiero, por ningún motivo, seguir haciendo esa vida frívola y superficial y bordeando siempre un abismito en el que un día, por puro fastidio, acabaría de caer. (*Cartas* 120)

> I don't want to keep living alone in Mexico City, among such unbalanced people, in a phony environment and playing an inauthentic and stupid role. I no longer, for any reason, want to keep living this frivolous and superficial life, always verging on that small abyss into which one day, out of sheer boredom, I'd end up falling.

Returning to Chiapas was saving herself, literally, from the alienation of modern life.

The indigenista aesthetic Castellanos first adopted in *Rescate* shifts the question of indigeneity away from the modernizing paradigm dominating revolutionary nationalist indigenismo and into an existential register of alienation and authenticity. The representation of indigenous people shifts accordingly. This shift is largely a question of perspective: nationalist indigenista policies involved a paternalist stance, looking *down* on Indians with benevolence, as if to help them rise up, whereas the perspective Castellanos assumed in *Rescate* looks *up* at them, as if she needed their help for herself. In both cases the Indian represents innocence of modernity and the changing world, but only in the latter case is this innocence conceived as wisdom, to which Castellanos's poetic "I" reverentially submits. In the act of submission, an icon is forged out of the subaltern, a process Spivak has discussed in describing the encounter between Western men and indigenous women ("A Literary Representation" 265).

Castellanos demonstrates its usefulness for "Western" women as well. In thinking about the relationship between the Doña Bárbara icon and the images of Indians in her poetry, it is hard not to suspect that we are seeing a substitution of one icon of indigeneity for another. The malevolent, domineering, wordly force of nature that is Doña Bárbara becomes the benign, domestic, earthy, and spiritually wise Maya washer-woman, weaver, harvester, etc. Adrienne Rich wrote once that "Re-vision — the act of looking back, of seeing with fresh eyes, of entering an old text from a new critical direction — is for women more than a chapter in cultural history: it is an act of survival" (167). Castellanos's re-vision — of Doña Bárbara as wise Indian woman — established a new iconography of indigeneity, one that allowed her to divorce indigeneity from the question of land, that is, to generate a sphere of belonging determined more by the presence of an individual's moral qualities and alternative perception than by primal, irrational, or collective/family forces. Indigeneity ceased to be a savage condition.

In light of *Balún Canán*, the autobiographical text she would go on to produce, the importance of this substitution should not be underestimated. Clothing indigenous women with wisdom and dignity and rhetorically standing before them in their new guise, she found another voice with which to speak of her home state. Castellanos was able to write of an inner connection to her originary place in terms of a process of enlightened self-discovery and moral self-improvement rather than as a succumbing to an irrational force. She thus plotted herself into the discourse of "lo mexicano" and set herself up as student — like her contemporaries Paz and Rulfo — of an alternative indigenous pedagogy. She found a way to "indigenize" herself, yet without adopting the role of Doña Bárbara, the female incarnation of dangerous indigeneity. This pedagogy intertwined utterly with a narrative of return home, not only in the sense of a return to origin, but also in the domestic sense, as a return inside, to interiority. One of her first steps in the process of self-domestication, of leaving Doña Bárbara behind, was to celebrate images of Indian craftswomen and set up a field of moral attributes centered around women's space and women's work.

In crafting her idealized visions of female domesticity, however, these early indigenista poems provide an inverted account of the social hierarchy of which Castellanos was a manifest beneficiary. In *Rescate,* she projected an "I" enthralled to the wisdom of those who were, in all likelihood, versions of her own female servants. One result was to distance herself from the culture she was raised in and bring herself a step closer to the fraught cultural politics of revolutionary nationalism. The indigenista iconography she developed in the early 1950s, shades of which can be found in *Balún Canán,* was part of a project of autobiographical self-invention undertaken in order to distance herself from her family past even as she was returning to the family home and confronting, ambivalently, her *latifundista* birthright.

This iconography thus emerges to mark her turn homeward as a transition or transformation rather than merely a return or a reinstatement. The Indian icon signals a very intimate divergence, serves as an interposition between her individual "mine" and her family's "ours." It allowed her to live in the latifundio house without becoming Doña Bárbara, providing a template for a domestic space of female craftsmanship imbued with moral virtues. These virtues had little in common with the mantle of sexual virtue assumed by ladino women in order to sustain an oligarchic race-class hierarchy, and this domestic space involved a moral geography distinct from that of the plantation home. Moving from Doña Bárbara to the Mayan craftswomen, Castellanos divorced indigeneity from savagery and began a process that *Balún Canán* would complete, that of divorcing female virtue from its metonymic association with land, with the blood-rights of patriarchal territorial possession, placing in its stead the virtues of authenticity, self-discovery, and self-improvement. In Chiapas, Castellanos proposed to learn how to be a better person, to civilize herself anew.

Grano de anís: The Marginal Voice

Notwithstanding Castellanos's frequent autobiographical statements and her interest in women's autobiography as a genre, the early Castellanos strongly resisted her own autobiographic impulses. As she herself liked to recount, even in her own girlhood diary she was too timid to write about herself: "A veces aparecía yo entre los renglones, con timidez y como pidiendo perdón" [Sometimes I appeared between the lines, timidly and apologetically] (Castellanos, "Rosario Castellanos" 91). She considered it a transgressive act. Like many other examples of women's writing, *Balún Canán* is a novel that thematizes its uncertainty about the value of

"I," as if reflecting its author's own considerable doubts about her substance. She writes about her childhood, "Sucede que era flaca y horrible. Pero tan flaca que ya casi no tenía yo cuerpo y entonces me sentía yo vagando por el aire como un puro fantasma" [I was thin and horrible. But so thin I had almost no body and so I felt myself floating through the air like a ghost] (*Cartas* 33). The memory dates to a few years before she began writing the novel. Initially, *Balún Canán*'s "I" is thin like that ghost, likely to be dispelled by strong light. But eventually, Castellanos acknowledges, she "fattened up": "Después engordé" (*Cartas* 33). So too does *Balún Canán*'s narrator, but not by eating. Rather, by taking in with her eyes and ears the world around her and refusing — Castellanos is almost literal about this — to open her mouth: she saves herself by keeping quiet. Secrets and silence nourish the self. In the end, through this narrative of the circuitous and perverse route to female self-empowerment under patriarchy, resistance to autobiography creates autobiography.

What is the significance of Castellanos's choice to create a marginalized and small female narrator? There is obviously here an inscription of her own self-image as "outsider," one that has become part and parcel of her posthumous canonization, and that many critics also understand as key to her feminist and indigenist social critique.[11] One begins then by interpreting it as a reflection of women's marginal social condition, a situation that increasingly came to preoccupy Castellanos in the 1960s and became the center of her intellectual endeavors in poetry, essays, and fiction. There is indeed a strong element of feminist critique in the novel, whose plot turns at key moments on the rebellious acts of girls and women who refuse to conform to expectations and pay heavily for this refusal. Such is the case of the spinster aunt who, after having an abortion, disappears forever into the jungle; or the girl-narrator who, fearing the wrath of God on the eve of her first communion, decides to sacrifice her brother in order to save herself and must live thereafter carrying the heavy burden of her own guilty conscience. Several generations of women readers have approached this novel as a testament to the impossible choices faced by Mexican women searching for self-expression. *Balún Canán* by this reading expresses in novelistic language sentiments that are at the center of Castellanos's most famous poem, a feminist motto of sorts, "Meditación en el umbral" [Meditation on the Brink]: "Debe haber otro modo...de ser humano y libre" (*Obras* 213) [There must be another way...to be human and free].[12]

But Castellanos understood marginality to be more than a negative condition of female oppression. It was also a consciously sought after and positive opportunity to develop an alternative way of seeing the world. Castellanos's intellectual interests in forms of expression that are not self-empowering but rather retiring and self-effacing also played a strong role in the construction of *Balún Canán*'s narrator. We can look, for instance, to her encounters with different modalities of politically engaged, ascetic, Christian femininity. In the year spent in Francoist Spain (1950–51) she lived with several young women who had committed themselves to the socially progressive Acción Católica (rival of the archconservative Opus Dei), and whom she declared her wish to emulate (*Cartas* 153, 160). In that same year she read Santa Teresa and was deeply moved by her humility, resolving to acquire the habit of humility herself (*Cartas* 117). She also read Simone Weil in the early 1950s, a thinker whose aphorisms she loved to quote and whose asceticism influenced her, so Castellanos tells an interviewer, in her decision to stay in Chiapas as an employee of the Instituto Nacional Indigenista (Carballo 420). One of Weil's earliest published books, *La pesanteur et la grâce* (Gravity and Grace) (1948), lays out the conditions for a spiritual asceticism that Castellanos found deeply compelling. Weil considered her self as absolutely without value (Weil 35), yet at the same time argued that our only true power in the world is the power to say "I," because everything else can be taken from us. Thus our only true act of freedom is to give "I" up, to destroy it by giving it to God (Weil 29). Castellanos shared this notion of the ego as an enemy, as a blockage to grace, and searched for a respite from "ese núcleo feroz de hambre y de desesperado egoísmo" [this core of ferocious hunger and desperate egotism] (*Cartas* 100).

It must have been in this spirit that she spoke of her autobiographical tendencies as a defect: "cuento mi autobiografía a la menor provocación o sin provocación" (*Cartas* 121) [I recount my autobiography at the slightest provocation or without any provocation]. What kind of auto-biographical practice is possible if one operates under these Weil-ian imperatives? *Balún Canán* can be considered, in part, an experiment in the possibility of writing about herself without turning "self" into an end in itself. To this end, Castellanos drew explicitly from modernist strategies of first-person narration in order to create a literary "I" of tenuous presence, a kind of witnessing "I," one composed as much by its liminal status, a mediator between different layers of daily experience, as by its direct self-expression. Castellanos was interested in conveying what she called the "nonsynchronicity" of subjective and objective worlds, of self to collective experience. It is the basis for a modernist perception of the enigma of social life, the disparity between inner and outer worlds:

> ...esta disparidad que podría ser quizás la misma de la que Proust hablaba en sus libros...la medición del tiempo externa es total-mente otra a la que se mide y rige los fenómenos internos de sensibilidad y de expresión. Es por eso que nos asombra, y lo deci-mos así, el hecho de que la vida y la obra sean tan no sincronizadas. (García Flores 7)

> ...that disparity which might perhaps be the same as the one that Proust spoke of in his books...the external measure of time is totally other to the measure of internal phenomena of sense and expression. That's why we are astonished, we say, by the fact that life and the work of art are so nonsynchronous.

The first extensive autobiographical narration of *Balún Canán* communi-cates this awareness of nonsynchronicity. It establishes both the childish voice of the narrator as well as her liminal position:

> No soy un grano de anís. Soy una niña y tengo siete años.... Y cuando me yergo puedo mirar de frente las rodillas de mi padre. Más arriba no. Me imagino que sigue creciendo como un gran árbol y que en su rama más alta está agazapado un tigre diminuto. Mi madre es diferente. Sobre su pelo — tan negro, tan espeso, tan cre-spo — pasan los pájaros y les gusta y se quedan. Me lo imagino nada más. Nunca lo he visto. Miro lo que está a mi nivel. Cier-tos arbustos con las hojas carcomidas por los insectos; los pupitres manchados de tinta; mi hermano. (9)

> I am not an anis seed. I'm a little girl and I'm seven years old.... And when I stand up straight I can see my father's knees just in front of me. But not higher. I imagine that he goes on growing like a big tree and that in its topmost branch a very small tiger is hiding. My mother is different. Birds wander through her hair — so black and thick and curly — and they like it there and they linger. I imagine it, that's all. I've never seen it. I see what's as high as myself. Some bushes, their leaves nibbled by the insects, the desks stained with ink, my brother. (13)[13]

Sight is primary to the girl-narrator's self-identification, particularly imaginative sight. The contrast to Jesús Lara's autobiographical section in *Surumi* is instructive. Lara's narrator is primarily defined in terms of the binary "I sense myself/I cannot sense myself," an opposition that differentiates free national subjects from serfs (automatons). The autobiographical narrator of *Balún Canán* meanwhile, oscilates between "I see/I do not see but can imagine." This division reveals a certain underlying framework, codified in the nineteenth century as part of industrial society's new division of spheres, positioning creative vision against empirical vision and within an aesthetic realm, itself positioned against the scientific realm.[14] The opening excursus on what the narrator can and cannot see is not presented to signal to the reader that this narrator's small stature makes her unreliable. On the contrary, she is extraordinarily self-conscious about the limits of her sight, locating exactly the point where her sight ends and her invention takes over. She knows that "what I see" and "what I imagine" are nonidentical, and are not to be confused. And she makes clear, as well, that the latter, composed of a wild garden of birds and tigers, is far more interesting than the former, composed of sickly bushes, old furniture, and her brother.

The bifurcation of the narrator's vision into two distinct registers, the seen and the imagined, reveals that she exists in two worlds simultaneously: a measurable, shared world; and a world only she can see, one formed by projecting her own creative imagination outward. Castellanos's narrator is a figure for the literary writer, dramatizing the slippage between empirical and imaginative perceptions of the object world, yet without undoing the terms of the binary itself. In this, she offers a portrait of the modern(ist) self that corresponds closely to the one painted by Charles Taylor. Regarding the subjects of Thomas Mann's *The Magic Mountain,* he writes: "The epiphanic and the ordinary but indispensable real can never be fully aligned, and we are condemned to live on more than one level — or else suffer the impoverishment of repression" (Taylor 480). Like the "nonsynchronous" Proustian subject Castellanos describes, the first-person narrator of *Balún Canán* situates herself at the boundary between subjective and objective worlds. Yet unlike the Proustian narrative, Castellanos's is far more concerned with the nonsentimental aspects of this boundary. The eye is its privileged mediating point, rather than more penetrating forms of sensory perception, such as taste or smell.

For this narrator, seeing is ideally a marginal and retiring practice, rather than a centered or dominating one. Its ideal form can perhaps best be appreciated in the narrator's wish, expressed early on, for a liminal space of contemplation: "Debe de ser tan bonito estar siempre, como los balcones, desocupado y distraído, sólo mirando" (11) [It must be nice to be like the balconies, always idle, absent-minded, just looking on (15)]. Thus Castellanos does not provide her with a classically perspectival stance, in the sense defined by John Berger as "European" perspective: "Every drawing or painting that used perspective proposed to the spectator that he was the unique centre of the world" (18). Disentangled and yearning toward aloofness, this narrator demonstrates Castellanos's resistance to the "narcissistic impulses of conventional autobiography," as Debra Castillo puts it (241). In *Balún Canán,* we can see Castellanos searching for the possibility of a subjective narration that is not subjectivist, a situated yet distracted quality of seeing.[15]

Another Way to See: Indigenous Insight and the Aesthetic Imagination

The development of this marginalized individuality intersected with Castellanos's growing commitment to nationalist indigenismo, for she enlisted this newfound sense of herself in the service of a critique of regional oligarchy. *Balún Canán*'s very composition is hostile to the regional society it describes. Its narrative voice expresses the critical distance from the family tradition that she had already begun developing in her poetry collection *El rescate del mundo.* As in the poetry collection, the narrator's critical distance and budding independence come from a special aesthetic perception of the world. Castellanos took the indigenous presence she found inside her and enlisted it to serve an aesthetic of marginalized interiority that brought her closer to the modernist writers she loved, from Proust to Gorostiza, and then linked that aesthetic, in turn, to the modernizing ideology of revolutionary nationalism.

By asserting the existence of a subjective interior world that cannot be seen — the world of her imagination — the girl-narrator is able to resist some aspects of ladino cultural hegemony. As Castellanos depicts it, the colonial structure of everyday social relations in Chiapas is sustained by an absurdly reductive visual epistemology. In a scene in the novel's first chapter, the girl expresses a desire to drink coffee just like her nana, but is told that only Indians drink coffee. White people drink milk. This dictum demonstrates that everyday racism is sustained by a kind of perception that must not exceed a superficial apprehension of the world: white people drink white things; dark people drink dark things. Over the course of the novel, the girl-narrator will develop her imaginative potential into an alternative sight that challenges the ideology of oligarchic social relations and brings her into a relationship of interethnic identification that would otherwise be impossible.

As in the poetry collection, that aesthetic perception develops under the tutelage of Maya Indian women, in this case, the narrator's nana. With the help of her nana, the narrator develops a special aesthetic perception of the world that breaks with the colonial inheritance and its survival into the everyday. That perception is of a visual nature that goes beyond the power of the eyes. Nana tells the girl that the earth has no eyes (10), meaning, it doesn't need them to see. Other scenes from the novel's early chapters further demonstrate this process, as when the girl accompanies her family to a field outside of Comitán to watch her brother compete in a kite flying contest. There, in a scene strongly reminiscent of Proust, she meets the wind, who moves across the plain with "liberty" and "brio." She enters his domain reverentially, with lowered eyes:

> nunca, hasta hoy, había yo venido a la casa de su albedrío. Y me quedo aquí, con los ojos bajos porque (la nana me lo ha dicho) es así como el respeto mira a lo que es grande. (23)

> never, before today, had I entered into the house of his will. And I stand here with lowered eyes because (Nana's said so) that is how humility gazes on greatness. (26)[16]

With her eyes downcast according to the wind's law, the girl misses her brother's victory in the kite-flying competition. Although she is a fool in her mother's eyes for such a transgression, she is rewarded with her nana's approval for having recognized one of the nine guardians of her people. That guardian, the wind, validates a distinct way of seeing. The girl is aware of the wind without looking at it; it cannot be seen directly, yet even so it is powerfully felt. It represents another mode of perception, one that Castellanos had earlier linked to the practice of poetry itself, which brings her out of the "dark world of men" and into another world. It contrasts starkly to the ladino world, which marshals the visible into a system of identity signs used to police social boundaries. In *El rescate del mundo*, Castellanos kneels before poetry, figured as the palm tree and the "lady of the wind." In *Balún Canán,* the girl-narrator reverentially approaches her own imaginative sight, figured as the lord of the wind.

I am tempted to call the wind's house by a *proper* name — "The House of the Wind" — not only to communicate its noble status but to adopt the conventions of Antonio Mediz Bolio's 1941 Spanish translation of the Maya Libro de Chilam Balam de Chumayel, a text with which Castellanos was familiar. This translation was in all likelihood the one Castellanos consulted for the epigraph she chose for Part Two.[17] Mediz Bolio, a Yucatec writer, used capital letters at a key moment to suggest the foundation of a new social order: "Entonces se comenzó a levantar la Casa Alta para los Señores y se comenzó a construir la escalera de piedra. Y entonces él se sentó en la Casa de Arriba, entre los *Trece Ahau,* llenos de majestad. Y comenzó a llegar la Ley, la gloria y el tiempo de *Ah Mex Cuc*" [Then the High House began to be erected for the Lords and the stone stairs began to be built. And then he sat down in the House Above, between the *Trece Ahau,* full of majesty. And the Law began to arrive, the glory and the time of *Ah Mex Cuc*] (Mediz Bolio 13). Although Castellanos herself does not resort to this convention, she shares Mediz Bolio's underlying vision of Mayan culture as one of noble grandeur.[18]

Figuring the wind as lord of a house, the girl endows him with a special legitimacy. He becomes a direct competitor to that other house, the one in which she lives with her family. Both become "Houses," noble seats of patriarchal power radiating dominion, their legitimacy perpetuated through lineage. Two Houses, two laws, two patriarchs. The competition between them will be confirmed later on, at a crucial moment in the novel's Part Two, when the narrator reveals that the Argüello's built their ancestral home at Chactajal in the wind's preferred spot: "Los ladinos... alzaron su casa sobre una colina favorecida de los vientos" (193) [The ladinos... set their house on a hill favored by the winds (181)].[19] The implication is that "los ladinos" have usurped the wind and taken its place. In consorting with the wind and its way of seeing the world, the ladino girl adopts the role of traitor to her house.

These houses, it should be understood, are not domestic spaces; they are largely alien, if not hostile, to the ideology of domesticity unevenly deployed across Mexico's late nineteenth and twentieth centuries. Borrowing Benedict Anderson's rough typology, one could say that these are *dynastic* or seignorial entities; they represent a system of social relations that has not yet been nationalized (19–22). In the spaces these dynastic entities enclose or control, social virtue is not accorded to individuals as such, nor is it determined by abstract, impersonal law. It is embodied in the representative of a bloodline — the patriarch — and disseminated through him to the members and allies of his house. The first half of *Balún Canán* depicts Chiapan society as if governed by dynastic law, with Castellanos offering it as a template for understanding all the socio-political forces in the novel. "House" in *Balún Canán* is a chronotope for patriarchal law, ruled by father-guardians: César Argüello, Lázaro Cárdenas, the wind, the priest. The female coming-of-age story narrated in this novel occurs in the midst of a war between these houses. From the perspective of the margins, there is not much difference between the patriarchs, except one: only the indigenous House validates a special way of seeing.

Castellanos was not the only indigenista author to celebrate Indians' alternative epistemology. Mediz Bolio himself, in a popular 1922 indigenista novel about Mayan Indians, works with a similar construction: "Envuelto en su triste oscuridad [el indio] va por todas partes, y ve. Ve lo que todo el mundo puede ver, y algo más. No se lo preguntes, porque no ha de decírtelo" [Shrouded in his sorrowful obscurity, the Indian goes everywhere, and he sees. He sees what everyone can see, and something more. Don't ask him what, because he won't tell you] (*Tierra* 29). Mediz Bolio's words suggest the extent to which Indian ways of seeing, native insights, were subject to a certain fetishization by modernizing intellectuals searching for "another way to be."

In Castellanos's novel, this alternative sight is initially associated with the will: the wind lives in the house of his will ("la casa de su albedrío"). This is not a coincidence: once again Castellanos employs the Indian figure in order to create a domain for the recovery of self-direction, separating her from the family sphere. This individualization, as in the *Rescate* poetry, has much to do with validating a quality of hers that her blood family undervalues: imaginative sight. Imaginative seeing is linked directly by Castellanos to the expression of agency. To stand in the house of the wind-guardian simultaneously implies, for "I," the possibility of distancing herself from her family and the affirmation of a special gift, the exercise of her imagination. This sight is the sign of a properly "intimate indigenismo," an indigenismo forged in an interethnic apprenticeship to a different kind of knowing. Castellanos's narrator brokers it with her nana in order to distance herself from an oppressive race-class formation and the dominant visual economy of social difference, just as did Castellanos herself, in the years prior to writing *Balún Canán*.

The Novel's Fracture in Perspective

Why did Castellanos choose to abandon that special perception, that marginal, witnessing "I" of the girl-narrator? Why supplement it, and in some sense cancel it out, with the omniscient narrator of the novel's Part Two? This other narrator adopts a god's-eye view, explicitly voicing its own clear sight. This is patently obvious in the very first lines of Part Two:

> El viento del amanecer desgarra la neblina del llano. Suben, se dispersan los jirones rotos mientras, silenciosamente, va desnudándose la gran extensión que avanza en hierba húmeda, en árboles retorcidos y solos, hasta donde se yergue el torso de la montaña, hasta donde espejea el río Jataté. (75)

> The wind of daybreak tears the mist from the moor. Its strands are broken and they rise and scatter while, silently, the great expanse is laid bare, out and out to the sodden grass and the twisted, lonely trees, to where the ribs of the mountain rise and the river Jataté shows clear. (75)

Significantly, here the wind appears again, yet far less personified than in the previous encounter with it as Maya guardian and "lord of a house of will." Castellanos has made the wind a symbol for clarity of vision: it clears the mist to offer a panoramic view. We might say that "I" has once again entered the wind's house, this time to tell of events that she cannot see in waking life. She sleeps as this narrative unfolds, so it holds for her the status of a dream. With this juxtaposition between an objective world that is a dream and a subjective world of penetrating insight, Castellanos seems to be continuing to reflect on the irreducible distinction between empirical and imaginative perception that so defines the girl-narrator. Yet in fact she has added a third term, omniscience, which leaves the initial distinction behind.

Some scholars have insisted, countering Castellanos's own confession, that the transition between Part One and Part Two does not challenge the novel's underlying coherence. In these accounts, the category of narrative voice or point of view has been replaced by the broader category of "discourse." Because heteroglossia permeates the entire novel, one critic argues that the distinction between first- and third-person is less significant than the fact that, in both cases, many voices and discourses are always present (O'Connell 83–84). Another points out that the at-times irreconcilable division between different narrative perspectives is merely a conscious illustration of social divisions (Messinger 6–7).

Other critics, however, have addressed the more destabilizing implications of these changes in perspective and argued that what is at stake in the shifts from first-person to third-person and back is what specific narrators are able to "see," that is, with questions of distance and perspective. Both Fabienne Bradú and César Rodríguez Chicharro have postulated that the break in narrative point of view demonstrates that the narrator of Part Two sees what the child narrator cannot (Bradú 96–97, Rodríguez C. "Reseña" 62). In different ways, both of these analyses bring out the element of instability in Castellanos's authorial enunciation. Bradú and Rodríguez Chicharro make an important point about the significance in the novel of "mood," to return again to Genette's term, the distance and perspective that regulate narrative information. It seems that between the novel's Part One and Part Two, Castellanos had a change of "mood," so to speak. Her decision to abandon, temporarily, the first-person narrator and bring in an omniscient third person, suggests that she wanted to communicate something that "I" couldn't see, that she was no longer content to let that thing remain invisible, even if unveiling it meant breaking the conventions with which she had begun the novel. What is it that "I" cannot see and why can she not see it?

Balún Canán's girl-narrator prefers to relate to the world as if it were a painting, standing at a distance and holding steady. A circus comes to town, to the joy of the children, who expect it to offer a living representation of their most exotic fantasies: "Ha de ser como esos libros de estampas iluminadas que mi hermano y yo hojeamos antes de dormir." (17) [It must be like those colored picture books my brother and I look at before going to sleep (20)]. These lines, spoken by the girl-narrator, echo Castellanos's meta-textual commentary on the novel several years after publishing *Balún Canán*, when she had occasion to refer to the first part of the novel as "una serie de estampas aisladas en apariencia pero que funcionan en conjunto" [a series of apparently isolated images that work together] (Carballo 418). The image of a reader leafing through a book and contemplating images, projected by the girl-narrator as an ideal pose, seems indeed to correspond to how she perceives the world, and to how Castellanos offered this world up to the reader: as a series of isolated images made available for contemplation.

But this desire for distance and steadiness cannot be fulfilled. An inkling of the destabilizations to come is provided in an early scene at the fair when she rides the Ferris wheel:

> Nos sientan en una especie de cuna.... Lentamente vamos ascendiendo. Un instante nos detenemos allá arriba. ¡Comitán, todo entero, como una nidada de pájaro, está a nuestras manos!... De pronto empezamos a adquirir velocidad. La rueda gira vertiginosamente. Los rostros se confunden, las imágenes se mezclan. (39)

> We sit in a kind of cradle.... We rise slowly skyward and for a moment are suspended there. All Comitán is within our grasp like a brood of chicks!... All of a sudden we gain speed. The wheel turns giddily. Faces swim together, things go higgedly-piggedly. (40)

The Ferris wheel allows only the briefest flash of clarity before the world becomes mixture and confusion. In motion, it captures a desire for change and self-transformation, and thus acts as a destabilizer; not only of the certainty of sight, but also of the existing social world. The narrator recounts how an Indian tries to move up in the world on this machine, literally so, only to be brought crashing down and socially humiliated. The wheel is an allegory for a stable world that has been set in motion, herald of impending changes that the narrator will ride out, enacting her own complicated rise and fall. It provides a lesson in the difficulty of maintaining the stance of distanced contemplation, of distracted seeing, given the bewildering consciousness of one's participation in a world in motion.

The clarity with which the girl began starts to crumble, as if she had entered the picture that she herself had framed for us to view. From reading the "book of images" that is the world, she becomes a part of this book-world, a character in it, and thus available to be read *by* it. As the narrative progresses, it becomes more difficult to distinguish between the two worlds, real and imagined, and thus to situate herself as an object in empty space. A pattern emerges: loss of vision is the girl's response to certain acts of violence, driving her to the refuge of darkness. And this violence has a name: Chactajal, site of the colonial entanglement.

Though Chactajal is at the very heart of the story that "I" will narrate, this contest remains for her a matter of significant ignorance, shrouded in a violence too awful for her to assimilate. Castellanos makes clear from the start that "I" refuses outright to *listen* when the nature of this violence is explained to her. Her very first words in the novel are a refusal to hear: "No me cuentes ese cuento, nana" (9) [Don't tell me that tale, Nana (13)]. Regarding the contest over Chactajal, she is, to all intents and purposes, deaf. It turns out that she is also nearly blind. The novel turns repeatedly to scenes that test the limits of her sight: what can she bear to see, and how does she see it? Her nana holds the conflict on her body in the form of a wound; she has been cursed by Chactajal's sorcerers for her allegiance to the enemy. When nana shows it to the girl, she sets off a cascade of troubled gazing:

> Mira lo que me están haciendo a mí. . . . Yo la miro con los ojos grandes de sorpresa. . . . Ahora lo miro [a mi padre] por primera vez. . . . Y no puedo soportar su rostro y corro a refugiarme en la cocina. (16)

> Just look what they've done to me. . . . I stare at her, eyes wide with surprise. . . . I see [my father] now for the first time. . . . I can't bear to look at him and run to take shelter in the kitchen. (19–20)

When the violence of Chactajal penetrates the domestic sphere in Comitán, it sets off another crisis of vision. An Indian from Chactajal, loyal to the Argüello family, is wounded and brought to Comitán to die in their house. Scarred by the sight of his bloodied corpse, the girl becomes unable to tolerate light (31). This violence can be seen only in darkness, and it can be seen only within: it has been interiorized. There is a low-intensity conflict brewing around her, but "I" can see it only if she closes her eyes. Dreams awash in blood, troubling memories, visions traumatically imprinted on the brain: these become the features of the girl's sight. She slowly enters a world of waking nightmare.

The girl's sight becomes blocked and blinded; her imagination darkens, becomes nightmarish. Her original clarity is undermined by ongoing violence, the conflict at the center of her social reality: the war between her family and "their" Indians over Chactajal, the family lands. Because Chactajal is at the center of this world, it seems that it is the colonial entanglement that confuses empirical sight and imagination, a confusion based on fear and a guilty conscience. For the girl, the window of distanced contemplation has been shut.

Like the Proustian subject Castellanos describes, the first-person nar-rator of *Balún Canán* situates herself at the boundary between subjective and objective worlds. But this boundary is placed under such pressure by events that it breaks, turning the imagination into a refuge from reality. This is Castellanos's depiction of a social world on the verge of collective insanity, the result of its refusal to see. This refusal reaches its apotheosis as Part One draws to a close. The family has left Comitán for Chactajal, bringing the narrator directly to the heart of the violence. And yet she is destined not to see it. She closes her eyes for 150 pages, cast into sleep by her nana, who guides her into the world of illusion. Distance and clarity can be achieved only by abandoning the first-person position.

The novel's Part One charts the loss of an ideal for relating to the world. It recreates a time of fear: of not seeing, of barely seeing, of not being able to bear seeing. But it also communicates to us, by having begun with the nana's story of dispossession, the essence of that which remains unseen: the contest over Chactajal. We might say that it is an "ideological" rendering of the first-person narration in the way described by Slavoj Žižek: " 'ideological' is a social reality whose very existence implies the non-knowledge of its participants as to its essence" (21). Yet in fact *Balún Canán*'s opening forces a rethinking of this understanding of social reality as governed by a shared unknown. The girl's nonknowledge of the violence within her home is certainly ideological in that way; it might be termed the essence of her social reality. But the nana *does* know about this violence. Does this mean she inhabits a different social reality, with a distinct "not-known" essence? Through the multiplicity of voices of Part One, its entangled stories, Castellanos forces us to ask about the nature of the social reality in which both girl and nana are participants: is there one such reality or are there many? The two characters seem not to share the same reality or to exist in a reality that has been so fractured that it would be impossible to find that singular "unknown" that Žižek suggests lies beneath.

Let us think of Chactajal as a kind of consciously embedded narra-tive blindspot: the closer one gets to it, the less it can be brought into focus. It brings us back to the point of entanglement between mine and yours, to the point of the original theft of words and lands. There is no way to be *in* the point of entanglement, at its heart, without losing one's balance, without losing one's sense of the difference between inner and outer worlds, empirical and imagined sight. It is a story that cannot be told from the perspective of the marginal individual, for it undoes all of the frames that order her existence. Castellanos's awareness of the colonial entanglement, of its capacity to impinge on the act of narration and on autonomous aesthetic perception, explains her change of "mood." It led her to seek another perspective through which to explain the nature of social relations in Chiapas.

The novel's omniscient second part makes strong use of free indirect style, interior monologue, and other narrative forms of communicating psychological immediacy. Though it is narrated from the third-person perspective, it is far more centered on the individual than the first-person Part One, which is voiced by an "I" with little if any self-possession and utterly marginal to the events she describes. Part Two, on the other hand, depicts social life built up out of a web of individuals' conflicting motives and desires, which become a motor force of history, driving events. Taking greater distance from the individual's perspective, Castellanos was paradoxically able to give individuality itself greater historical significance.

The novel's Part Two plots a single narrative of social entanglement in terms of interiorization, of individuals caught in the net of collective history through their sentimental affinities. Yet *Balún Canán* reenacts what might be called the paradox of domestic fiction, as Nancy Armstrong has defined the genre, namely, that the social entanglements it describes — the psychic internalizations of normative social relations — in fact represent new possibilities of individual *disentanglement* from traditional social bonds. This is how Castellanos's novel formalizes one of its own themes: the fall of a great house and the dissolution of a regional society in which politics is a family or tribal affair, and the rise, in its stead, of a social order far more centered on the rational individual. Castellanos's novel is thus akin to the British domestic fiction Armstrong describes, for it is key to introducing "a whole new vocabulary of social relations, terms that attac[h] precise moral value to certain qualities of mind," rather than to birth or status (Armstrong 4). The novel genre participated in the creation of a gendered domain of privacy which promised, Armstrong argues, "that individuals could realize a new and more fundamental identity and thus free themselves of the status distinctions organizing the old society" (98). In Part Two of the novel, Castellanos will express the laws of this society in the voice of a character made bitter by the realization that his fate was determined at birth: "No va a cambiar nuestra situación. Indio naciste, indio te quedás. Igual yo" (160) [Our circumstances won't change. Born an Indian, always an Indian. Me too].[20] The novel's very ability to give voice to this ironic commentary signals the author's distance from the society she depicts and of which she once was a part.

However, unlike in Part One of the novel, that distance is not enabled by the alternative epistemology of indigenous ways of seeing. Instead, it is enabled by Castellanos's growing attachment to state indigenismo. Less than a year after writing those words in the novel, Castellanos would reproduce them almost exactly, transposing them to one of the didactic plays she produced for the INI's Teatro Petul, a traveling puppet theater that presented the indigenista message to indigenous communities of Chiapas. Castellanos wrote the scripts for plays about hygiene, education, national history, and the like. The following is from her dramatic recreation of the life of Benito Juárez, taken from a dialogue between the young Benito and his uncle Bernardino, who fears his nephew's ambitions will land him in trouble:

> *Bernardino:* Te van a castigar por alzado. Indio naciste, indio tienes que morir.
>
> *Benito Juárez:* Soy indio y no tengo porque avergonzarme de mi raza. Pero ser indio no quiere decir ser tan infeliz como nosotros.
>
> *Bernardino:* ¿Y qué quieres? ¿Ser igual que las gentes de razón?
>
> *Benito Juárez:* Sí, saber lo que saben los ladinos. (*Teatro Petul* 8–9)

> *Bernardino:* They will punish you for being uppity. Born an Indian, you'll die an Indian.
>
> *Benito Juárez:* I am an Indian and I don't have to feel ashamed of my race. But to be an Indian doesn't mean having to be as wretched as we are.
>
> *Bernardino:* So what do you want? To be the equal of "gentes de razón" [literally, "rational people," i.e., non-Indians, Europeans]?
>
> *Benito:* Yes, to know what the white people know.

Read retroactively from the perspective of the Teatro Petul, Castellanos's novel comes to seem the expression of an institutional indigenismo committed to liberalism. The words "indio naciste, indio te quedas," "born an Indian, always an Indian," both in the play and in the novel, are designed to convey a sense of profound injustice — the young Benito Juárez would like to become something else, something better, and disentangle himself from stifling traditions. Justice, then, comes to be conceived as a matter of social mobility and equality through education, here made out to be the essence of revolutionary change and democratization.

Castellanos's adoption of the omniscient perspective was clearly meant to be temporary, for she returned to the first-person narrator to finish out the novel. Yet the first-person narrator who appears in Part Three is far more self-possessed, far more individualistic, than she was in Part One. Although the narrators of Parts One and Three share the same perspective, something fundamental has changed between them. Though the girl continues to remain marginal, her narration changes to reflect a new sense of self-possession. Gone is her tenuousness, her tendency to be displaced by the indigenous narrator, to be "read" by the world rather than to read the world herself. Gone is the power of the blindspot — Chactajal — to decenter her, to drive her to nausea and nightmares. Though the world around her remains divided by conflict, though Chactajal itself literally burns, it does not fundamentally destabilize her perspective. It does not displace "I." In Part Three, Castellanos crafted numerous scenes designed to express her narrator's decision to place herself at the center of events and to repudiate both the wind and her family. She imagines herself gazing on the wind directly, refusing to keep her eyes lowered and thus defiantly contravening his law, "mirando para siempre" (245) [looking forever (230)]. She imagines herself willing to sacrifice her brother in order to protect herself from damnation, declaring: "me salvaré yo sola" (279) [I'll save myself alone (260)]. Her allegiance is to herself, and to "the names she tells, in her own words, with her words or with her silence, with her own truth that is the product of her imagination" (Castillo 238). Gone is the conflicted time and space of the colonial entanglement, when the nana, in telling her story, tells the narrator's story as well, but in words she refuses to recognize. The girl has disentangled her story from the stories around her — not completely, perhaps, but far more so than she had before. Enough so that she can begin to write on the walls of her father's house, as she does at the novel's close, rather than be written out by them. Despite Castellanos's return to the first-person narrator in the novel's Part Three, a more profound shift in mood seems to have taken place. The novel has internalized the civilizing mission of indigenismo and uses it as a feminist instrument, as a justification for female autonomy and self-discovery. Underlying the shifts between first- and third-person narration is a more fundamental and significant shift in the author's orientation to the power of the nation-state and the power of the indigenous House.

In Part One of *Balún Canán,* no common ground exists on which to build an interethnic consensus. One side's theft is another's rightful possession. Impossible to disentangle mine from yours if we have no consensus for determining the legitimate boundary between them. By voicing Indian history at its opening, the novel writes against what might be called the ladino consensus, one that collectively disavows Indian claims to land. But there is no ground between the ladino and indigenous consensus, except the shifting alliances of dependent subjects, those on the margins of both norms: women, children, bastard sons, Indians. Castellanos depicts a lawless world, not because there are no laws, but because there are too many, emanating from institutions around whose legitimacy there is no consensus. The nana introduces the existence of a Chactajal law before which she has been deemed transgressive and literally stigmatized, marked with a wound. This law proclaims: "Es malo querer a los que mandan, a los que poseen. Así dice la ley" (16) [It's wicked to love those who give orders and have possessions. That's what the law says (19)]. Later, a letter from Mexico City arrives and proclaims the institution of a new law: "Se aprobó la ley según la cual los dueños de fincas, con más de cinco familias de indios a su servicio, tienen la obligación de proporcionarles medios de enseñanza, estableciendo una escuela y pagando de su peculio a un maestro rural" (45) [A law has been passed by which propietors of farms with more than five familes of Indians in their service must provide facilities for teaching, by establishing a school and paying the salary of a rural master (45)]. And then the narrator must confront the law that says that only male children shall inherit the family papers and the ownership rights that these provide (60). Each law is the subject of dispute and resistance; none has widely recognized legitimacy, and the narratives of injustice that swirl around them cannot be subordinated into one overarching story. There is no single story that can be told of this conflict. This explains why "I" remains so off-balance as a narrator, with other stories constantly intruding on hers.

Yet the narrator of Part Two suffers from no such imbalance. This narrator becomes itself a mediator or unifier, weaving one complex story. It creates a collectively shared reality, drawing a multitude of characters into one single time-space. This shared time-space is the nation, strung together through a series of implicit "meanwhiles," as Anderson argues:

"simultaneity is, as it were, transverse, cross-time, marked not by pre-figuring and fulfillment, but by temporal coincidence, and measured by clock and calendar" (24). Individual national subjects, though they may never meet in person, are nevertheless connected to one another "in their steady, anonymous, simultaneous activity" (26). Not surprisingly, the "House" chronotope begins to wane into this portion of the novel, as the very nature of the conflict described undergoes a profound trans-formation. What had been a war between different houses eventually transforms into a struggle between house and nonhouse, that is, law and lawlessness. What was once a complex zone of conflict among multi-ple patriarchs, each a law unto itself, is progressively simplified over the course of the novel's Part Two until the field has been reduced to two competing entities: the force of law and the force of lawlessness.

The key scene revealing this underlying simplification occurs toward the end of Part Two. The tension between the rancher and his workers has reached a breaking point, and Chactajal erupts in flames. The narrator here becomes fully omniscient, abandoning the mediating voice of inte-rior monologue and free indirect discourse and taking on the solemn tone reserved for epic history. The narrative voice recapitulates centuries of events: the arrival and settlement of the first inhabitants of the land, their dispossession by newcomers, the growth of rural industry, the arrival of the cane mill, the fire. The subject of this narration is an impersonal force, Chactajal, the land itself:

> Todo Chactajal habló en su momento. Habló con su potente y temible voz, recuperó su rango de primacía en la amenaza.
> Las indias temblaban en el interior de los jacales. Arrodilladas imploraban perdón, clemencia. Porque alguien, uno de ellos, había invocado a las potencias del fuego y las potencias acudieron a la invocación, con sus caras embadurnadas de rojo, con su enorme ca-bellera desmelenada, con sus fauces hambrientas. Y con su corazón *que no reconoce la ley.* (198, emphasis added)

> All Chactajal was speaking now, speaking in a powerful, fear-inspiring voice, regaining its old supremacy under threat.
> The Indians inside their huts trembled. They fell on their knees to implore forgiveness and mercy. For somebody, one of them-selves, must have invoked the powers of fire, and the powers had gathered in council with red-bespattered faces, their long hair

> dishevelled, their jaws hungry, and their hearts *ignorant of law.* (185, emphasis added)

This indigenous force, the originary land, has become entirely overtaken by tropes of savagery. Gone is the idea, implicit in the nana's first narration, that the originary land is a word-memory enveloping its inhabitants and binding them to a collective history. It has become simply savage nature: the wild. What of the house of the wind and the other guardians of indigeneity, lords of Chactajal? They are part of that which *acknowledges no law.*

At this moment, the law is revealed to be a single, unitary system that some people acknowledge and others do not. "Law" has become at this point in the novel the law of the impersonal state, the only legitimate law. Castellanos depicts a social field now neatly divided in two: those who adhere to the principle of law and those who do not. This drastic simplification of the world depicted in the novel reveals that Castellanos has found a disentangled perspective from which to narrate, one that speaks with a stronger voice and verges on the monolithic. It proclaims the existence of only one law and one history. The indigenous world, by this point in the novel, has ceased to be a moral order; it has become, rather, savage disorder, outside the law.[21] This is how the state becomes rhetorically embedded at the level of narrative voice, the state understood not as one interest, one position, among a group of competing interests and positions, but as their ultimately disinterested arbiter; it normalizes social relations.

When Castellanos narrated the story of Indian dispossession omnisciently in Part Two, projecting the voice of Chactajal in its savage glory, she must have thought she was merely voicing anew the story of dispossession told by the nana. Lienhard indeed argues that the entire novel pretends to occupy this position, that Castellanos framed the novel as one among several indigenous texts (Lienhard 214). If so, then Castellanos reproduced a fallacy of revolutionary nationalism, namely, that its version of Mexican history is the same as indigenous versions, and that the revolution has sutured the wound of colonization. In fact when the indigenous history of dispossession offered by her nana meets the history of indigenous dispossession narrated by the revolution, they do not conjoin into a continuous line, but rather clash and break. This is because it is not possible to tell only one story of the Conquest. What Castellanos knew on the first page of her novel, she "forgot" on page 198.

Our sense of this forgetting is compounded by Castellanos's later comments on the novel. Nearly a decade after completing *Balún Canán*, she spoke again about the perspectival changes in the novel and explained that her turn to an "objective" third-person narration reflected her search for a more "adult" and less indigenous depiction. She explained that, in Parts One and Three of the novel, the childish perspective and the indigenous perspective were extremely close if not interchangeable:

> Este mundo infantil es muy semejante al mundo de los indígenas, en el cual se sitúa la acción de la novela. (Las mentalidades de la niña y de los indígenas poseen en común varios rasgos que las aproximan). Así, en estas dos partes la niña y los indios se ceden la palabra y las diferencias de tono no son mayúsculas. El núcleo de la acción, que por objetivo corresponde al punto de vista de los adultos, está contado por el autor en tercera persona. (Carballo 419)

> This childhood world is very similar to the Indians' world, in which the novel takes place. (The mind-sets of the girl and the Indians possess several traits in common that draw them close together). Thus, in these two parts the girl's words give way to those of the Indians, and those of the Indians to hers, without a major difference in tone. The heart of the action — which, because it is objective, corresponds to the adult point of view — is narrated by the author in the third person.

She underscored the point again in her "Tentativa de autocrítica" [Attempt at Self-Criticism] noting,

> cuando traté por primera vez de escribir una novela — *Balún Canán* — no fui armada de rigor sino de efusividad. Las metáforas resplandecían por todas partes, pero yo me salvaguardaba de una condenación arguyendo que me había propuesto rescatar una infancia perdida y un mundo presidido por la magia y no por la lógica. Pero el equilibrio se rompía cada vez que este mundo me planteaba la exigencia de ser comprendido y explicado y no simplemente descrito. A esta exigencia he ido cediendo paulatinamente en mis relatos posteriores. (*Obras* 992–93)

> when I tried to write a novel for the first time — *Balún Canán* — I was not armed with rigor, only profuseness. Metaphors glittered everywhere, but I saved myself from condemnation, arguing that I

had intended to retrieve a lost childhood and a world presided over by magic and not by logic. But the balance would be thrown off each time this world demanded an understanding and an explanation from me and not merely a description. I have gradually yielded to this demand in my subsequent narratives.[22]

Effusiveness, poetry, childhood, magic, on one side; rigor, logic, adulthood, explanation, on the other. Magic is a phase one outgrows, she all but states, unless of course one is an Indian; one then has to be specially convinced to leave it behind. Although the transition to Part Two may appear as the continuation of the novel's search for a different way of seeing, Castellanos's own words suggest a repudiation of what came before. It is a repudiation of the Weil-ian "I," whose site is the balcony, who is contemplative and distanced; and of the indigenized "I," who shares an intimate time-space with her nana, who listens carefully to the voice of the wind and sees her imagined world around her. And it is a repudiation of the entangled narrative of the colonial encounter that emerged through this unwordly, off-center "I," who is spoken by another as much as by herself.

To be sure, Castellanos incorporated this repudiation into the novel as a theme, by depicting the narrator's repudiation of her Mayan nana. The depiction is deeply ironic; we know that in reality the girl is grieving the loss of her caretaker and teacher and that her racism is a cover for her interior sadness and disappointment. Yet at the same time, Castellanos normalized this loss by linking it to the inevitable process of growing up (eventually, all children outgrow their nannies) and by implying that it is the price to be paid for one's adult autonomy. The narrator may have lost her nanny, but it is this loss that enables the emergence of a new voice and a new measure of independence. Castellanos adopted the conventional wisdom of her day: the girl's melancholic abandonment of her indigenous teacher is a sign of *progress*.

Debt and Disentanglement

A fundamental shift in Castellanos's way of approaching indigeneity occurred while she was composing the novel. In an interview conducted ten years after the novel was published, Castellanos explained that in composing *Balún Canán* she had arrived at a new social consciousness:

> Desde mi infancia, alterné con los indios. Después de adquirir una perspectiva, me di cuenta de cómo eran los indios y de lo que deberían ser. Me sentía en deuda, como individual y como clase, con ellos. Esa deuda se me volvió consciente al redactar *Balún Canán*. Asumirla trajo como resultado otros libros y la actividad de dirigir el teatro guiñol en el centro que el Instituto mantiene en San Cristóbal. (cited in B. Miller 136)

> Ever since my childhood, I've mixed with Indians. After acquiring a perspective, I realized what Indians are and what they should become. I felt indebted to them, as an individual and a member of a social class. I became aware of that debt while composing *Balún Canán*. Taking on that debt led to other books and to the work of directing the INI's puppet theater in San Cristóbal.

Her words are striking in light of what we know about the years leading up to *Balún Canán* and indeed in light of the novel itself. First, the statement about her childhood contact with Indians is not as straightforward as it seems. It is the result of a certain framing of her autobiography that she acquired only after her travels in Europe. Second, Castellanos talks here of "acquiring a perspective" through writing the novel, perspective in the singular. Yet in the novel there are multiple perspectives present. These include, of course, the perspective of the first-person and the third-person narrators. But this multiplicity also derives from the construction of the first-person narrator herself, as someone who straddles two worlds that cannot be reconciled, the seen and the imagined, and as someone whose story about herself clashes with, and cannot completely silence or override, the story her nana tells about that origin. Castellanos's reference here to a singular perspective falls in line with her other repudiations of the novel's experiments in perspective.

Third, although Castellanos here communicates her sense of entanglement with Indians, she uses a language that normalizes disentanglement, calling forth the legal and ethical imperative to pay off a debt. How could Castellanos ever pay off this debt? In what *currency* does this transaction occur? The existence of a debt reveals an underlying shared economy of the law, one into which Castellanos brings herself and Indians. Castellanos thus advanced the possibility of creating a singular story of encounter, of unifying the multiple threads of the colonial "point of entanglement" into one narrative. The idea of debt, we might say, rationalizes a situation that had remained, until then, out of control.

Furthermore, the relationship of debt creates a sphere of exchange that straddles intimate and public worlds. As Nietzsche shows, debt and guilt are related: "the central moral concept of 'guilt' originated from the very material concept of debt" (44). Castellanos found a way to transmute her guilt into revolutionary nationalism and thus synchronize her personal search for authenticity with the reigning political ideology. Castellanos aligned herself with the state, for she paid her debt in the currency it offered: institutional indigenista action. In so doing, she brought herself more fully into the public sphere. In imagining herself indebted to Indians, Castellanos reflected her awareness of her own entitlement: only those considered creditable can contract a debt. Positing her relationship to Indians as one of indebtedness, Castellanos signaled her emancipation from a discredited position, the position of woman-as-nature. In writing *Balún Canán* and then joining the INI, she laid the ghost of Doña Bárbara to rest.

But the notion of interethnic relations as debt did not accomplish the same for Indians — it did not bring them further into the public sphere, but rather further into the interior sphere of affective, intimate relations. Castellanos posed her relationship to Indians as a debt that she proposed to pay by civilizing them, for the INI's puppet theater was a didactic one. Castellanos thus attributed to Indians a paradoxical kind of authority, one that does not affirm their power but rather their need. In the act of recognizing the moral authority of Indians, she simultaneously takes it away. Indeed, Mexican indigenismo did not recognize Indians as fully empowered subjects before the law. When INI published the book *Indigenismo* in 1958 to explain the institution's mission and achievements, its director, Alfonso Caso, somberly explained the reason behind the official posture of treating Indians as children: "Nada hay más peligroso que considerar iguales ante la Ley, a quienes no lo son por su situación social y económica" [Nothing is more dangerous than to consider as equals before the Law those people who are not, by virtue of their social and economic situation] (Caso, *Indigenismo* 27).

The transaction between Castellanos and Indians, the loan they offered her, thus takes place in part in a private realm that the state does not officially recognize as legitimate. Turning repeatedly to this inner realm of intimate connection, Castellanos was able to deny her full coevalness to the materialism of cosmopolitan modernity. She manifested not only her marginality with respect to the everyday world, but also a profound attachment to the idea of marginality, proof to her that modern subjects, though saturated by instrumental reason, have not yet become machines. But that attachment to aesthetic marginality, crucial to developing her autonomy and her literary art, came at the price of denying coevalness to Indians yet without endowing them with its accompanying autonomy.

Finally, in the passage I quoted above, Castellanos turns the novel into an instrument of a larger purpose — national progress — rather than an end in itself. This move allowed her to join together her literary vocation and her indigenista vocation into a single narrative of female enlightenment and moral self-improvement. The writing of *Balún Canán* thus contributed to forging Castellanos's attitude to writing as both a deeply personal and a deeply political act, one that has much to do with the process of female — and feminist — self-invention and discovery. She considered writing to be, among other things, a form of therapy: writing soothes, releases, changes oneself.[23] She had in mind a scene from Proust's *A la recherche du temps perdu,* when a young boy's writing serves as a kind of balm to soothe his anguish. Writing, she wrote, is capable of producing "una modificación liberadora" on the author, "a liberating modification" ("Escrituras tempranas" 994). In her case, she wrote, the purpose had much to do with individualizing herself, through a process of self-objectification and self-reflection:

> Soy yo misma la que quiero verme representada para conocerme, para reconocerme. ¿Pero cómo me llamo? ¿A quién me parezco? ¿De quién me distingo? Con la pluma en la mano inicio una búsqueda que ha tenido sus treguas en la medida en que ha tenido sus hallazgos, pero que todavía no termina. ("Escrituras tempranas" 997)

> I am the one who wants to see myself represented in order to know myself, to recognize myself. But what is my name? Who do I look like? Who am I different from? With pen in hand, I begin a search that has had its moments of respite, to the extent that it has had its discoveries, but that still remains unfinished.

If *Balún Canán* is understood as an example of this kind of writing, as I think it must be, then it follows that its point of enunciation did not remain steady over the course of its composition. Somewhere in the present of writing, along the way, the "now" of the author's first enunciation got left behind, overtaken by events: by writing as an event. Is it possible to perceive this event in *Balún Canán*? To accept this aspect of *Balún Canán*, its nature as a testament to a process of individual change, not just at the level of representation but also at the level of enunciation, seriously destabilizes critical analysis of it. Castellanos changed while writing it and because of writing it, which in turn changed what she wrote as she was writing. And these changes mean that the novel's status as an object has been challenged: for which *subject* is this book an *object* that has been carefully and conscientiously created and molded, for the author who started writing it or the author who finished it? One must speak, in this case, of at least two authors and two books. Where does one book begin and the other leave off?

I believe this transition left its traces in the move from Part One to Part Two of the novel. Paradoxically enough, by leaving behind the personal, autobiographical "I" of the novel's Part One, Castellanos made her authorial presence more strongly felt. Striving for objectivity and an adult perspective, she revealed the tenuous nature of her attachment to the idea that the indigenous Book represents a moral order to which she must remain subject. Judith Butler, paraphrasing Freud, writes that "conscience is a passionate attachment to prohibition" (*Psychic* 68). She means that it is an attachment to prohibition as such; it reveals the subject's dependence on renunciation before the law, its "turning back" on its own desire. In light of *Balún Canán,* one is tempted to pluralize this vision of prohibition. Rather than a singular or abstract principle of prohibition, there exist multiple, overlapping, competing prohibitions, differently embodied, mutually antagonistic, and subject to historical transformation. Adopting the autobiographical pose, fictionalized as it was, and choosing the revolution as her backdrop, Castellanos placed a female "I" before these various laws as if testing the possibilities of each to authorize her self-possession. But in the end she settled on one in particular: the civilizing mission of revolutionary indigenismo. Castellanos's internalization of indigenismo thus had a liberating and empowering effect on herself as a Mexican woman. Indeed, in an essay honoring Lázaro Cárdenas, she thanked him for enabling her to lead a life that was "the most responsible, the fullest, and the most human" ("A Man" 235). Her trajectory signals the possibilities of individual self-transformation opened by indigenista nationalism. It also signals how that self-transformation becomes most meaningful when it is harnessed to an ideology of progress and civilization that marginalizes and infantilizes Indians.

Conclusion

Listening to Small Voices

Two major threads constitute "national time" in the production of in-digenista novels. One of these threads is a form of re-presentation of the unified or synchronous temporal experience of nationality. As Bene-dict Anderson suggests, the novel, by positing that events which occur in different spaces are simultaneous with one another, unifies disparate ex-periences into a singular and coherent entity, into a "solid community" moving as one through history. Underlying it is "homogenous, empty time . . . marked . . . by temporal coincidence, and measured by clock and calendar" (24). This view of national time allows us to consider indi-genista novels as symbolic representations of the indigenista dream of culturally unified national consciousness and solidarity.

But the simultaneity of the clock and the calendar is only one of a number of possible apprehensions of national time. Indigenista novels also represent national time in the confessional mode. They point to it as a redemptive, egalitarian space of inner self-encounter, one that counteracts and overwhelms the oppressive, hierarchical space of oli-garchical daily life, marked by slavery, injustice, self-repudiation and shame. The time of the confessional is national time, the time of human-ity, recognition, communication, and love, of self-affirmation through self-sacrifice. Hierarchy, though still existent, has been inverted: now it is the figure of an indigenous teacher who presides benevolently over the community.

Speaking about the inner structure of the novel, Bakhtin writes that the "pivotal axis of the novel" is constituted by "the sequence guilt — punishment — redemption — purification — blessedness" (128). Intimate indigenismo attempts to transform the isolating experience of modern individuality into one of shared communication, a collective experience. But this collective does not move "up or down history" and across the empty time of the clock. Rather, it charts a shared passage or journey across Bakhtin's axis, where the end point is a better individual self and a better collective life. The nation, understood this way, is not an end in itself, but rather a means to liberation from the past. It is redemptive.

Jesús Lara and José María Arguedas entered "the lettered city," Angel Rama's figure for the Latin American state, only at the cost of significant self-violence, for they had to learn to view their mother tongue as stigma. They entered the lettered city as guilty subjects. Castellanos entered it, meanwhile, by adopting a distanced stance toward the stigma of femininity, honing the double-voiced irony of the feminist who prefers subversion from within (Perus 1093). Amidst the fragments of the Republican form this lettered city had adopted in the nineteenth century, the populist lettered city of the mid-twentieth century offers a complex time-space of aesthetic creation.[1] Martin Lienhard has traced the existence of written texts whose form belongs neither to subaltern textual production nor to criollo or elite production (15). This "neither-nor" category, forming what he calls "an other history" of Latin American literature, suggests that the lettered city or republic might be subject to mapping, and that it might be possible to seek out its distinct spaces, identifying suburbs and frontiers. Perhaps one might also speak of distinct time zones. All of these zones generate writing practices bespeaking their authors' relative social and political power. Yet not all of them are synchronized to the time of the state; or rather, the state, which is not a monolith, may itself keep different times.

The confessional time-space of intimate indigenismo addresses multiple instances of authority, social laws that are both residual and emergent, institutionalized and informal. Most importantly, it appeals to a new indigenous figure of the law, having converted the Indian, fetishistically, into a norm. Judith Butler writes, "Norms do not unilaterally act upon the psyche; rather, they become condensed as figures of the law to which the psyche returns" (*Antigone's Claim* 30). Indigenista narratives participate in the symbolic labor necessary for such condensations, toward which their authors turn in the search for new legitimacy, a new *normalcy*. Although they were initially oppositional, indigenista rhetorical strategies such as the ones I have examined here, which configured the nation as an intimate sphere writ large and as a form of redemption from a colonial legacy experienced concretely in the form of individual shame, rapidly became hegemonic. Yet despite their power, their role in the national-populist regimes of the mid-twentieth century has been downplayed.

Anthropologist Claudio Lomnitz, in his study of Mexican national culture, suggests that the contemporary prevalence of "intimate stories" may be a reflection of nationalism on the wane rather than an expression of nationalism itself. In a piece originally published in the year 2000 he writes,

> Current tastes reflect weariness with the epic visions of revolutionary nationalism: today the intimate world of Frida Kahlo is of greater interest than the epic grandiloquence of Diego Rivera; even when they distill nationalism, as with the narratives of Poniatowska and Monsiváis, intimate chronicles are consumed with more interest than the comprehensive national epics of a Carlos Fuentes. This situation is symptomatic of the crisis of old nationalism: the longing for community and an inheritance continues, but the state definitions of those communities are almost as weak as they were in the nineteenth century. (*Deep Mexico* 55–56)

Without disputing these claims about current shifts in aesthetic taste, this vision of the "old nationalism" and the narrative genre most associated with it call for further scrutiny. The relationship Lomnitz posits between epic and intimate genres is primarily one of antagonism, and it is plotted along a devolutionary scale: intimacy is what happens once epic forms become weak and old. It suggests that intimacy is proper to a state in ruins, but a ruin that one should not mourn. Such is the case when, at the end of Juan Rulfo's novel *Pedro Páramo,* the state that is personified in the cacique, a law unto himself, quietly collapses into a mound of small stones.[2] It seems that the image of the revolutionary state as stern yet benevolent father — "el estado papá," as historian Alan Knight puts it — imposes a particular finality even on those who are critical of that state and its self-image: the father ages, weakens, and finally collapses. For decades now, this anthropomorphic telos of the state has been made coextensive with a narrative of political liberation, for its end stage is "democratic Mexico." Thus, although Lomnitz does not say it here explicitly, there is nevertheless an implicit association of intimacy, and the feminine, with freedom from an overly strong state.

Yet how truly marginal are these realms to Mexican revolutionary nationalism, or to the revolutionary nationalisms of other states, or indeed to other forms of strong national sentiment? The emblematic voices and bodies of Kahlo and Poniatowska, injured, small, and childlike when compared to the towering figures of Rivera, Fuentes, and "el estado papá," have always been invested with a certain kind of power. This power is, in part, one that accrues to those who, in helping the weak, benefit from the portrait in contrasts which they themselves have staged. But it is also the power that accrues, paradoxically enough, through the attribution of political powerlessness to certain kinds of people, such as the injured, women, and, most importantly for mestizo nationalism, indigenous people. Following from Wendy Brown's account, which draws from Nietzsche's *On the Genealogy of Morals,* one could say that this power appears as the more enduring, stronger power of Truth and Good over material power. Truth and Good, being uncorrupted, are hence perfectly suited to reproach power from a position apparently outside it (Brown 46–47).

A paradigmatic example of the enactment of this power can be found in the political style of Lázaro Cárdenas who, as Majorie Becker writes, "was the first Mexican head of state since the hapless Maximilian to listen to campesinos as they detailed their troubles" (248). Listening to them, he endowed them with a certain power over himself, sentimental yet nonetheless profound. In that pose, he was meant to be understood as listening to his own tender heart. In Bolivia, meanwhile, as Josefa Salmón has argued, the Movimiento Nacional Revolucionario, the political party that came to power in the 1952 revolution, constructed its modernizing program on the dichotomy between industrial mining and "la tierra india" [Indian land or earth], which must be nationalized through economic integration. This discourse perpetuated the metonymic association of Indians with nature while also denying, through the strategic use of the word "virgin" in conjunction with this rural space, that it was already a site of intense indigenous political mobilization (125–30). Laura Gotkowitz, in her study of regional discourses of citizenship in Bolivia in this prerevolutionary period, makes a similar point, showing how indigenistas demonized indigenous activists by inserting them into a cultural script in which "activism" and "indigeneity" were made mutually incompatible cultural features (201ff).

Finally, in Peru, Marisol de la Cadena demonstrates that while certain oppositional indigenista sectors of the 1920s supported indigenous activism in the countryside, this tendency was offset by an equally powerful tendency toward presenting Indians as incapable of studied political action, and hence morally innocent of the violence attributed to them (de la Cadena 110–18). Arguing that Indians were "primitive and innately harmless, but ferocious if provoked" (de la Cadena 111), some indigenistas claimed that the Indians' political violence was the result of a collective delirium, and hence they were not morally responsible for their actions. This logic was used to defend Indians against their powerful accusers, but it had the effect of denying them the capacity for taking their political destiny into their own hands. Indigenous activism was symbolically equated with insanity.

The work of indigenismo, and of its offspring, mestizo nationalism — both of them the ideological glue transforming revolutionary nationalisms into populist hegemonies in Mexico and the Andes — can be understood from this vantage point as a mechanism for the state to accrue power through listening to small voices, voices whose virtue resides precisely in their smallness vis-à-vis the powerful. Indigenismo attributes political powerlessness to those who, at one time or other, have actively risen up against the state. Rebellious bodies, rebellious words: they represent the political energies unleashed by a revolutionary moment that must subsequently be recontained and subordinated to a new configuration of power. As Lisa Lowe and David Lloyd argue, "the moment of anticolonial struggle is generally very productive of 'emancipatory' possibilities far in excess of nationalism's own projects" (9). In order to accomplish this recontainment, indigenista-inflected nationalist thought set about identifying and then naturalizing the existence of certain indigenous cultural attributes that recent events themselves belied, attributes such as political quietude, stoic suffering, passive victimization, and innocence of power. It symbolically transformed their insurgency into quiet virtue by validating as heroic precisely those behaviors that epic history ignores or forgets; it made their quiet virtue heroic, while actively erasing their insurgency, and the alternative nationalisms around which these indigenous mobilizations often coalesced, from the collective memory. "México no es una nación" [Mexico is not a nation], declares an indigenista functionary in 1940, because its Indians lack the concept of nation (Cruz Ramírez 40) — this, a mere twenty years after Zapatismo! These discursive maneuvers justified indigenista claims about the urgent need to nationalize Indians. Such claims attempted to contain the power of prior indigenous mobilizations, many of them already strongly oriented nationally, by positing Indian subjects as thoroughly outside the course of national development.

The populist hegemonies constructed by indigenista-oriented nationalisms thus project a powerless voice, which they then incorporate into the concept of the nation, and posit the existence of a small voice at the nation's core, a forgotten voice to which one must carefully listen in order to be true. That small voice — so often an Indian voice — lies at the core of mestizo authenticity and political autonomy. It is what distinguishes Bolivia from Spain, according to Tamayo's 1910 *Creación de una pedagogía nacional* (143–45); or Mexico from the United States, as José Vasconcelos says in *La raza cósmica* (1925), couching mestizaje as an expression of love (96). It is what makes us properly "American," proclaims Peruvian indigenista Uriel García (8).

Rather than speaking of intimate narratives as those that rise up from below once the state, doddering about in senile confusion, can no longer generate an epic monument in its own image; rather than seeing intimate narratives as those that have been unleashed from the fragments of the body that once was Pedro Páramo, I would suggest we see them as enabling a particular mode of state interpellation, one in which state power has been masked as its opposite. The earnest listening pose adopted by indigenistas, and the practice of indigenista anti-positivism more broadly, would then be examples of "everyday forms of state formation," to use the phrase coined by the historians Joseph and Nugent, a state formation that derives its legitimacy through discourses about the vulnerability and innocence at the core of national selves.

To a certain extent, this kind of indigenista discourse participated in the formation of a limited or qualified version of what Lauren Berlant has termed, referring to a vastly different time and place, the "intimate public sphere." This sphere is occupied by identity narratives that respond to the "paradox of partial legibility," a paradox that arises from "the experience of social hierarchy." Berlant writes, "The experience of social hierarchy is intensely individuating, yet it also makes people public and generic: it turns them into *kinds* of people who are both attached to and underdescribed by the identities that organize them" (Berlant 1). Rather than calling on the abstractions of liberal citizenship to resolve these paradoxes, the identity narrative found in the intimate indigenista archive seeks instead to make explicit "the vulnerability of personal existence to the instability of capitalism and the concretely unequal forms and norms of national life" (Berlant 4).

This vulnerability comes to the fore in stories that recount how the individual has suffered exclusion before the law, whether because of ethno-racial ancestry, linguistic heritage, gender, or regional location. Lara's Indian narrator protests against the stigma of race that he carries like a burden while at school, much as Lara himself protested about the stigma of race he carried by virtue of his indigenous mother tongue. Arguedas's autobiographical narratives contain numerous references to similar formative experiences. Moving from the Quechua-infused world of his childhood to the reactionary Hispanism of Lima or the provincial colegio, this author-narrator oscillates between resentment at his exclusion and appeals to another world of restitution and redemption. Castellanos, meanwhile, found herself in dialogue with concepts of women's inferiority that had been strongly internalized and that were intimately bound up with the negative image of the regional oligarchy — of which Castellanos was an heir — put forward by Mexican revolutionary-nationalist ideologies.

Under certain political conditions, that narrative of overcoming stigma comes to take on a powerful collective significance: it constitutes the shared ground of nationality, part and parcel of populist hegemonies. Though limited to a minority, this kind of indigenismo, I would argue, provided a discursive space for rendering visible what Bolivian historian Silvia Rivera has termed "the invisible violence of self-imposed cultural change" ("La raíz" 79), and for reflecting on its costs, and it was crucial to bringing that reflection into discourses of national identity. To an extent, then, intimate indigenista narratives can be read as instances of a phenomenology of social mobility, one that reflects the particular contradictions of modernization in Mexico and the Andes.[3]

The potential of these identity narratives to provide a critical perspective on their times, however, is offset by the fact that they contributed to furthering national-populist ideologies that kept indigenous people subordinate. Intimate indigenismo wielded the language of a struggle for liberation — liberation from shame, from prejudice, from silence and self-denial — that became instrumental to consolidating a new status quo, one that attempted to delegitimize other, potentially more threatening kinds of liberation struggles, such as those emanating from organized workers and indigenous peasants. Intimate indigenismo remained anchored in the broader indigenista project of consolidating modern state power and played a role in generating the emotional appeal crucial to the consolidation of populist hegemonies.

I follow Neil Larsen's definition of populism as the political regime that results when "the consensual stability of civil society must be sought through the direct control of . . . non-state circuitries [e.g., peasants, the church, armed insurgents] rather than through the traditional atomizing approach of the liberal metropolitan states (constitution of the modern 'citizen')" (Larsen 63). What is the image of the nation that results from the hegemonic process Larsen describes? Claudio Lomnitz has argued that it is different from the "fraternal" community emphasized by Benedict Anderson: "regardless of the actual inequality and exploitation that may prevail in each, the nation is always conceived as a deep, horizontal comradeship" (Anderson 7). Lomnitz proposes, rather, that the Mexican nation-as-community is in fact imagined as unequal and heterogeneous: "it systematically distinguishes full citizens from part citizens or strong citizens from weak ones (e.g., children, women, Indians, the ignorant). . . . The fraternal bond is critical, but so are what one might call the *bonds of dependence* that are intrinsically a part of any nationalism" (*Deep Mexico* 12, original emphasis). Lomnitz thus redefines the nation as "a community that is conceived of as a deep comradeship among full citizens, each of whom is a potential broker between the national state and weak, embryonic, or part citizens who he or she can construe as dependents" (13). Put another way, we might say that the sovereignty of certain national selves depends in turn on the lack of sovereignty of others, but also that the relationship between these two kinds of national person defines the imagined community, and finally that the "full citizen" who has been interpellated into such a system has internalized that relationship: the relationship between partial citizens and full citizens is analogous to the relationship between one's self and the outside world. The core of the self feels a deep kinship with embryonic citizens such as Indians.

Indigenista policies characteristically treat Indians as dependents, as if they were children before a benevolent father. Yet at times we see that it is the indigenista who places himself or herself in the dependent position, attributing to Indians a moral innocence to which a certain authority has come to be attached. In effect, embryonic citizens can be envisaged as more human than full citizens, just as Las Casas's Indians would now appear to us as more human than were their tyrannical oppressors. A modern example of the attribution of greater "humanness" to Indians can be found in Octavio Paz's essay "Los hijos de la Malinche," from *Laberinto de la soledad* (The Labyrinth of Solitude) (1950). Paz built his arguments about Mexican national character on the contrast between

Mexicans and industrial workers. The latter had lost their irreducibility, had become transparent, abstract, and entirely instrumentalized by their labor (73–77). Paz claimed that Mexicans were able to resist this instrumentalization by holding on to the enigmatic opacity at the core of the Mexican character — an enigma that resulted in part from Mexicans' ambiguous relationship to their indigenous heritage. And yet, the moral authority — the greater humanity — that is attributed to Indians, both in Paz and in indigenista discourses, has nothing to do with the social laws of the state. As embryonic citizens, Indians were considered by indigenistas to be too incomplete to stand before such laws without benefit of special protection.

What happens to those who rhetorically "enter" the sphere of the "indigenous soul" at the core of the self? Like indigenista discourse more generally, intimate indigenismo posed a challenge to existing moral economies of race and culture. Thus, the turn to this intimate sphere authorized subjects who were previously considered transgressive. It turned racial stigmas into virtues and helped turned "partial" citizens into full citizens. The personal transformations enabled by such indigenista invocations are significant. Lara, Arguedas, and Castellanos were full citizens who carried within themselves the memory of having once been treated as part citizens, Lara and Arguedas by virtue of their indigenous tongue, Castellanos by virtue of her sex. Indigenismo was thus for them a way to be rid of those stigmas, to change the mark of apartness into the sign of social esteem. It provided them with a new entitlement.

The indigenista concept of being beholden to Indians, of owing them a debt, contributed paradoxically to this self-authorization. As I discussed in chapters 2 and 4, both Lara and Castellanos spoke of their relation to Indians in the language of debt: they claimed to owe something to Indians. Intimate indigenismo thus operated for them as a confessional sphere, for "such is the object of confession: to elicit from the convert a voiced acknowledgment of what he or she owes to the Father" (Rafael 94). Their indigenista action, including the practice of literature, was expiatory, an attempt to pay off that debt to a newly formed authority, the nation personified in the Indian. In assuming their relationship to Indians as one of indebtedness, however, Lara and Castellanos also demonstrated that they themselves are creditable, and thus possessed of a certain kind of honor. In other words, by affirming their indebtedness, they affirmed themselves as "full citizens." The civilizing mission of indigenismo was thus invested with the power to protect or liberate indigenistas themselves from different forms of constraint: the alienation of instrumental reason and the stigma of the sub-human that might have marked them.

Yet it did not provide the same entitlement to their creditors. The language of debt has a masking function and becomes a powerful ideological alibi. It asks us to imagine a negotiation of sorts, an exchange or a contract entered into among equals. In effect, in order to adopt such a language, the indigenista has to imagine Indian servitude through the centuries as a loan. Transforming slavery into sacrifice and the slave into a lender or a creditor, this gesture effectively suppresses the fact that the colonized could not freely dispose of their will. But it is also another gesture of indigenista hypocrisy: ironically, the free will attributed to the indigenous "lender" is not sufficient to make of him or her a full citizen. The transaction, such as it is, thus takes place in a private realm that the state does not officially recognize as legitimate.

Yet the transaction or conversation that takes place in that private realm nevertheless binds subjects to the state more thoroughly, through the almost ritual exercise of transforming guilt into innocence that takes place within it. Thus intimate indigenista speech not only involves self-authorization and liberation, freeing people from the burdens of the past. It can also be considered part of the process of subjection to the modernizing nation-state. Distinguishing authentic from inauthentic selves on the basis of their affinity for Indians and their capacity to hear an inner indigenous voice, indigenismo displaces other forms of identity in order to make national identity the primordial truth of the self. That truth becomes a power to which one willingly submits — in part because it is a benevolent power, an authority that has been symbolically linked to Indians and indigeneity and therefore appears paradoxically innocent of power, and in part because in submitting one also proves oneself to be similarly innocent. Such submission, enacted in an Indian-ized sphere, becomes effective proof of one's humanity; it has a cleansing function.

The attribution of political powerlessness is a particularly effective way to destigmatize. Associated with the Good and the True in the indigenista moral economy, it has an immediate cleansing effect, stripping its object of inherited guilt and rendering it innocent. The small voices whispering among the pantheon of national giants, I would suggest, are those that national subjects have been encouraged, at some level, to recognize as themselves, in themselves, part of themselves — and this particular form of self-recognition is necessary to being recognized by the state.

In this sense, there is a strong link between the confessional sphere affirmed by Las Casas as proof that the colonized are human, and the sphere of national belonging into which indigenistas metaphorically enter. The indigenista-inflected national self-descriptions are enunciated from a confessional site, as the rhetorical structure of their autobiographical statements repeatedly makes clear. In positing an inner, Indian truth that must be heard, intimate indigenismo would then involve a discursive practice similar to the sexualized confessional of seventeenth- and eighteenth-century Europe that Michel Foucault describes:

> The confession is a ritual of discourse in which the speaking subject is also the subject of the statement; it is also a ritual that unfolds within a power relationship, for one does not confess without the presence (or virtual presence) of a partner who is not simply the interlocutor but the authority who requires the confession, prescribes and appreciates it, and intervenes in order to judge, punish, forgive, console, and reconcile; a ritual in which the truth is corroborated by the obstacles and resistances it has had to surmount in order to be formulated; and finally, a ritual in which the expression alone, independently of its external consequences produces intrinsic modifications in the person who articulates it: it exonerates, redeems, and purifies him; it unburdens him of his wrongs, liberates him, and promises him salvation. (*History* 61–62)

The modern encounter with an indigenous voice within an intimate sphere suggests that there is an element of national subjectivity that functions according to the disciplinary logic of the confessional. Expressing the racialized truth of the national self enacts a moral transformation: of guilt into innocence, of stigma into belonging, of the less-than-human or liminally human into the fully human. The confessional, racialized as a result of its role in Spanish imperial conquest (and "reconquest"), survives into the twentieth century embedded in the very language of nationality.

In order to understand the subjectifying effects of indigenista nationalism, it is necessary to consider the possibility that it might be an ideology rather than merely a set of ideas or myths. Though perhaps no one would dispute that "mestizaje," heavily promoted by indigenista nationalism, has become a profoundly ideological term, it is often treated as if it were an intellectual concept or a mirage, the figment of a small elite's imagination or a convenient fiction served up by state propaganda to cover

over the existence of profound social inequalities within the nation.[4] This critique is immensely powerful to the extent that it questions whether the national "I" is as indigenista or mestizo nationalists claim it to be, and examines the political and economic interests motivating such a projection. But because this critique associates indigenismo primarily with the repressive nation-states of the mid-to-late twentieth century, it has obscured the more subtle ideological effects of indigenismo, those which cannot be accounted for in terms of repression, silencing, objectifying, and othering. It has also obscured the nature and extent of indigenismo's challenge to the racial status quo in the first half of the twentieth century in Mexico, Bolivia, and Peru. Finally, it has downplayed the historical power of indigenista-inflected nationalist ideas for creating new collective identities by mistaking their incompleteness for a lack of substance and effect. In other words, because the national reality does not live up to an often coercively projected national image, that image has been taken as nothing more than an insubstantial myth or empty rhetoric. To the extent that critics question whether such a national subject exists at all, except as a form of false consciousness or propaganda, a murk that can be cleared away when brought into the light of rational historical inquiry, they may perhaps underestimate the ideological effects of the modern nation-state. How to account for the profound interpellating power of indigenista nationalism and the mestizo national identity that it promotes, for its wide and enduring appeal?

In her analysis of Bolivian mestizo nationalism, Silvia Rivera suggests that its success is to due to its appeal to certain social sectors, and she turns to an existential account of modernization in order to explain its power. She speculates that it responds to the needs of the descendants of deterritorialized indigenous people to establish new forms of belonging as they work their way up the social ladder; it counteracts their "uprootedness," "insecurity," and "deculturation" ("La raíz" 85). Rivera suggests, in effect, that a state apparatus and a form of social hegemony, however fragile or temporary, were created out of the existential need of a minority group only recently invested with social power. Yet one senses that Rivera implicitly rejects her own hypotheses, or at least refuses to consider them seriously. She refers to "el carácter imaginario de la comunidad que se construyó en torno a la identidad mestiza" [the imaginary nature of the community that was constructed around mestizo identity] (85). She means "imaginary" in the sense of nonexistent, a mirage by which, through the rhetorical arts of a powerful minority, a majority Indian nation comes to appear as shimmeringly other to itself. She thus dismisses the mestizo nation as a compensatory fiction.

What if one lent greater power to this compensatory fiction? Rivera may effectively be right: the idea of a mestizo nation may indeed be compensatory for the self-violence of cultural assimilation, and thus one should treat it with a measure of suspicion because it leads to a potentially reactionary cultural politics. But that doesn't mean it isn't real, only that it forms modern subjects in a problematic way: through their consciousness of their own "state of injury," as Wendy Brown would say. This consciousness of injury lends them an identity crystallized around a "history of suffering" to which they remain attached, even when their own position has substantially changed for the better. Thus, although they protest against the fiction of the ideal universal citizen by keeping alive the memory of their past experience of exclusion from it, they also continue to strive for that ideal and impose it on others as norm. It remains a sign of liberation from stigma (Brown 52–76).

Intimate indigenista narratives repeatedly betray a longing to become unmarked. Liberation is thus understood in part as a matter of freedom from particularity.[5] In Villoro's phenomenological account, this freedom from particularity is the end-goal of intimate indigenista action: "para salvar al indio habrá que acabar por negarlo en cuanto tal indio, por suprimir su especificidad. Pues en la comunidad sin desigualdad de razas, no habrá ya 'indios' ni 'blancos' ni 'mestizos,' sino hombres que se reconozcan recíprocamente en su libertad" [to save the Indian it will be necessary to end up negating him qua Indian, to suppress his specificity. Because in a community with no racial inequality, there will be no "Indians" or "whites" or "mestizos," but men who mutually recognize themselves in their freedom] (278). His words suggest the presence of an unacknowledged liberal horizon operating within revolutionary populism.

The growing power of indigenous social movements has definitively changed the Latin American political landscape.[6] One effect has been to put the status of indigenismo into ever greater question. Modern indigenista institutions in Mexico and the Andes are currently in the process of being reformed or dissolved. In July 2003, Mexico's INI, the Instituto Nacional Indigenista, ceased to exist after half a century of operation. It was replaced by the Comisión Nacional para el Desarrollo de los Pueblos Indígenas (CDI) [National Commission for the Development of

Indigenous Peoples], whose stated aim is to guarantee full expression of Mexico's political, religious, and cultural plurality. The commission's director explicitly contrasts its mission to the integrating mission of the now-defunct INI. She writes:

> Aún hace falta trabajar para reconocer y aceptar las muchas identidades que hay en mi país. Implica que todos los ciudadanos reconozcamos la diversidad, y que esta aceptación se convierta en nuevas acciones y políticas públicas que nada tienen que ver con las viejas políticas integracionistas o asimilacionistas, sino con el respeto a todos los derechos de los pueblos indígenas y sus integrantes. La acción pública de las instituciones federales, estatales y municipales debe tomar en cuenta a las autoridades e instituciones indígenas. (Gálvez)

> We still need to work to recognize and accept the many identities that exist in my country. This implies that all citizens recognize diversity, and that this acceptance be transformed into new actions and public policies that have nothing to do with the old integrationist or assimilationist policies, but rather to do with respect for all the rights of indigenous peoples and their members. The public actions of federal, state, and municipal institutions have to take indigenous authorities and institutions into account.

Meanwhile, in Bolivia, President Evo Morales has dismantled the Ministerio de Asuntos Indígenas y Pueblos Originarios [Ministry of Affairs for Indigenous and Originary Peoples]. He calls it "racist and discriminatory," arguing that "los indígenas y las mujeres serán ministros, por tanto, no hay por qué crear un ministerio de la mujer o un ministerio indígena... sería como crear un ministerio de k'aras (blancos)" [indigenous people and women will be ministers, thus, there is no reason to create a ministry of women or an indigenous ministry... that would be like creating a ministry of whites] (cited in Gómez).

These developments appear to confirm French anthropologist Henri Favre's predictions about the fate of indigenismo. In his book *Indigenismo* (originally published in 1996), he hypothesizes that indigenismo is destined to disappear: "Hoy en día, la 'globalización' y su tribalización hacen caduco cualquier proyecto nacional. La mundialización hace pasar al indigenismo a la historia" [Today, "globalization" and its tribalization have rendered any national project outdated. Globalization has consigned indigenismo to history] (149–50). However, a decade later, things have not come to pass in exactly this way. As I write, indigenista-oriented populisms have reemerged in Mexico and the Andes. This resurgence suggests the contemporary relevance of older indigenista paradigms. Certain indigenista ideals continue to hold strong appeal, such as the idea that the nation is essentially Indian, and that resistance to global capital — decolonization — involves national self-perception as Indian.[7]

Nationalist indigenismo has always spoken, whether cynically or earnestly, as if in the embattled and defiant position of the stigmatized subject, even when that subject has come to gain tremendous social power. What of the enemies indigenismo called on — the cruel and corrupt oligarchs, the soulless and greedy foreign capitalists, the shaming internalization of racial inferiority — in order to mobilize support for the journey toward redemption, toward an authentically national land? Although these features of populist rhetoric are signs of the cynical exercise of political self-legitimacy, they refer to a global situation that is far from spectral. Even after it becomes hegemonic, indigenismo continues to provide a discursive sphere in which to reflect on a national modernity that is arrythmic, uneven, colonized.

Contemporary populisms contain elements of the intimate indigenista discourse I have traced in this book. For example, Mexican populist leader Andrés Manuel López Obrador has had occasion to refer to his indigenista awakening as one of the most important moments of his political career. In public interviews, he discusses how his work in the 1970s with Chontal indigenous communities in his natal state, Tabasco, led him to become aware that these communities had been forgotten by the state's authorities, their existence officially denied (Thompson). And in his political autobiography, he recounts what happened when the INI wanted to establish a Centro Coordinador Indigenista Chontal en Tabasco (a parallel to the institute where Castellanos worked in San Cristóbal in the 1950s): Tabasco's governor insisted there was no need for such a center because there were no Indians in the state (López Obrador 27). But the Chontales, López Obrador will later rectify, represent "the most intimate reality of Tabasco" (cited in Thompson). A true son of the state must "enter" that intimate reality as if he were entering his own house, his own soul, and listen to the voices that reside there. López Obrador's political discourse gives new vitality to the indigenista legacy of Lázaro Cárdenas.

Peruvian presidential candidate Ollanta Humala also revitalized indigenista discourse during the elections of 2006, though his popularity has since greatly declined. Humala and his political party, the Peruvian Nationalist Party (PNP), claimed Mariátegui as an inspiration, located the origins of Peru in the Incan empire, and exalted the anti-colonial struggles of Manco Inca and Tupac Amaru II. Humala and his party spoke of the need to incorporate Indians into the nation-state and, like the intimate indigenismo of José María Arguedas, believed that justice involves "strengthening our self-esteem" through national policies that recognize the importance of indigenous cultures (Partido).

In Bolivia, Evo Morales, the first indigenous president of Bolivia, draws on the discursive legacy of intimate indigenismo in order to appeal to non-Indians. In his inaugural speech, delivered on assuming the presidency in January 2006, he directly addressed intellectuals, professionals, businesspeople — the Bolivian middle class — and encouraged them to feel pride in indigenous people: "les invito a ustedes que se sientan orgullosos de los pueblos indígenas que es la reserva moral de la humanidad" [I invite you to feel proud of indigenous peoples, who are humanity's moral reserve] (Morales). Like indigenista thinkers before him, Morales attributes greater moral authority to indigenous people and transubstantiates their value: once physically and materially valuable as an enslaved labor force, they are now spiritually valuable as moral exemplars to the world community.

It is common to consider indigenismo as ideological in the sense of offering ideas that justify a particular state policy or practice. Indigenismo has been examined as a weapon in the consolidation of a centralized nation-state against regional elites, in the case of Mexico (Knight 83), or, on the contrary, as a weapon in the regionalist bid for autonomy vis-à-vis the centralizing state, in the case of Peru (Deustua and Rénique). With regards to both Mexico and Bolivia, it has been seen as providing the justification for economic protectionism with respect to foreign investment and the nationalization of industry (Lomnitz, *Exits* 278; Salmón 119). These accounts are entirely accurate, yet, as I have argued, the ideological work of indigenismo can also be seen as operating on levels other than the more or less cynical exercise of justifying official power. It has also been, historically, profoundly involved in the ideologies that define individual subjects in relation to political and religious authority and makes distinctions between these subjects. I have suggested that at the core of the indigenous subject so defined lies a dialectic of innocence and guilt that remains tied to the very category of the human. It can be resolved in favor of innocence only on the condition that this individual subject not seek out power in the wider social body. This subject, when he or she becomes a citizen, remains embryonic and must rely on the appeal of innocence in order to launch any political demands "within" the system. The dilemmas of such a position also apply to other political subjects of populism, where they are reenacted in the symbolic performance of intimate indigenismo.

In the process of strengthening the icon of Indian authority, indigenismo disempowers Indians politically: that irony is part and parcel of indigenista normalization. Indigenismo seriously contested existing social boundaries and promoted a reconfiguration of the experience of national belonging to include Indians. However, this inclusion took a highly ambiguous and paradoxical form. On the one hand, indigenismo invested Indians with positive symbolic attributes as signs of the nation's territorial indivisibility and historical continuity. Yet on the other, these attributions nevertheless remained subordinate to a notion of citizenship understood as the exercise of reason over nature. If these positive symbolic attributions posited Indians as the true essence of nationality, its most essentially virtuous core, the dominant notion of citizenship posited Indians and other subjects as incomplete citizens because of their deficient exercise of reason. Although it might seem counter-intuitive, it is in fact the dominant notion of citizenship that has historically provided Indians and other incomplete citizens with a language that they can reclaim and transform into a series of political demands on the state. The "intimate" form of indigenismo that I have analyzed here, meanwhile, has provided far fewer openings to Indian participation in the state, despite its nominally egalitarian, anti-racist vision.

Is the time of indigenismo definitively over? Favre argues that indigenismo has given way to indigenous discourse proper (Favre 127), but I remain skeptical about marking too clear a break with the indigenista past. Clearly there has always been an indigenous discourse, but it was either repressed or not recognized as such. Favre does not mark a shift from the absence to the presence of indigenous discourse, but rather a shift in the relative balance of power between indigenous people and state institutions (and their intermediaries), a shift from "speaking for" to "listening to" the Indian. But there are different ways to listen and different ways of offering one's words to the listener. I believe some of these contemporary ways of "listening to" indigenous people are continuous with the "intimate indigenismo" I have described here, though they involve new social actors and respond to new contradictions, such as those engendered by a far more globalized national experience. The turn to that interior, confessional space that opened onto interethnic communication, and that promised self-improvement through the emulation of virtuous behaviors associated with indigenous ways of life and states of mind, continues to be understood as a radical and redemptive form of behavior. Perhaps the most salient difference between this contemporary "intimate indigenismo" and the one I have described in this book, however, lies in the fact that indigenous people have seized hold of it themselves as an instrument in their struggles for greater social and political power.

Notes

Introduction

1. There is a wealth of literature offering systematic demystifications of indigenismo, all of which have profoundly influenced my approach. Regarding Bolivia, see works by Mamani, Paz Soldán, Reinaga, Rivera, Salmón, Sanjinés, Stephenson. Regarding Peru, see works by Cornejo, de la Cadena, Degregori et al., Deustua and Rénique, Kristal, and Lauer. Regarding Mexico, see works by Bartra, Bonfil Batalla, de la Peña, Hernández Castillo, Knight, Medina, Monsiváis, Sommers, and Warman. For broad Latin Americanist approaches, see Beverley, de Castro, Lienhard, Miller, Mires, and Muyulema.

2. The translation of Favre's text is my own. All translations here are my own unless otherwise indicated.

3. The phrase "carnal knowledge" alludes to Ann Stoler's *Carnal Knowledge and Imperial Power: Race and the Intimate in Colonial Rule*. Her contentions, both in that book as well as in her *Race and the Education of Desire*, about the role of race in the normalization of European state power in the nineteenth-century — a strong revisionist reading of volume 1 of Foucault's *History of Sexuality* in light of the history of European colonialism — has been very useful for my thinking. Notwithstanding the substantially different history of race and bourgeois culture in nineteenth century Spanish America — tied more to positivism than to liberalism and the site of intense ideological conflict rather than a unitary policy or vision, as Brooke Larson has argued (*Trials* 63) — Stoler's claim that the discourses of sexuality formative of modern European identity "were refracted through the discourse of empire and its exigencies, by men and women whose affirmations of a bourgeois self, and the racialized contexts in which these confidences were built, could not be disentangled" (*Race* 7), has a very strong resonance for Latin America. For an excellent extended analysis of the intertwining of race, sex, and gender in nationalist discourses of modern Bolivia, see Stephenson.

4. Roberto Paoli was perhaps the first critic to point out this aspect of contemporary indigenista literary criticism, namely, that it takes an attribute of indigenismo — its non-Indian enunciation — to be the central defining essence of indigenismo (Paoli 258).

5. The notion of indigenismo as a "destigmatizing" discourse is entirely indebted to the work of anthropologist Marisol de la Cadena. In her study of the development of Cuzco indigenismo, *Indigenous Mestizos*, she demonstrates that urban provincial indigenistas worked to remove some of the negative attributes associated with Indianness. I will refer to her work further below.

6. On the importance of militias in the formation of new kinds of subjects, see Florencia Mallon, *Peasant and Nation.*

7. On the reinstatement of Indian tribute in Bolivia, see Brooke Larson, *Trials.*

8. I refer here to the work of anthropologists and social historians such as Nancy Appelbaum, Marisol de la Cadena, Laura Gotkowitz, Brooke Larson, Claudio Lomnitz Adler, and Silvia Rivera Cusicanqui, among others, who have been very important for demonstrating the multiplicity of cultural and racial discourses in Spanish America and who have substantially influenced my thinking.

9. This is one of the reasons why indigenismo is different from Orientalism. Another difference is that indigenismo is a method of social control over a potentially threatening yet necessary political and military ally: the indigenous peasant, who plays a role in the struggles for regional control that take place when liberal oligarchies enter crisis in the first decades of the twentieth century. Indigenismo can be considered a hegemonic discourse in the sense defined by Florencia Mallon: the "end point" to a power struggle, a kind of temporary stasis point involving a "dynamic or precarious balance, a contract or agreement . . . reached among contesting forces" ("Reflections" 70). Indigenismo can become a "language of contention," to use Brooke Larson's phrase, one shared by elite and popular sectors (*Trials* 13). Larson offers the example of nineteenth-century Bolivia, when both elites and Indians participated in discourses of Indianness (*Trials* 69). Alcida Ramos makes a similar point about Brazilian indigenismo: "Indians are equally agents in the country's indigenist project, no matter how constrained their agency may be. Moreover, when Indians seize the notion of 'culture,' an artifact of Western thinking about the Other, to further their cause for ethnic recognition and self-determination, they contribute significantly to the design of Indigenism" (7). From this perspective, "indigenista" and "indígena" discourses may at times become very similar to one another and participate in a shared discursive ground. How, whether, and when indigenismo becomes "hegemonic" varies enormously in each country/region, however. See also O'Connell for a thoughtful discussion of indigenismo as Orientalism (51–52).

10. A number of recent studies provide good overviews and regional case studies of this intellectual "cult." See de Castro; Miller; Sanjinés.

11. Indigenismo, as a state discourse, thus acts to establish "a common discursive framework that sets out central terms around which and in terms of which contestation and struggle can occur" (Joseph and Nugent 20).

12. The origins of the novel form have been traced to various kinds of confessional practices, which in turn become novelistic tropes: the novel offers a complex staging of the subject before the law, whether spiritual or secular — or antedating such a division, as in the case of the Inquisitorial tribunal. For such literary genealogies, see González Echevarría (43–92) and Gómez-Moriana.

1. Anatomy of Indigenismo

1. Fabian writes apropos of the colonial expansion that generates the denial of coevalness: "It is not difficult to transpose from physics to politics one of the most ancient rules which states that it is impossible for two bodies to occupy the

same space at the same time. When in the course of colonial expansion a Western body politic came to occupy, literally, the space of an autochthonous body, several alternatives were conceived to deal with that violation of the rule.... Most often the preferred strategy has been simply to manipulate the other variable — Time. With the help of various devices of sequencing and distancing one assigns to the conquered populations a *different* Time" (Fabian 29–30, original emphasis). The denial of coevalness is thus *"a persistent and systematic tendency to place the referent(s) of anthropology in a Time other than the present of the producer of anthropological discourse"* (31, original emphasis). Nationalist discourse clearly draws on this element of anthropological discourse. The creation of coevalness, meanwhile, involves the "sharing of present Time" (Fabian 32). For a systematic analysis of the spatial and historical discourses and technologies making the "denial of coevalness" central to Spanish colonization of the Americas, see Mignolo.

2. For a more detailed examination of these liberal and positivist racial discourses, see Larson, *Trials;* Demelas; Knight; Stabb.

3. See Brading, "Manuel Gamio," for a thorough account of Gamio's intellectual formation. See Knight for more on his impact on Mexican revolutionary ideology.

4. See Alcides Arguedas's *Pueblo enfermo* (1909); Tamayo's *Creación de la pedagogía nacional* (1910), which I discuss below; Medinaceli's essays collected in *Estudios críticos;* Lara's *Viaje a Incallajta* (1927). Francovich, Paz Soldán, Salmón, and Sanjinés all provide overviews of these tendencies in Bolivian thought.

5. For detailed and critical analysis of Peruvian elite perceptions of indigenous participation in the war against Chile, see Florencia Mallon, *Peasant and Nation;* Brooke Larson, *Trials* (178–201).

6. On Peruvian indigenismo and regionalism, see Mariátegui's essay "Regionalismo y descentralización," in *Siete ensayos* (175–205); also de la Cadena's extended analysis in *Indigenous Mestizos,* a book devoted to this topic. For indigenismo and the aesthetic avant-gardes in Peru, see Lauer, Vich, and Wise.

7. For a discussion of the development and effects of this notion of the Indian origin of nationality in Bolivia, see Salmón 119–20. For Mexico, see Brading, *Origins;* Franco, "The Return of Coatlicue."

8. This was part of Latin American intellectuals' response to the biological determinisms of European racial thinking. Latin Americans tended to stress looser forms of determinism, such as resulted from the physical environment or history, rather than biology (Appelbaum et al. 3–13).

9. Regarding the understanding of mestizaje as "fictive ethnicity," I draw in general terms from Gareth Williams's analysis of populist hegemony in Spanish America. Williams is concerned with "transculturation" rather than mestizaje or indigenismo, and he uses the term "transculturation" idiosyncratically to refer to both mixed-culture and mixed-class identities. Thus he considers Peruvian national-populism and Argentine national-populism as expressions of the same phenomenon, namely, the adoption of "transculturation" as a political ideology by modernizers (Williams 24–70). However, Williams's retroactive application of the term "transculturation" to national-populists who embraced mestizaje before

the term "transculturation" itself was coined in 1940 — as he does with Mexico's revolutionary thinkers and Peruvian and Bolivian indigenismo through the 1930s — has the effect of diminishing the historical complexity and development of racial and cultural discourses in Spanish America. These ideologies of mestizaje, I would argue, are not reducible to Fernando Ortiz's concept of cultural transformation, even if his thinking was incorporated over the years.

10. Carlos Alonso offers an extended examination of the discourse of "cultural auctochtony," focusing on its "rhetorical artifice" (Alonso 1–37). See also Sanjinés's examination of this discourse in Bolivia (32–65).

11. Yet unlike most of his contemporaries, Mariátegui did not propose to substitute these colonial forms of possession with national ones, strictly speaking. His project was socialist, and thus he insisted on the land as an exclusively economic question. See the essay "El problema de la tierra" (*Siete ensayos* 46–93). He understood Indian culture to be defined by its particular mode of production, the ayllu system, rather than by its originary relationship and privileged affiliation to particular lands or regions. Mariátegui's way of conceiving the "Indian problem," it bears noting, has been explicitly rejected by indigenous groups such as the Taller de Historia Oral Andina. Members of the group point out that Mariátegui circumscribed indigenous social movements to the narrow question of survival and ignored the broader processes of self-definition and self-determination that were also occurring (Taller 28).

12. Mediz Bolio's words were recalled by Alfonso Reyes in his prologue to the second edition of Mediz Bolio's novel *La tierra del faisán y el venado*, which was originally published in 1922. Martin Lienhard offers a more extended analysis of Mediz Bolio's indigenista work, showing how the author constructs Maya culture outside "historical time" (203–5).

13. The idea of nationality as a sentimental education owes much to Doris Sommer, especially her analysis of the role of the romance novel in forging "passionate patriotism" (*Foundational Fictions* 30–51). For an analysis of revolutionary nationalism in particular as a form of "moral education," see Tapia.

14. Modern indigenismo tends to eschew the language of race in favor of cultural relativism. Latin American anthropology followed Boas in asserting "culture" over "race," as D. A. Brading has argued for Mexican indigenista anthropologist Manuel Gamio, for example ("Manuel Gamio" 79; see also Gamio, *Forjando Patria* 23–26). However, such a transition does not represent as great a rupture as might be surmised from the difference in terminology. Strong disclaimers to the contrary notwithstanding, "culture" remained a strongly racialized category to the extent that it incorporated essentialist ideas of "folk" and "spirit" inherited from Romantic concepts of race (de la Cadena 2–3).

15. See the essays collected in Larson and Harris, *Ethnicity, Markets, and Migration,* which explore and refute the longstanding idea in the Andes that Indians do not participate in market relations, indeed, that those who do can no longer be considered Indians.

16. "Encomenderos" refers to Spanish colonizers to whom the crown granted the right to collect tribute from one or more Indian communities in exchange for

providing religious instruction to the Indians and protecting their welfare (Klein 37; Larson, *Cochabamba* 402).

17. See also José Rabasa's extensive analysis of the significance of early tropings of "America" foregrounding its/her "nakedness" (23–48).

18. Their innocence of worldly matters, except sex: Las Casas always mentions that they are totally naked *except* for genitals, thus proving that they have a concept of original sin (108).

19. It must be noted that Las Casas, in later texts, provided a different basis for his defense of Indians, one that marks an emergent ethnological perspective. As Anthony Pagden points out, Las Casas's *Argumentum apologiae* (1550) and his *Apologética historia* (1551–), both responding to Sepúlveda, claimed that indigenous governments were legitimate, though tyrannical, because they "fulfilled all of Aristotle's requirements for a true civil society" (Pagden 121), and followed custom and law (Pagden 132). Though Las Casas admitted they were "barbarian" because they were not Christian, he also distinguished among various types of barbarity, Pagden argues, so as to demonstrate the Indians' perfectibility.

20. In establishing this common sphere, Las Casas was conveniently omitting the fact that Indians had strongly resisted entering it, to the great frustration of missionaries. The confession was imposed, as Jorge Klor de Alva argues, in order to destroy indigenous culture and its moral economy, and it had as an effect, he further argues, the implantation of more intense forms of colonial control. Entering it was thus, for the Indians, tantamount to committing ethnocide (Klor de Alva 72–76).

21. Michel Foucault has argued that the confessional, in seventeenth- and eighteenth-century Europe, increasingly makes this submission a matter of sexual renunciation through self-examination which, paradoxically, heightens the power of sexuality to determine the truth of oneself (*History* 58–65). But the confessional as used in the Spanish colonies takes on another function as well: it is an evangelical device, a means of transforming the colonized into "New Christians" of a sort. The practices of self-examination it imposes on the colonized have as a consequence, not only the transformation of desire into the core truth of the self, as Foucault argues, but also, and more importantly, the demonstration that racial claims regarding the bestial nature of the colonized are false. One might say, then, that confessional practices in the colonial context transform "humanity" into the core truth of the self, one to which a knowledge-producing apparatus is henceforth directed to seek out and investigate. This humanity is established through the racialized concepts of innocence and guilt.

22. Guillermo de la Peña provides a nuanced account of other competing visions of the Indians' nature, especially in New Spain, with reference not only to Las Casas and Sepúlveda, but also Vasco de Quiroga, the bishop of Michoacán; and Juan de Zumárraga, first bishop of Mexico (286–96).

23. Because converted Indians were a kind of "New Christian," "they had to be watched by the Spaniards, and they could legitimately be made to pay for their spiritual debt through tribute and labor" (Lomnitz, *Exits* 264).

24. In Mexico, by contrast, the "nación criolla" already nascent in the early seventeenth century, distanced itself rhetorically from the Crown by invoking its indigeneity, epitomized in the Virgin of Guadalupe, rather than by simply

206 • Notes to Chapter 1

asserting its rights to dominate the Crown's indigenous subjects. For a discussion of nascent criollo nationalism in New Spain, see D. A. Brading's *The Origins of Mexican Nationalism*. I thank Iván Reyna for directing my attention to the Millones text.

25. The category "mestizo" emerges in the colonial period to describe subjects who, by reasons of birth, pertained neither to the "República de Indios" nor to the "República de Españoles." As such, they occupied a distinct juridical and fiscal identity within the colonial administration and were ambiguously positioned with respect to prevailing notions of purity, understood here as a matter of both race and religion, as discussed above on the matter of "limpieza de sangre." In the postcolonial period, the term underwent substantial transformations — as did its relational terms, "indio," "criollo," "cholo," "misti," etc — across liberal and positivist political regimes and distinct regional subcultures. "Mestizaje" became a widespread political ideology linked to nationalism and promoting massive social transformation only in the beginning of the twentieth century in Mexico, closer to the middle of the century in Bolivia and Peru. One might say that the ethnogenesis and ethnocide that were once byproducts of world-historical events — colonization, Christianization, and globalization more broadly — in the twentieth century come to be framed as social necessities and seen as the base upon which the success of national modernization depends. Ideologies of mestizaje are thus linked to the transformation of rural life through the political-economic logic of modern progress.

26. For images and analyses of mestizos as unlawful or inauthentic, see Alcides Arguedas (*Pueblo enfermo* 71–81); Reinaga (*La 'inteligentsia' del cholaje boliviano* is dedicated entirely to unveiling the hypocrisies of those whom he called "intellectual cholos"); Valcárcel (*Tempestad* 38–40); Harris (364–67); and Paz (the essay "Los hijos de la Malinche" in *Laberinto de la soledad* elaborates a theory of Mexican identity as the historical product of Mexicans' rejection of their underlying mestizo illegitimacy).

27. See also Alan Knight's immensely useful article "Racism, Revolution, and *Indigenismo*: Mexico, 1910–1940," which likewise argues for the importance of racial paradigms in indigenista thought. For a historical overview of how Andean intellectuals responded to European racial discourses, see de la Cadena, 12–29; Larson, *Trials*. For a broader Latin Americanist account, see Stepan's fundamental history; Appelbaum et al.

28. Cornejo first presented "heterogeneous literature" in a talk he gave at Casa de las Américas in 1977. It was the fruit of his discussions with prominent critics who, like himself, were attempting to break with the triumphalism that permeated the response to the phenomenal success of writers such as Cortázar, Fuentes, Vargas Llosa, and García Márquez. This triumphalism was one facet of the tendency that Idelber Avelar calls "the substitution of aesthetics for politics," represented by a host of writers and critics who presented Latin America's literary achievements as "surrogates" for the region's instability and poverty — as if literary success compensated for failures in other areas (Avelar 11–12; for more on the politics of the literary culture that developed around the "boom," see Doris Sommer 1–6; Avelar 22–38). Insisting on a far more critical stance toward Latin

American modernity, Cornejo argued that the most representative Latin American narratives were those that reflected the region's state of crisis, its continuing inability to resolve its most pressing social problems. The notion of "heterogeneous discourse" insisted on cultural conflict as the ongoing motor force of Latin American history, counteracting both the complacency of certain novelists as well as the propaganda of Peru's military governments, which claimed that through mestizaje and national unity, the country's colonial legacy was finally being put to rest. As Alberto Moreiras writes, the main function of Cornejo Polar's concept of heterogeneity is to signal the fact that "from the point of view of what was heterogeneous to the dominant social articulation, for instance, indigenous ethnicities in Peru, transculturation was a powerfully threatening instrument of social subordination, not of redemption" (265).

29. Angel Rama's *Transculturación narrativa* also accomplished a similar displacement of indigenismo away from reductive aestheticism and formulaic typologies around much the same period as Cornejo, though toward different ends; his aim was to show that indigenismo, like other regionalist literary traditions, was central, not marginal, to the development of the most technically complex and celebrated examples of the "nueva novela" (158–72).

30. For approaches to indigenista literature that measure it according to its degree of verisimilitude with respect to ethnographic accounts of indigenous culture, see Rodríguez Chicharro and Bigas Torres.

31. Cornejo developed his ideas about the conflict between orality and literacy through a fascinating account of the events at Cajamarca in 1532, when Pizarro's army defeated the Inca Atahualpa. See his article "Heterogeneidad y contradicción en la literatura andina" as well as his book *Escribir en el aire* (20–43).

32. William Rowe has also offered a recent revision of Cornejo's orality-writing dualism, though from a somewhat different perspective from my own. Rowe is interested in showing the limits of what he terms "the myth of the oppressive letter," which silences all those voices marginalized by "the lettered city" ("Sobre" 226). He argues that the divide between writing and orality idealizes and narrows the latter, occluding the "dense relations" it maintains with a variety of textual and visual practices, such as the Andean quipu (225).

33. Ultimately, what heterogeneous literature reenacts is not a flawed nationality in the sense meant by Mariátegui, but rather a fracture that nationality itself cannot and should not heal. This is because nationality, as it is traditionally understood, involves subordinating internal social differences to a more primal difference between the foreign and the native; and this subordination would signal, in effect, a refusal to acknowledge that the primordial feature of Peruvian identity is the ongoing fracturing effect of the Conquest. One might say that heterogeneous literature reenacts the limits of nationality itself as the collective self-image of a multi-ethnic society. Peru's fractures remain for Cornejo both a necessary and a tragic condition of national life, an ambiguity that can be summed up in the phrase he uses to describe the nation: "un pueblo quebrado y heteróclito" [a broken and anomalous nation] (*Escribir* 195). Cornejo undertook a complex theorization of this problematic in his work on the nation as a "contradictory totality." Using this concept of "contradictory totality," Cornejo

described the logic underlying Peru's division into separate and autonomous cultural systems that nevertheless formed a whole, an integral entity within which these separate cultural systems interacted and were mutually defined (see his "Literatura peruana: totalidad contradictoria").

34. Regarding Bolivian census categories, see Rivera, *Oprimidos* (15).

2. The Voice of the Son in Jesús Lara's Surumi

1. The question echoes the title of Denise Riley's 1988 book, an examination of "feminism and the category of women." The problematic she describes is roughly parallel to the one Rivera discusses, namely, a system in which names serve to naturalize the social hierarchy and perpetuate it rather than merely describe categories within it.

2. "Cholo" and "chola" generally refer to urbanized Indians and/or to Indians who engage in market relations. "Pongo" is the name given to hacienda Indians who are rotated into uncompensated domestic labor in the homes of hacienda owners. Throughout the nineteenth and into the twentieth century, "pongueaje" (the practice of pongo labor) and other forms of forced labor (and tribute as well) were legally abolished in Bolivia and then subsequently reinstated various times. As late as 1945 it was once again formally abolished by President Villaroel. Nevertheless, despite these legal attempts to abolish it, the practice continued to flourish until 1952. See Reyeros (127–50).

3. The account of his travel to the Inca ruins near Pocona first appeared serially in 1926 in the newspaper *El Republicano*, and then in 1927 as a book, *Viaje a Incallajta*.

4. His first major book was *Repete* (1937), an account of the Chaco War based on his front line diary. In the 1920s Lara had already published several works, including two "novelas cortas" in popular format, *Predestinados* (1922) and *El estigma* (1923), and a book of poetry, *Cantigas de la cigarra* (1919). Lara also had written *Wiñay Urpi*, in 1930, a drama set in Inca times at Incallajta, an outpost on the empire's eastern frontier, written in Spanish verse, which to this day remains unpublished.

5. Laura Gotkowitz explains the Cochabamba institution of "colonos": "*Colono* refers to the rural population that held parcels of hacienda land in usufruct and had rights to graze their animals on hacienda lands, in exchange for labor on the hacienda and in-kind payment. To carry out required labor on hacienda lands, colonos were obligated to provide their own tools and animals. Further, they had to use their own animals to transport goods produced on the hacienda to the market. In addition, the colono and his family were required to provide domestic services in the house of the landowner, either on the hacienda itself or in the town or city (*pongueaje*). Specific rules and obligations varied from one large property to another" (265, note 21).

6. Note that Lara used the term "race" to denote what post-Boas anthropology would call "culture." Lara used the term "culture," meanwhile, as a synonym for "civilization" in the nineteenth-century sense of the term, i.e., culture as the overcoming of barbarism.

7. Stephenson demonstrates that Bolivian nationalism "correlates modernization with miscegenation" (1), and she examines the variety of social institutions bent on transforming indigenous people, literally and symbolically, into suitable marriage partners — always feminized — for the country's upper and middle classes. Fostering the development of independent-minded, authority-questioning Indians, the process with which Lara was most centrally concerned in *Surumi*, was not on most reformers' agendas.

8. The term "nationalist," when speaking of mid-twentieth-century Bolivia, connotes a rather more highly partisan political position than is usually the case when referring to Latin America. The nationalists of the 1940s had recently formed their own political party, the Movimiento Nacionalista Revolucionario (MNR), and proclaimed themselves nationalists in contraposition to an entrenched liberal oligarchy, which they referred to as the "anti-nation," as well as in contraposition to a number of Marxist political parties, with some of whom it eventually formed political alliances. Without going so far as to capitalize the term — "Nationalists" vs. "nationalists" — the distinction between lower-case and upper-case nationalists is useful nevertheless to explain Jesús Lara's political position during the years before he joined the Communist Party in 1953. Because he never joined the MNR, and indeed remained one of its harshest critics from the Left after the MNR came to power in 1952, he would have to be considered a lower-case nationalist, one who shared with the "Nationalists" certain strong elements of socio-political vision: anti-liberal, anti-oligarchic, and believing in the Indian root of Bolivian nationality.

9. For a provocative discussion of this rejection, see Sanjinés's analysis of Katarismo as "mestizaje upside down" (149–89). For an in-depth analysis of the expansion of "civilizing" institutions in this period targeting indigenous populations and subjecting them to new forms of social control through the disciplinary work of school, clinic, domestic science, and labor management, see Stephenson.

10. The testimonies and analyses collected in Gordillo reveal that, in Cochabamba's Valle Bajo, peasants allied themselves with miners, who were themselves only one generation removed from agricultural labor (87). I would add that this makes it difficult to capture the insurgents of the Cochabamba region for an iconography of the subaltern, when the subaltern is understood as a heroic interruption or dislocation of national hegemony, or as that which national hegemony excludes (Sanjinés 8–9; Williams 11).

11. I use the terms "provincial-metropolitan" instead of "rural-urban," in part to emphasize that these are symbolic spaces above all, inscribing a hierarchical relation between two parts of a whole; in part to underscore the importance of intermediary spaces that the urban-rural dichotomy tends to render invisible, such as the provincial small towns where Lara and a host of other national-populist figures grew up, including at least two Bolivian presidents (Gualberto Villaroel, military president 1943–46, was from Muela, the same as Lara; and René Barrientos Ortuño, military president 1964–69, was from Tarata).

12. Peluffo's article, "El poder de las lágrimas," examines the ideological work of sentimentalism in Clorinda Matto de Turner's nineteenth-century novel *Aves sin nido*.

13. The possibility of colono laborers to gain independent access to the internal regional market was a historical feature of the Cochabamba area (Larson, *Cochabamba* 202–6; Rivera, *Oprimidos* 59–60).

14. Notable examples include Lara's own *Repete* (1937); Augusto Guzmán, *Prisionero de guerra* (1937); Oscar Cerruto, *Aluvión de fuego* (1935); Augusto Céspedes, *Sangre de mestizos* (1936).

15. In fact Lara wrote the first part of *Surumi* while in hiding in the countryside, in 1939, to escape political persecution at the hands of the Quintanilla regime (Lara and Antezana 15).

16. Some of the most important works on Indian education of the 1940s are Anaya, *Indianismo*, and Guillén, *La educación del indio*. For illuminating critical perspectives, see Choque et al. (especially 79–98) and Stephenson (111–41).

17. José Gordillo refers to this propaganda campaign as a veritable "Dirty War" against Leftist leaders (22).

18. The rebellion depicted in *Yanakuna* was based on the Ayopaya rebellion of 1947, at the haciendas Yayani and Parte Libre. The rebellion's leaders were tried in Cochabamba in 1949 in a very public event (see Dandler and Torrico for an account of the rebellion).

19. "Chicha" is an alcoholic beverage made from corn. Gustavo Rodríguez O. and Humberto Solares S. provide a thorough analysis of the effects of the chicha economy in constituting Cochabamba society during the liberal era.

20. In the traditional elaboration of chicha, an early and crucial step involved the moistening of corn meal with saliva; this is "muk'eo." The young women who engaged in this form of labor were "muk'eras"; they introduced small amounts of meal into their mouths, rolling it around until small saliva-coated spheres had formed, the starter material for the fermentation process.

21. Brackets indicate that I have modified the translation of this verse, sacrificing its rhythm in order to clarify certain significant elements, namely, that the "meat" refers to women and that the "land of the devil" is in fact the city. Special thanks to Luis Morató Peña for assistance with the translation of this verse.

22. In making the name "Pongo" such a crucial part of the novel, Lara showed how attuned he was to the political debates of those years. Throughout the 1930 and 1940s, Indians in the valleys of Cochabamba presented numerous petitions requesting the abolition of pongueaje as the question of Indian labor came to play a central role in contemporary debates (Gotkowitz 220–34). Only two years after the novel's publication, pongueaje would be the main topic at the Congreso Nacional Indígena (1945), in a discussion couched in the same vocabulary as *Surumi*: "The keyword at this extraordinary encounter according to one participant was the end of 'slavery'" (Gotkowitz 168).

23. Significantly enough Lara was himself an archivist of sorts: he was for many years the director of the Cochabamba Municipal Library. This was, it bears noting, a political appointment, its fortunes shifting with each political change in the municipality. Thus at one point Lara was removed from the job during Villaroel's presidency and accused of stealing books when political rivals came to power; he was subsequently reinstated when Villaroel's regime fell in 1946.

24. Lara would himself become an important scholar of this play. He "discovered" and published a manuscript version of the play dating back to the nineteenth century (known as the "Chayanta" version for its place of origin). When he first published *La poesía quechua,* however, he knew only of the version collected by Bolivian writer Mario Unzueta, who in 1943 saw the play performed in Cliza, a Cochabamba valley town.

25. Garcilaso recounts a story, now famous, of two Indian servants whose fetishistic misunderstanding of writing lands them in trouble (263–64). "Wáskar" was of course Atahualpa's half-brother, defeated, captured, and then murdered in 1532 during their war of succession. Garcilaso was related, on his mother's side, to Wáskar's kinship group, and offered a highly critical portrayal of Atahualpa in the *Comentarios reales,* especially Book 9, chapters 32–40.

26. Analysis of an early draft of *Surumi,* still penciled in the author's own hand, suggests that this confusion about "when" to place the "writing I" was present for Lara at all stages of his own writing process. The draft contains sentences that situate the narrator's in a more distant present vis-à-vis his schooldays, but they were subsequently crossed out, as if Lara were unsure about whether to include them (*Surumi* ms. n.p.).

27. For fuller discussions on the significance of Montenegro's historicist obsession, see Tapia (n.p.); Sanjinés (122–36).

28. The Virgin Surumi appeared in Arani, 3 km from Lara's hometown Muela (now Villa Rivero); Lara attended primary school in Arani. Regarding the novel's title, Raúl Botelho González, one of the editors of the nationalist journal *Kollasuyu,* told Lara in a letter that writer Augusto Guzmán thought it should be titled "Pongo Puma" instead of "Surumi" (Botelho González). The suggestion makes sense, given the relative weight accorded these two characters in the novel. It is thus significant that Lara would have stuck to his original title, choosing explicitly to privilege Surumi symbolically even if foregrounding the voice and experience of her son.

29. *La poesía quechua* was substantially revised and then reissued in 1961 under a new title, *La literatura de los Quechuas.* The changes Lara made to the text are extensive: the inclusion of Quechua prose, the expansion of the anthology, the elimination of certain sections of the essay, particularly those sections that most polemically engaged the political context of the 1940s. A comparison of the two versions would yield a very fruitful study of the significant changes in the political landscape of Bolivia in the intervening years, most notably the advent of the 1952 revolution, and Lara's own engagement with the Communist Party.

30. Lara refers here to, among others, Gabriel René Moreno, one of the most important intellectual figures of Bolivia's late nineteenth century, and Nataniel Aguirre, a writer whose novelistic account of Cochabamba's role in the wars of Independence, *Juan de la Rosa* (1885), is a foundational classic of Bolivian literature.

31. Notable examples of Quechua anthologies, drawn from Lara's own bibliography, include: J. M. B. Farfán, *Poesía folklórica quechua;* Rigoberto Paredes, *El arte folklórico de Bolivia;* Ricardo Rojas, *Himnos quechuas;* Luis Alberto Sánchez, *Historia de la literatura americana.*

32. Early scenes from *Paqarin,* volume one of Lara's autobiography, make this differentiation explicit. In the very first chapter he recounts his misadventures with the "indiecito" [little Indian] his mother had hired to care for him while she worked. Everything in Lara's description of this boy suggests that he belonged to a different social class than Lara's family. Lara's use of the term "indiecito," furthermore, with its complex flavor of affection and condescension, communicates his distance from those to whom the townspeople of Muela referred to as "Indians."

3. José María Arguedas and the Mediating Voice

1. All English translations of this essay by Arguedas, as well as of the novels *Los ríos profundos* and *Yawar fiesta,* and the speech "No soy un aculturado," are taken from the published translations by Frances Barraclough, unless otherwise noted. Parenthetical page references following the English refer to her texts.

2. *Transculturación narrativa* appeared in 1982, but key chapters had already been published in journals from the mid-seventies on.

3. Luis Leal, for instance, wrote of Arguedas's *Los ríos profundos,* in 1971, that it offered the Indian's point of view (289).

4. Key texts for the dissemination of these aspects of his autobiography include the 1950 essay "La novela y el problema de la expresión literaria en el Perú" and the public declarations he offered at the Primer Encuentro de Narradores Peruanos in 1965. An "ayllu" is "the basic kin unit of Andean native society" (Larson 401).

5. I have made small changes to Barraclough's translation of this passage.

6. Virtually all of Cornejo's work revolves around the refutation of mestizaje and other notions of harmonious cultural synthesis, but see especially the Introduction to *Escribir en el aire* (5–17). See also Lienhard (92–94); Moreiras (184–207); Beverley (41–64).

7. Regina Harrison has done much the same thing in her analysis of Arguedas's translations of Quechua hymns, elaborating on his "art of translation."

8. For example, in a letter to Manuel Moreno Jiménez about a friend's criticism of *Yawar fiesta,* Arguedas complained that he was treated "como si fuera una criatura principiante" [as if I were a novice child] (Forgues, *La letra* 128).

9. For example, as can be in found in the nineteenth century Bolivian novel *Juan de la Rosa,* which opens with a letter from the presumed author to his publisher asking the latter to please print the following account of his life as a youth for the edification of his fellow citizens.

10. Rama would be in agreement on this point: regarding the circumstances, life, customs, and education of the adult narrator, writes Rama, "Arguedas guarda estricto silencio" [Arguedas keeps a strict silence] (276).

11. This article, as with many other published throughout Arguedas's lifetime, was not a scholarly publication; he began publishing these pieces in order to add to his income, and they were intended for a general audience. He published them in two daily newspapers, Lima's *El comercio* and Buenos Aires's *La prensa.* His longer, more scholarly pieces were published in more academic

venues and did not begin appearing until the mid-1950s. The later scholarly articles were compiled by Angel Rama in the collection *Formación de una cultura nacional indoamericana*. Many of the shorter articles published in daily newspapers were compiled posthumously in several different collections (*Señores e indios*, ed. Angel Rama; *Indios, mestizos y señores*, ed. Sybila Arredondo de Arguedas; and *Nosotros los maestros*, ed. Wilfredo Kapsoli).

12. Arturo Escobar has argued that such a notion of community also circulates in El Inca Garcilaso de Vega's *Comentarios reales* (*Lenguaje* 155).

13. The presence of an integrated world in *Los ríos profundos* has been extensively analyzed, and often taken as an attribute of the novel's underlying mythic cosmology. See Rowe (*Mito* 88–102); Rama (*Transculturación* 194–206), for this view. Cornejo Polar offers an analysis of the integration that does not attribute it to a magical or mythical Quechua worldview (*Universos* 152–61).

14. Nuckolls provides the following definition of sound symbolism: "The term sound symbolism is used when a sound unit such as a phoneme, syllable, feature or tone is said to go beyond its linguistic function as a contrastive, non-meaning bearing unit, to directly express some kind of meaning" (228). See especially Bruce Mannheim's work on Quechua iconicity, which includes a reading of this passage from *Los ríos profundos* (184–85).

15. I have omitted a short phrase from this translation by Barraclough, signaled by [. . .]. The phrase does not appear in the novel's first edition, here cited; Barraclough translated a later edition of the novel.

16. This Spanish text is quite difficult to translate into English because the reader can't distinguish properly between poetic license and unconscious error. This has lead me to a perhaps overly literal translation. Overall I have tried to communicate the ambiguity of the phrasing, the complex and fragmented syntax, and the strongly literary tone infusing this school composition.

17. There is a question here about the original text: Arguedas says that Quechua "resume en su lenguaje," but context suggests that he meant "rezuma," hence my translation as "oozes" (Forgues, *La Letra* 90 n. 50).

18. For a detailed compare-and-contrast account of language in the different published versions of *Yawar fiesta*, see Rowe's very useful analysis (*Mito* 49–59).

19. Alberto Flores Galindo makes a similar point: "Hay ocasiones en que [Arguedas] insiste en las imágenes del puente. Arguedas se presenta a sí mismo como una suerte de puente entre el mundo indio y el mundo español, entre el mundo occidental y el mundo andino" [There are times when Arguedas insists on images of bridges. Arguedas presents himself as a kind of bridge between the Indian world and the Spanish world, between the occidental world and the Andean world] (*Dos ensayos* 39)

20. Cornejo (*Escribir* 192–95), Rama (*Transculturación* 255), and Landreau (217–19) offer contrasting interpretations of this significant scene.

21. See "¡Ay siwar k'enti!" (76), sung by the mestizas who serve in the chicherías; "Kausarak'mi kani" (237), sung by the master harpist Oblitas, also in the chichería. See also, most especially, "Chaynallatak'mi wak'an ninki/Dile que he llorado," which Arguedas published and translated in *Canto kechwa* and which has almost an identical theme, including the line addressed to the bird: "Quiero darte un encargo: mi amada está lejos, picaflor siwar llévale esta carta"

[I want to give you an errand: my beloved is far away, hummingbird *siwar,* carry her this letter] (*Canto kechwa* 20–21).

22. The poem is included in anthologies by Lara (*La poesía quechua* 158) and Hillman (16–17), in addition to Arguedas's. Bendezú includes it as well, but uses Arguedas's translation and thus reproduces the mistake (7).

23. In fact Arguedas made a mistake in his morphological reconstruction of the original Quechua text. Arguedas saw the word "tuyanqui," which he re-transcribed as "tuyanki," using the standardized Quechua alphabet approved in 1951 by the Primer Congreso de Peruanistas. He then translated "tuyanki" into Spanish as "calandriarás" ("Himnos" 122–28). This Spanish word is a poetic invention; the closest equivalent in English might be "you will sing larkingly." Regarding the Quechua word "tuyanki," I have not found it in any dictionar-ies. Itier and other translators, meanwhile, differ from Arguedas in that their morphological reconstructions render the word in question "suyanki," meaning "esperarás" [you will wait], which is apparently the more accurate rendition of the original.

24. And indeed the iconography of pre-Conquest Andean art suggests the link between the figure of the Inca and birds. But it is, far more frequently, a figure of religious syncretism, the result of missionary translations of scripture (Gisbert 150–73).

4. Rosario Castellanos at the Edge of Entanglement

1. This and all following English translations of *Balún Canán* are Irene Nicholson's, unless otherwise noted. Regarding English translations of other texts by Castellanos, when available, I have used the translations by Maureen Ahern and others compiled in Ahern's *A Rosario Castellanos Reader.* All other translations are my own unless otherwise noted.

2. I have modified Nicholson's translation substantially here. For example, I use the verb "to rob" rather than "to confiscate" to communicate that an illegal action has taken place.

3. Glissant's understanding of the legacy of conquest emerges from intellec-tual debates in the French Caribbean, and my transposition of his concepts to Mexico and Spanish America requires a brief comment. Glissant's work responds critically to the Nègritude movement's turn to Africa, which Glissant termed a "detour," a distraction from the heterodox, foundation-less condition of Car-ibbean culture. Glissant opposes those who insist on recreating the precolonial singularities of distinct peoples. His critique of those who assert collective cul-tural singularity, however, cannot be so easily transposed to Mexico or other areas of strong indigenous survival in the Americas. When indigenous people in-sist on their cultural singularity, it is not always in the name of a prelapsarian time or place to which they propose figuratively to return, but often in order to underscore an injustice that is ongoing and whose stakes may be territorial. The turn to origins is part of a juridical discourse of rights, the foundation for self-determination movements, and as such cannot be dismissed as wishful think-ing or nostalgia; it is rather one of the means by which indigenous groups relate

to the institutions of the state. For an analysis of how territoriality, singularity, and indigenous self-determination are intertwined in the discursive space of Indian-state relations, see Rappaport, *The Politics of Memory*; Mamani, *Taraqu*.

4. Of course the first such words to serve this signal function are "Balún Canán" in the novel's title, since they refer to the indigenous name for the place ladinos call "Comitán." Regarding the name "Balún Canán" for "Comitán," however, it should be understood that some ladinos proudly adopted the indigenous name for the town as part of the construction of a regional identity. The fact that Castellanos chose a title composed of indigenous words thus does not in and of itself constitute a contestatory position vis-à-vis ladino cultural hegemony in Chiapas. An epic poem published in 1937, recounting events from 1863, when Chiapas participated "heroically" in the wars of the Reforma while also defending the territorial integrity of the nation against incursions by Guatemala, refers to Comitán as "balún canán" (Cruz Robles 42).

5. For a thoroughly critical account of the self-image of Mexico as melancholic, see Roger Bartra's *La jaula de la melancolía*.

6. I draw here from Lowe and Lloyd's discussion of how the state-form, in this case the Mexican revolutionary state, requires compliance with normative concepts of social identity (Lowe and Lloyd 7).

7. Elena Poniatowska recounts that Castellanos gave these lands away, in order better to escape the role her parents had assumed as "amos" [masters] (112). For more details regarding this aspect of her biography, see Steele, "María Escandón."

8. See Knight's "Racism, Revolution, and Indigenismo" for a fuller account of the role of indigenismo in the federal government's war against regionalism.

9. "Ladino" is the term used for non-Indians in Chiapas and Guatemala.

10. This view of women victimized by the church was espoused by revolutionary feminists as well. An article published in 1916 in the feminist journal *La mujer moderna* places Mexican feminist struggles squarely in the context of this negative association between the Catholic Church and women's anti-revolutionary politics. The author, Salomé Carranza G., calls on the feminist movement to work to counteract the influence of the church on women's minds. She attacks the church for keeping women "sumida[s] en la superstición y el fanaticismo" [sunk in superstition and fanaticism]. Women are "víctimas del egoísmo y el atraso" [victims of the egotism and backwardness] of the church (quoted in Rocha 245). Carranza advocates for women's rights, yet she shares the same attitudes as her anti-feminist opponents about women's inability to act politically in a rational manner because they are captive to the false consciousness inculcated by the church.

11. Eduardo Mejía, editor of the two-volume "Collected Works of Rosario Castellanos," stresses this point in his introductory essay, titled "Rosario Castellanos, la voz del extranjero" [Rosario Castellanos, the Voice of the Stranger] (7). For other analyses of the uses to which Castellanos put her marginal or "outsider" position, see Lavou (31), Castillo (216).

12. English translation of this poem by Maureen Ahern (111).

13. I have modified Nicholson's translation to emphasize Castellano's use of the verb "to imagine."

14. I draw from Andreas Huyssen's argument, in "Mass Culture as Woman," concerning the formation of an independent sphere of aesthetic creation in nineteenth-century Europe.

15. There may also be a hidden polemic underlying her desire to find this subjective-distracted position. This desire conforms closely to a literary consensus openly disapproving of feminine sentiment, of writing that is *too* subjective. To what extent was Castellanos looking to the negative example provided by "bad" women writers, to the view that subjectivism led to "low" forms of literature? In a contemporaneous article the female critic María Elvira Bermúdez railed against "la proliferación de obras de carácter subjetivo" [the proliferation of works of a subjective nature] by Mexican women writers, arguing that the result was "banal," "monotonous," and ultimately "embarrassing" (22). Bermúdez wrote, "constituyen todavía una excepción las escritoras que se apartan de personales obsesiones para atender a vidas ajenas que demandan una comprensión desinteresada" [those women writers who distance themselves from personal obsessions to pay attention to other lives that require a disinterested understanding are still an exception] (21). In composing *Balún Canán*, how much did Castellanos take these words to heart?

16. Again, I have modified Nicholson's translation slightly.

17. The passage she cites can be found verbatim in Mediz Bolio's translation (25), leading me to believe that his was the version she had read. Other evidence suggesting that she drew from his version is the presence of the Mayan word "Dzules" in his text, in the paragraph immediately preceding the one Castellanos excerpted for the epigraph: "No quisieron esperar a los *Dzules,* ni a su cristianismo. No quisieron pagar tributo" [They didn't want to wait for the *Dzules,* nor for their Christianity. They didn't want to pay tribute] (Mediz Bolio 25). This word may be at the origin of the word "dzulúm," which Castellanos uses frequently in *Balún Canán* to refer to a mythical savage beast responsible for the disappearance of desperate ladina women; they are lured to the forest by his call and never seen again (*Balún Canán* 21). Castellanos's childhood friend and biographer Oscar Bonifaz has argued that "dzulúm" is her invention, on the basis of the claim that the phoneme "dz" does not exist in Mayan languages (cited in Lavou 201). However, the presence of the word "Dzules" in numerous transcriptions of the Chilam Balam — though not always using the same transliteration — suggests otherwise. It is interesting to note that, although Mediz was a native speaker of Yucatec Maya, he did not translate "Dzules" into Spanish; in fact there are numerous Mayan words left untranslated in his version of the book, suggesting perhaps that he himself did not know their meaning. As in the case of Arguedas and Lara, twentieth-century speakers of indigenous languages were usually ignorant of the colonial versions of the same language and were often unaware of the many distinctions between colonial and contemporary versions. An English translation of the *Chilam Balam de Chumayel* renders "dzules" as "foreigners," in a passage clearly referring to the Spaniards (Roys 83). This is quite ironic, since Castellanos uses her version of the term to refer to an entirely indigenous mythic creation.

18. Lienhard, too, notes Mediz Bolio's tendency to "capitalize" the Maya Indian, part of the "ideological construction" of contemporary Yucatec writers who considered themselves the heirs of Maya civilization (205).

19. I have slightly modified Nicholson's translation.

20. This is entirely my translation.

21. See also Steele's analysis of Castellanos's tendency to recur to "the image of Savagism" reminiscent of nineteenth-century nation-building discourses ("The Fiction" 66).

22. Translation by Laura Carp Solomon (in Ahern 227).

23. See also Poniatowska on this point: "No creo que Rosario Castellanos se haya propuesto legar una imagen de plañidera. Lo que pasa es que Rosario usó la literatura como todavía la usamos la mayoría de las mujeres, como forma de terapia. Recurrimos a la escritura para liberarnos, vaciarnos, confesarnos, explicarnos el mundo, comprender lo que nos sucede.... Pocos escritores mexicanos han proporcionado tanta información acerca de su persona, pocos lo han hecho tan emotivamente" [I don't think Rosario Castellanos decided to bequeath an image of a mournful weeper. What happened is that Rosario used literature like the majority of us women use it, as a kind of therapy. We turn to literature to free ourselves, pour ourselves out, confess ourselves, explain the world to ourselves, to understand what is happening to us.... Few Mexican writers have provided so much information about themselves; few have done it so emotionally] (57).

Conclusion

1. Regarding the fragmentary and uneven nature of Latin American modernity from the nineteenth century onward, see Julio Ramos (41–77).

2. For more on ruins and collapse in Rulfo's novel, see Aguilar Mora (10–13) and García Moreno's "Desencanto." For a discussion of this novel as emblematic of the masking operations of Mexican populism, see Larsen (49–71).

3. Angel Rama, in his *Transculturación narrativa en América Latina,* also considered the socially mobile origin of the indigenista enunciation to be quite significant; it explains the essentially mediatory role adopted by the indigenistas and, more importantly, their more successful offspring, the "transculturators" (Rama 139–57). See the essays collected in Degregori et al. for an extended discussion of indigenismo as a class phenomenon.

4. For mestizaje as myth, see works by Rivera ("La raíz"); Bonfil Batalla; Bartra; Cornejo, "Cultura nacional."

5. The idea of "freedom from particularity" comes from Brown's analysis of liberalism (7). A contemporary example of desire for this freedom brought under the purview of the intimate is Leonardo García Pabón's *La patria íntima,* which offers an illuminating analysis of several Bolivian literary texts. The prologue announces a desire to discover the "flesh and bone" Bolivian, whom the "sciences of man," charged with categorizing and quantifying human experience, still do not recognize (1). This Bolivian inhabits "the intimate country" of García Pabón's title.

6. See Yashar for an extended analysis of the causes and effects of contemporary indigenous movements in Latin America.

7. See Canessa for a fascinating account of the relationship between contemporary indigenous discourses and old-style indigenismo in Bolivia, although I consider his account of indigenismo overly simplified. This leads him to downplay the links between current and past discourses on Indianness.

Bibliography

Aguilar Mora, Jorge. "Prólogo: El silencio de Nellie Campobello." In *Cartucho: Relatos de la lucha en el norte de Mexico,* by Nellie Campobello, 9–43. Mexico: Ediciones Era, 2000.

Ahern, Maureen, editor. *A Rosario Castellanos Reader.* Edited and with a critical introduction by Maureen Ahern. Translated by Maureen Ahern and others. Austin: University of Texas Press, 1988.

Albó, Xavier. *El futuro de los idiomas oprimidos en los Andes.* Lima: Universidad Nacional Mayor de San Marcos – Centro de Investigación de Lingüística Aplicada, 1977.

Albro, Robert. "As Witness to Literary Spectacle: The Personality of Folklore in Provincial Bolivian Politics." *Journal of Latin American Cultural Studies* 9, no. 3 (2000): 305–32.

Alonso, Carlos. *The Spanish-American Regional Novel.* Cambridge: Cambridge University Press, 1990.

Althusser, Louis. "Ideology and Ideological State Apparatuses (Notes towards an Investigation)." In *Lenin and Philosophy and Other Essays.* Translated by Ben Brewster, 127–86. New York: Monthly Review Press, 1971.

Anaya de Urquidi, Mercedes. *Indianismo.* Buenos Aires: Sociedad Editora Latino-Americana, 1947.

Anderson, Benedict. *Imagined Communities.* Revised edition. London: Verso, 1991.

Appelbaum, Nancy P. *Muddied Waters: Race, Region and Local History in Colombia, 1846–1948.* Durham, N.C.: Duke University Press, 2003.

Appelbaum, Nancy P., Anne S. Macpherson, and Karin Alejandra Rosemblatt. "Introduction: Racial Nations." In *Race and Nation in Modern Latin America,* edited by Nancy P. Appelbaum, Anne S. Macpherson, and Karin Alejandra Rosemblatt, 1–31. Chapel Hill: University of North Carolina Press, 2003.

Arguedas, Alcides. *Historia general de Bolivia.* La Paz: Gisbert y Cia, 1975 [1922].

———. *Pueblo enfermo.* La Paz: Editorial Juventud, 1996 [1909].

Arguedas, José María. "Acerca del intenso significado de dos voces quechuas." In *Indios, señores y mestizos,* edited by Sybila Arredondo de Arguedas, 147–49. Lima: Editorial Horizonte, 1989.

———. "El arte popular religioso y la cultural mestiza de Huamanga." *Revista del Museo Nacional* 37 (1958): 139–94.

———. "La canción popular mestiza en el Perú: Su valor documental y poético." In *Indios, señores y mestizos,* edited by Sybila Arredondo de Arguedas, 49–56. Lima: Editorial Horizonte, 1989.

———. *Canto Kechwa*. Lima, 1938.

———. *Deep Rivers*. Translated by Frances Horning Barraclough. Austin: University of Texas Press, 1978.

———. "Los doce meses." In *Indios, señores y mestizos*, edited by Sybila Arredondo de Arguedas, 29–36. Lima: Editorial Horizonte, 1989.

———. "Entre el kechwa y el castellano la angustia del mestizo." In *Indios, señores y mestizos*, edited by Sybila Arredondo de Arguedas, 25–28. Lima: Editorial Horizonte, 1989.

———. *Formación de una cultura nacional indoamericana*. Edited by Angel Rama. Mexico: Siglo XXI Editores, 1975.

———. *The Fox from Up Above and the Fox from Down Below*. Edited by Julio Ortega. Translated by Frances Horning Barraclough. Pittsburgh: University of Pittsburgh Press, 2000.

———. "Los himnos quechuas católicos cuzqueños." *Folklore Americano* 3, no. 3 (1955): 121–232.

———. "I Am Not an Acculturated Man . . . " In *The Fox from Up Above and the Fox from Down Below*, edited by Julio Ortega, 268–70. Translated by Frances Horning Barraclough. Pittsburgh: University of Pittsburgh Press, 2000.

———. "Un método para el caso lingüístico del indio peruano" [1944]. In *Nosotros los maestros*, edited and introduced by Wilfredo Kapsoli, 39–44. Lima: Editorial Horizonte, 1986.

———. "No soy un aculturado." In *El zorro de arriba y el zorro de abajo*, edited and introduced by Eve-Marie Fell, 256–58. Colección Archivos 14. Madrid: CSIC, 1990 [1971].

———. "The Novel and the Problem of Literary Expression in Peru." *Yawar Fiesta*. Translated by Frances Horning Barraclough, xiii-xxi. Austin: University of Texas Press, 1985.

———. "La novela y el problema de la expresión literaria en el Perú." *Yawar Fiesta*, 165–74. 2nd edition. Buenos Aires: Editorial Losada, 1977.

———. *Poesía quechua*. Buenos Aires: Editorial Universitaria de Buenos Aires, 1965.

———. *Pumaccahua: Trabajos de los alumnos del Colegio Nacional de Sicuani*. Sicuani, Peru: Colegio Nacional "Mateo Pumaccahua," 1940.

———. *Los ríos profundos*. Buenos Aires: Losada, 1998 [1958].

———. *Señores e indios*. Edited by Angel Rama. Buenos Aires: Arca, 1976.

———. "El wayno y el problema del idioma en el mestizo." In *Nosotros los maestros*, edited by Wilfredo Kapsoli, 35–38. Lima: Editorial Horizonte, 1986.

———. *Yawar Fiesta*. 1st edition. Lima: CIP, 1941.

———. *Yawar Fiesta*. Translated by Frances Horning Barraclough. Austin: University of Texas Press, 1985.

———. *El zorro de arriba y el zorro de abajo*. Edited and with an introduction by Eve-Marie Fell. Colección Archivos 14. Madrid: CSIC, 1990 [1971].

Armstrong, Nancy. *Desire and Domestic Fiction: A Political History of the Novel*. New York: Oxford University Press, 1987.

Avelar, Idelber. *The Untimely Present: Postdictatorial Latin American Fiction and the Task of Mourning*. Durham, N.C.: Duke University Press, 1999.

Bakhtin, M. M. *The Dialogic Imagination: Four Essays.* Edited by Michael Holquist. Translated by Caryl Emerson and Michael Holquist. Austin: University of Texas Press, 1981.

Balibar, Etienne, and Immanuel Wallerstein. "The Nation Form: History and Ideology." In *Race, Nation, Class: Ambiguous Identities,* 86–106. Translated by Chris Turner. London: Verso, 1991.

Bartra, Roger. *La jaula de la melancolía: Identidad y metamorfosis del mexicano.* Mexico: Grijalbo, 1996 [1987].

Becker, Marjorie. "Torching La Purísima, Dancing at the Altar: The Construction of Revolutionary Hegemony in Michoacán, 1934–1940." In *Everyday Forms of State Formation: Revolution and the Negotiation of Rule in Mexico,* edited by Gilbert M. Joseph and Daniel Nugent, 247–64. Durham, N.C.: Duke University Press, 1994.

Bendezú Aybar, Edmundo, editor. *Literatura Quechua.* Caracas: Biblioteca Ayacucho, 1980.

Benjamin, Walter. "The Storyteller." In *The Theory of the Novel (A Critical Anthology),* edited by Michael McKeon, 77–93. Baltimore: Johns Hopkins University Press, 2000.

Berger, John. *Ways of Seeing.* London: BBC/Penguin Books, 1972.

Berlant, Lauren. *The Queen of America Goes to Washington City: Essays on Sex and Citizenship.* Durham, N.C.: Duke University Press, 1997.

Bermúdez, María Elvira. "Discurso sobre la literatura femenina." *Las Letras Patrias* 3 (1954): 20–38.

Beverley, John. *Subalternity and Representation: Arguments in Cultural Theory.* Durham, N.C.: Duke University Press, 1999.

Beyersdorff, Margot. *Historia y drama ritual en los andes bolivianos (siglos XVI–XX).* La Paz: Plural Editores, 1998.

Bigas Torres, Sylvia. *La narrativa indigenista mexicana del siglo XX.* Guadalajara: Editorial Universidad de Guadalajara, 1990.

Brading, David A. "Manuel Gamio and Official Indigenismo in Mexico." *Bulletin of Latin American Research* 7, no. 1 (1988): 75–89.

———. *The Origins of Mexican Nationalism.* Cambridge: Center of Latin American Studies, 1985.

Bonfil Batalla, Guillermo. *México profundo: Una civilización negada.* Mexico: Grijalbo, 1987.

Borges, Jorge Luis. "The Argentine Writer and Tradition." In *The Total Library: Non-Fiction 1922–1986,* edited by Eliot Weinberger, 420–27. Translated by Esther Allen, Suzanne Jill Levine, and Eliot Weinberger. New York: Penguin Books, 1999.

Botelho González, Raúl. Letter to Jesús Lara. November 4, 1942. Jesús Lara Personal Archive. Cochabamba, Bolivia.

Bradú, Fabienne. *Señas particulares: Escritora.* Mexico: Fondo de Cultura Económica, 1987.

Brown, Wendy. *States of Injury: Power and Freedom in Late Modernity.* Princeton, N.J.: Princeton University Press, 1995.

Butler, Judith. *Antigone's Claim: Kinship between Life and Death.* New York: Columbia University Press, 2000.

———. *The Psychic Life of Power.* Stanford: Stanford University Press, 1997.

Capdevilla, Arturo. "El poema de Khatira y Ariwaki y su poeta." *Khatira y Ariwaki: Egloga quechua,* by Jesús Lara, 65–71. Cochabamba: Editorial Canelas, 1964.

Canessa, Andrew. "Todos somos indígenas: Towards a New Language of National Political Identity." *Bulletin of Latin American Research* 25, no. 2 (2006): 241–63.

Carballo, Emmanuel. "Rosario Castellanos." In *19 protagonistas de la literatura mexicana del siglo XX,* 411–24. Mexico: Empresas editoriales, S.A., 1965.

Caso, Alfonso. *La comunidad indígena.* Prologue by Gonzalo Aguirre Beltrán. Mexico: SEP/Diana, 1980.

———. *Indigenismo.* Mexico: Instituto Nacional Indigenista, 1958.

———. *¿Qué es el INI?* Mexico: Instituto Nacional Indigenista, 1965.

Castellanos, Rosario. *Balún Canán.* Mexico: Fondo de Cultura Económica, 1957.

———. *Cartas a Ricardo.* Prologue by Elena Poniatowska. Mexico City: Consejo Nacional para la Cultura y las Artes, 1994.

———. "Escrituras tempranas." In *Obras completas* vol. 2: *Poesía, teatro y ensayo,* edited by Eduardo Mejía, 993–97. Mexico: Fondo de Cultura Económica, 1998.

———. "A Man of Destiny." In *A Rosario Castellanos Reader,* edited and with a critical introduction by Maureen Ahern, 232–35. Translated by Maureen Ahern et al. Austin: University of Texas Press, 1988.

———. *The Nine Guardians.* Translated by Irene Nicholson. New York: Vanguard Press, 1960.

———. *Obras completas,* vol. 2: *Poesía, teatro y ensayo,* edited by Eduardo Mejía. Mexico: Fondo de Cultura Económica, 1998.

———. "El Padre Las Casas." *El uso de la palabra.* Prologue by José Emilio Pacheco, 144–46. Mexico: Ediciones de Excélsior, 1974.

———. "Rosario Castellanos." In *Los narradores ante el público.* Vol. 1. By Rafael Solana et al. Mexico: Joaquín Mortiz, 1966.

———. *Teatro Petul 2.* Mexico: Instituto Nacional Indigenista, 1961.

———. "Una tentativa de auto-crítica." In *Obras completas,* vol. 2: *Poesía, teatro y ensayo,* edited by Eduardo Mejía, 991–93. Mexico: Fondo de Cultura Económica, 1998.

Castillo, Debra. *Talking Back: Towards a Latin American Feminist Literary Criticism.* Ithaca, N.Y.: Cornell University Press, 1992.

Castro-Klaren, Sara. *Escritura, transgresión y sujeto en la literatura latinoamericana.* Puebla, Mexico: Premia Editora, 1989.

Céspedes, Augusto. "Carlos Montenegro: Un desconocido." *Selecciones Bolivianas* 7 (1953): 58–65.

———. *El presidente colgado.* Buenos Aires: Editorial Jorge Alvarez, 1966.

Choque, Roberto, et al. *Educación indígena: ¿Ciudadanía o colonización?* La Paz: Ediciones Aruwiyiri (THOA), 1992.

Cohn, Dorrit. *The Distinction of Fiction.* Baltimore: Johns Hopkins University Press, 1999.

Cornejo Polar, Antonio. "La cultura nacional: Problema y posibilidad." *Letras* (Lima) 94 (1997): 121–29.

————. *Escribir en el aire: Ensayo sobre la heterogeneidad socio-cultural en las literaturas andinas*. 2nd edition. Lima: CELACP/Latinoamericana Editores, 2003.

————. "Heterogeneidad y contradicción en la literatura andina (Tres incidentes en la contienda entre oralidad y escritura)." *Nuevo Texto Crítico 5*, nos. 9/10 (1992): 103–11.

————. "El indigenismo y las literaturas heterogéneas: Su doble estatuto socio-cultural." *Revista de Crítica Literaria Latinoamericana 7–8* (1978): 7–21.

————. "La literatura peruana: Totalidad contradictoria." *Revista de Crítica Literaria Latinoamericana 18* (1983): 37–50.

————. *Los universos narrativos de José María Arguedas*. Buenos Aires: Losada, 1973.

Cresta de Leguizamón, María Luisa. "En recuerdo de Rosario Castellanos." *La Palabra y el Hombre 19* (1976): 3–18.

Cruz Ramírez, Darío. *Hacia una legislación tutelar para las clases indígenas de México*. Mexico: Primer Congreso Indigenista Interamericano, Departamento de Asuntos Indígenas, 1940.

Cruz Robles, Galileo. *Chiapas, Baluarte de México: La guerra de Ortega. Episodios de la Reforma al Segundo Imperio 1863. Poema heroíco en IX cantos y en verso*. Mexico: Editorial de Izquierda de la Cámara de Diputados, 1937.

Dandler, Jorge, and Juan Torrico A. "From the National Indigenous Congress to the Ayopaya Rebellion: Bolivia, 1945–1947." In *Resistance, Rebellion, and Consciousness in the Andean Peasant World*, edited by Steve Stern, 334–78. Madison: University of Wisconsin Press, 1987.

de Castro, Juan E. *Mestizo Nations: Culture, Race and Conformity in Latin American Literature*. Tucson: University of Arizona Press, 2002.

de la Cadena, Marisol. *Indigenous Mestizos: The Politics of Race and Culture in Cuzco, Peru 1919–1991*. Durham, N.C.: Duke University Press, 2000.

de la Peña, Guillermo. "Orden social y educación indígena en México: La pervivencia de un legado colonial." In *La heterodoxia recuperada: En torno a Angel Palerm*, edited by Susana Glantz, 285–320. Mexico: Fondo de Cultura Económica, 1987.

Degregori, Carlos Iván, et al., editors. *Indigenismo, clases sociales y problema nacional: La discusión sobre el "problema indígena" en el Perú*. Lima: Ediciones Centro Latinoamericano de Trabajo Social, 1978.

Demelas, Marie-Danièle. "Darwinismo a la Criolla: El Darwiniso Social en Bolivia." *Historia Boliviana 1/2* (1981): 55–82.

Derrida, Jacques. *Archive Fever: A Freudian Impression*. Translated by Eric Prenowitz. Chicago: University of Chicago Press, 1995.

Deustua, José, and José Luis Rénique. *Intelectuales, indigenismo y descentralismo en el Perú 1897–1931*. Cuzco: CERA, 1984.

Emery, Amy Fass. *The Anthropological Imagination in Latin American Literature*. Columbia: University of Missouri Press, 1996.

Escobar, Arturo. *Arguedas o la utopía de la lengua*. Lima: Instituto de Estudios Peruanos, 1984.

————. *Lenguaje y discriminación social en América Latina*. Lima: Editorial Milla Batres, 1972.

Fabian, Johannes. *Time and the Other: How Anthropology Makes Its Object.* Foreword by Matti Bunzl. New York: Columbia University Press, 2002.

Favre, Henri. *El indigenismo.* Translated from the French by Glenn Amado Gallardo Jordán. Mexico: Fondo de Cultura Económica, 1998.

Fell, Eve-Marie. "Introducción." In *El zorro de arriba y el zorro de abajo,* by José María Arguedas. Edited by Eve-Marie Fell, xxi–xxvii. Colección Archivos 14. Madrid: CSIC, 1990 [1971].

Flores Galindo, Alberto. *Buscando un inca: Identidad y utopia en los Andes.* Lima: Instituto de Apoyo Agrario, 1987.

———. *Dos Ensayos sobre José María Arguedas.* Lima: Casa SUR, 1992.

Forgues, Roland. *José María Arguedas: La letra inmortal. Correspondencia con Manuel Moreno Jiménez.* Lima: Ediciones de los Ríos Profundos, 1993.

———. "El mito del monolingüismo quechua de Arguedas." In *José María Arguedas: Vida y obra,* edited by Hildebrando Pozo and Carlos Garayar, 47–58. Lima: Amaru Editores, 1991.

Foucault, Michel. *The History of Sexuality.* Vol. 1. Translated by Robert Hurley. New York: Vintage, 1978.

Franco, Jean. *Plotting Women: Gender and Representation in Mexico.* New York: Columbia University Press, 1989.

———. "The Return of Coatlicue: Mexican Nationalism and the Aztec Past." *Journal of Latin American Cultural Studies* 13, no. 2 (2004): 205–19.

Francovich, Guillermo. Letter to Jesús Lara. September 17, 1947. Jesús Lara Personal Archive. Cochabamba, Bolivia.

———. *El pensamiento boliviano en el siglo XX.* 2nd edition. Cochabamba: Los Amigos del Libro, 1984.

Gálvez Ruiz, Xóchitl. "México Pluricultural: Los pueblos indígenas de México." Comisión Nacional para el Desarrollo de los Pueblos Indigenas. March 12, 2006. www.cdi.gob.mx/index.php?id_seccion=1066.

Gamio, Manuel. *Consideraciones sobre el problema indígena.* Mexico: Instituto Indigenista Interamericano, 1948.

———. *Forjando Patria.* Mexico: Porrúa, 1982 [1916].

García, José Uriel. *El nuevo indio.* Lima: Editorial Universo, 1973 [1930].

García Flores, Margarita. "Rosario Castellanos: La lucidez como forma de vida." *La Onda,* supplement of *Novedades.* August 18, 1974: 6–7.

García Moreno, Laura. "Desencanto y melancolía en *Pedro Páramo.*" *Revista Canadiense de Estudios Hispánicos* 30, no. 3 (2006):497–519.

García Pabón, Leonardo. *La patria íntima: Alegorías nacionales en la literatura y el cine de Bolivia.* La Paz: CESU/Plural Editores, 1998.

Garcilaso de la Vega, Inca. *Comentarios reales.* Edited by Enrique Pupo-Walker. Madrid: Cátedra, 1996.

Genette, Gérard. *Narrative Discourse: An Essay in Method.* Ithaca, N.Y.: Cornell University Press, 1980.

Gisbert, Teresa. *El paraíso de los pájaros parlantes: La imagen del otro en la cultura andina.* La Paz: Plural Editores, 1999.

Glissant, Edouard. *Le discours antillais.* Paris: Seuil, 1981.

Goffman, Erving. *Stigma: Notes on the Management of Spoiled Identity.* Englewood Cliffs, N.J.: Prentice-Hall, 1963.

Gómez, Luis A. "Morales anuncia que desaparecerá 'por racista' el Ministe-rio de Asuntos Indígenas." *La Jornada* January 20, 2006. March 12, 2006 www.jornada.unam.mx/2006/01/20/035n1mun.php.

Gómez-Moriana, Antonio. "Autobiographie et discours rituel: La confession autobiographique au tribunal de l'Inquisition." *Poétique* 56 (1983): 444–60.

González Echevarría, Roberto. *Myth and Archive: A Theory of Latin American Narrative*. Durham, N.C.: Duke University Press, 1998.

González Prada, Manuel. "Discurso en el Politeama." In *Antología*, edited by Luis Alberto Sánchez, 63–69. Lima: Biblioteca Básica del Perú, 1996.

Gordillo, José M., editor. *Arando en la historia: La experiencia política campesina en Cochabamba*. La Paz: CEP/CERES/PLURAL, 1998.

Gotkowitz, Laura. "Within the Boundaries of Equality: Race, Gender and Citi-zenship in Bolivia (Cochabamba 1880–1953)." Diss. University of Chicago, 1998.

Guillén Pinto, Alfredo. *La educación del indio*. La Paz: González y Medina Editores, 1919.

Gutiérrez, Gustavo. *Entre las calandrias: Un ensayo sobre José María Arguedas*. Lima: Instituto Bartolomé de las Casas, 1990.

Hanke, Lewis. *All Mankind Is One*. Dekalb: Northern Illinois University Press, 1974.

Harris, Olivia. "Ethnic Identity and Market Relations: Indians and Mestizos in the Andes." In *Ethnicity, Markets, and Migration in the Andes: At the Cross-roads of History and Anthropology*, edited by Brooke Larson and Olivia Harris, with Enrique Tandeter, 351–417. Durham, N.C.: Duke University Press, 1995.

Harrison, Regina. "José María Arguedas: El substrato quechua." *Revista Ibero-americana* 49, no. 122 (1983): 111–32.

Hernández Castillo, Rosalba Aída. "Esperanzas y desafíos de las Chiapanecas ante el siglo XXI." *Doble Jornada*, March 3, 1997, 18–20.

Hillman, Grady, with Guillermo Delgado-P. *The Return of the Inca: Translations from the Quechua Messianic Tradition*. Austin: Place of Herons, 1986.

Huyssen, Andreas. "Mass Culture as Woman: Modernism's Other." In *Stud-ies in Entertainment: Critical Approaches to Mass Culture*, edited by Tania Modleski, 188–207. Bloomington: Indiana University Press, 1986.

Icaza, Jorge. *Huasipungo*. Edited by Teodosio Fernández. Madrid: Cátedra, 1997.

Itier, César. "Estudio y comentario lingüístico." In *Relación de antiguedades deste reyno del Piru*. By Joan de Santa Cruz Pachacuti Yamqui Salcamaygua. Edited by Pierre Duviols and César Itier, 129–78. Cuzco: IFEA/Centro de Estudios Regionales Andinos Bartolomé de las Casas, 1993.

Jameson, Fredric. *The Political Unconscious: Narrative as a Socially Symbolic Act*. Ithaca, N.Y.: Cornell University Press, 1981.

Joseph, Gilbert M., and Daniel Nugent. "Popular Culture and State Formation in Revolutionary Mexico." In *Everyday Forms of State Formation: Revolution and the Negotiation of Rule in Mexico*, edited by Gilbert M. Joseph and Daniel Nugent, 3–23. Durham, N.C.: Duke University Press, 1994.

Klein, Herbert. *Bolivia: The Evolution of Multi-Ethnic Society.* New York: Oxford: Oxford University Press, 1982.

Klor de Alva, J. Jorge. "Contar vidas: La autobiografía confesional y la reconstrucción del ser nahua." *Arbor* 515–16 (1988): 49–78.

Knight, Alan. "Racism, Revolution, and *Indigenismo*: Mexico, 1910–1940." *The Idea of Race in Latin America, 1870–1940,* edited by Richard Graham, 71–113. Austin: University of Texas Press, 1990.

Kristal, Efraín. *The Andes Viewed from the City: Literary and Political Discourse on the Indian in Peru 1848–1930.* New York: Peter Lang, 1987.

Landreau, John C. "Hacia una relectura de la leyenda autobiográfica de José María Arguedas." In *Indigenismo hacia el fin del milenio: Homenaje a Antonio Cornejo-Polar,* edited by Mabel Moraña, 211–22. Pittsburgh: Instituto Internacional de Literatura Iberoamericana, 1998.

Lara, Jesús. "Bolivia tiene ahora un sitio en la literatura Americana." *Tribuna* February 1, 1950, 3.

———. *Paqarin.* Cochabamba: Los Amigos del Libro, 1974.

———. *La poesía quechua: Ensayo y antología.* Cochabamba: Universidad Mayor de San Simón, 1947.

———. *Qheshwataki — Poesía popular quechua.* Cochabamba: Los Amigos del Libro, 1993 [1956].

———. *Sasañan.* Cochabamba: Los Amigos del Libro, 1975.

———. *Surumi* ms.

———. *Surumi.* 1st edition. Bueno Aires: Librería Perlado, 1943.

———. *Surumi.* 2nd edition. Cochabamba: Los Amigos del Libro, 1988 [1950].

———. *Viaje a Incallajta: Impresiones.* Cochabamba: Editorial López, 1927.

———. *Wichay uray.* Cochabamba: Los Amigos del Libro, 1977.

———. *Yanakuna.* La Paz: Editorial Juventud, 1952.

Lara, Jesús, and Luis H. Antezana. *Tapuy jayniy. Entrevistas:* Cochabamba: Los Amigos del Libro, 1980.

Lara, Jesús, and Mario Lara López. *Wiñaypaj.* Cochabamba: Los Amigos del Libro, 1986.

Larsen, Neil. *Modernism and Hegemony: A Materialist Critique of Aesthetic Agencies.* Foreword by Jaime Concha. Minneapolis: University of Minnesota Press, 1990.

Larson, Brooke. *Cochabamba, 1550–1900: Colonialism and Agrarian Transformation in Bolivia,* expanded edition. Durham, N.C.: Duke University Press, 1998.

———. "Indios redimidos, cholos barbarizados: Imaginando la modernidad neocolonial boliviana (1900–1910)." In *Visiones de fin de siglo: Bolivia y América Latina en el Siglo XX,* edited by Dora Cajías, Magdalena Cajías, Carmen Johnson, and Iris Villegas, 27–48. La Paz: Coordinadora de Historia/IFEA, 2001.

———. *Trials of Nation Making: Liberalism, Race, and Ethnicity in the Andes, 1810–1910.* Cambridge: Cambridge University Press, 2004.

Las Casas, Bartolomé de. *Brevísima relación de la destrucción de las indias.* Edited by André Saint-Lu. Madrid: Cátedra, 1992.

Latorre, Roberto. Letter to Jesús Lara. March 1948. Jesús Lara Personal Archive. Cochabamba, Bolivia.

Lauer, Mirko. *Andes imaginarios: Discursos del indigenismo 2.* Cuzco: Centro de Estudios Rurales Andinos Bartolomé de las Casas. Lima: Casa SUR, 1997.

Lavou Zoungbo, Victorien. *Mujeres e indios, voces del silencio.* Rome: Bulzoni Editore, 2001.

Leal, Luis. *Breve historia de la literatura latinoamericana.* New York: Knopf, 1971.

Lienhard, Martín. *La voz y su huella: Escritura y conflicto étnico-cultural en América Latina 1492–1988.* Lima: Horizonte, 1992.

Lloyd, David. *Nationalism and Minor Literature: James Clarence Mangan and the Emergence of Irish Cultural Nationalism.* Berkeley: University of California Press, 1987.

———. "Nationalisms against the State." In *The Politics of Culture in the Shadow of Capital,* edited by Lisa Lowe and David Lloyd, 173–97. Durham, N.C.: Duke University Press, 1997.

Lomnitz Adler, Claudio. *Deep Mexico, Silent Mexico: An Anthropology of Nationalism.* Minneapolis: University of Minnesota Press, 2001.

———. *Exits from the Labyrinth: Culture and Ideology in the Mexican National Space.* Berkeley: University of California Press, 1992.

López Obrador, Andrés Manuel. *Entre la historia y la esperanza: Corrupción y lucha democrática en Tabasco.* Mexico: Grijalbo, 1995.

Lowe, Lisa, and David Lloyd, editors. "Introduction." In *The Politics of Culture in the Shadow of Capital,* 1–30. Durham, N.C.: Duke University Press, 1997.

Macías, Ana. *Against All Odds: The Feminist Movement in Mexico to 1940.* Westport, Conn.: Greenwood Press, 1982.

Mallon, Florencia E. *Peasant and Nation: The Making of Postcolonial Mexico and Peru.* Berkeley: University of California Press, 1995.

———. "Reflections on the Ruins: Everyday Forms of State Formation in Nineteenth-Century Mexico." In *Everyday Forms of State Formation: Revolution and the Negotiation of Rule in Mexico,* edited by Gilbert M. Joseph and Daniel Nugent, 69–106. Durham, N.C.: Duke University Press, 1994.

Mamani Condori, Carlos. *Los aymaras frente a la historia: Dos ensayos metodológicos.* La Paz: Aruwiyiri/THOA, 1992.

———. "Restitución, reconstitución de la identidad y derechos de los pueblos indígenas de los Andes: Historiografía y política aymara." Unpublished manuscript.

———. *Taraqu, 1866–1935: Masacre, guerra y "Renovación" en la biografía de Eduardo L. Nina Qhispi.* La Paz: Ediciones Aruwiyiri, 1991.

Mannheim, Bruce. *The Language of the Inka since the European Invasion.* Austin: University of Texas Press, 1991.

Mariátegui, José Carlos. *Peruanicemos al Perú.* Ediciones populares de las obras completas 11. Lima: Amauta, 1970.

———. *Siete ensayos de interpretación de la realidad peruana.* Mexico: Ediciones Era, 1979 [1928].

Mediz Bolio, Antonio. *La tierra del faisán y el venado.* Prólogo de Alfonso Reyes. Mexico: Editorial Mexico, 1934 [1922].

———, translator. *Libro de Chilam Balam de Chumayel.* Mexico: Ediciones de la Universidad Autónoma, 1941.

Medina, Andrés, and Carlos García Mora, editors. *La quiebra política de la antropología social en México: Antología de una polémica.* Vol. 2. Universidad Nacional Autónoma de México, Instituto de Investigaciones Antropológicas, 1983.

Medinaceli, Carlos. *Estudios Críticos.* 2nd edition. Cochabamba: Los Amigos del Libro, 1969.

Merino de Zela, Mildred. "Vida y Obra de José María Arguedas." In *José María Arguedas: Veinte años después; Huellas y horizontes 1969–1989,* edited by Rodrigo Montoya, 99–144. Lima: Escuela de Antropología de la Universidad Nacional Mayor de San Marcos, 1991.

Messinger Cypess, Sandra. "*Balún-Canán:* A Model Demonstration of Discourse as Power." *Revista de Estudios Hispánicos* 3 (1985): 1–16.

Mignolo, Walter D. *The Darker Side of the Renaissance: Literacy, Territoriality, and Colonization.* Ann Arbor: University of Michigan Press, 1995.

Miller, Beth, and Alfonso González. "Rosario Castellanos." In *26 autoras del México actual,* 115–38. Mexico: B. Costa Amic, 1978.

Miller, Marilyn Grace. *The Rise and Fall of the Cosmic Race: The Cult of Mestizaje in Latin America.* Austin: University of Texas Press, 2004.

Millones, Luis. "Prólogo." In *Reflexiones sobre la violencia,* edited by Moises Lemlij, i–xii. Lima: Biblioteca Peruana de Psicoanálisis/SIDEA, 1994.

Mires, Fernando. *El discurso de la indianidad: La cuestión indígena en América Latina.* Quito: Ediciones Abya-Yala, 1991.

Molloy, Sylvia. *At Face Value: Autobiographical Writing in Spanish America.* Cambridge: Cambridge University Press, 1991.

Monsiváis, Carlos. "Versiones nacionales de lo indígena." *Cultura y derechos de los pueblos indígenas de México,* 55–74. Mexico: Archivo General de la Nación/Fondo de Cultura Económica, 1996.

Montenegro, Carlos. *Nacionalismo y coloniaje.* La Paz: Juventud, 2002 [1943].

Morales Ayma, Evo. "Discurso inaugural." January 22, 2006. April 16, 2006. http://ukhamawa.blogdiario.com/i2006-01.

More, Ernesto. Letter to Jesús Lara. July 5, 1955. Jesús Lara Personal Archive. Cochabamba, Bolivia.

Moreiras, Alberto. *The Exhaustion of Difference: The Politics of Latin American Cultural Studies.* Durham, N.C.: Duke University Press, 2001.

Muyulema, Armando. "De la 'cuestión indígena' a lo 'indígena' como cuestionamiento: Hacia una crítica del latinoamericanismo, el indigenismo y el mestiz(o)aje." In *Convergencia de tiempos: Estudios subalternos/contextos latinoamericanos; Estado, cultura, subalternidad,* edited by Ileana Rodríguez, 327–63. Amsterdam: Rodopi, 2001.

Nietzsche, Friedrich. *On the Genealogy of Morals.* Translated by Douglas Smith. Oxford: Oxford University Press, 1996.

Nuckolls, Janice. "The Case for Sound Symbolism." *Annual Review of Anthropology* 28 (1999): 225–52.

O'Connell, Joanna. *Prospero's Daughter: The Prose of Rosario Castellanos.* Austin: University of Texas Press, 1995.

Ortega, Julio. *Texto, comunicación y cultura: Los ríos profundos de José María Arguedas.* Lima: Centro de Estudios para el Desarrollo y la Participación, 1982.

Ortiz, Fernando. *Contrapunteo cubano del tabaco y el azúcar.* Caracas: Biblioteca Ayacucho, 1978 [1940].

Pachacuti Yamqui Salcamaygua, Joan de Santa Cruz. In *Relación de antiguedades deste reyno del Piru*, edited by Pierre Duviols and César Itier. Cuzco: IFEA/Centro de Estudios Regionales Andinos Bartolomé de las Casas, 1993.

Pagden, Anthony. *The Fall of Natural Man: The American Indian and the Origins of Comparative Ethnology.* Cambridge: Cambridge University Press, 1986.

Paoli, Roberto. "Sobre el concepto de heterogeneidad: A propósito del indigenismo literario." *Revista de Crítica Literaria Latinoamericana* 6, no. 12 (1980): 257–63.

Partido Nacionalista Peruano. "Ideario." October 3, 2005. April 16, 2006. www.partidonacionalistaperuano.com/ideario.htm.

Pastor, Beatriz. *Discursos narrativos de la conquista: Mitificación y emergencia.* Hanover, N.H.: Ediciones del Norte, 1988.

Paz, Octavio. *El laberinto de la soledad.* Mexico: Fondo de Cultura Económica, 1994 [1950], 72–97.

Paz Soldán, José Edmundo. *Alcides Arguedas y la narrativa de la nación enferma.* La Paz: Plural Editores, 2003.

Peluffo, Ana. "El poder de las lágrimas: Sentimentalismo, género y nación en *Aves sin nido* de Clorinda Matto de Turner." In *Indigenismo hacia el fin del milenio: Homenaje a Antonio Conejo-Polar*, edited by Mabel Moraña, 119–38. Pittsburgh: Instituto Internacional de Literatura Iberoamericana, 1998.

Perus, Françoise. "Sobre la narrativa de Rosario Castellanos y *La espiral parece un círculo* de A. López." *Nueva Revista de Filología Hispánica* 39, no. 2 (1991): 1083–95.

Poniatowska, Elena. *¡Ay Vida, no me mereces!* Mexico: Joaquín Mortiz, 1985.

Povinelli, Elizabeth. "Consuming Geist: Popontology and the Spirit of Capital in Indigenous Australia." In *Millenial Capitalism and the Culture of Neoliberalism*, edited by Jean Comaroff and John L. Comaroff, 241–70. Durham, N.C.: Duke University Press, 2001.

Pozas, Ricardo. "La educación." In *Memorias del Instituto Nacional Indigenista.* Vol. 4: *Métodos y resultados de la política indigenista en México*, edited by Alfonso Caso, Silvio Zavala, et al., 245–58. Mexico: Ediciones del Instituto Nacional Indigenista, 1954.

Primer Encuentro de Narradores Peruanos 1965: Arequipa, Perú. Lima: Casa de la Cultura del Perú, 1969.

Rabasa, José. *Inventing America: Spanish Historiography and the Formation of Eurocentrism.* Norman: University of Oklahoma Press, 1993.

Rafael, Vicente. *Contracting Colonialism: Translation and Christian Conversion in Tagalog Society under Early Spanish Rule.* Ithaca, N.Y.: Cornell University Press, 1988.

Rama, Angel. *The Lettered City.* Translated by John Charles Chasteen. Durham, N.C.: Duke University Press, 1996.

———. *Transculturación narrativa en América Latina.* Mexico: Siglo XXI Editores, 1982.

Ramos, Alcida Rita. *Indigenism: Ethnic Politics in Brazil.* Madison: University of Wisconsin Press, 1998.

Ramos, Julio. *Divergent Modernities: Culture and Politics in Nineteenth-Century Latin America*. Translated by John D. Blanco. Durham, N.C.: Duke University Press, 2001.

Rappaport, Joanne. *The Politics of Memory: Native Historical Interpretation in the Colombian Andes*. Durham, N.C.: Duke University Press, 1998.

Reinaga, Fausto. *La "intelligentsia" del cholaje boliviano*. La Paz: Ediciones PIB (Partido Indio de Bolivia), 1967.

Reyeros, Rafael A. *El pongueaje: La servidumbre personal de los indios bolivianos*. La Paz, 1949.

Reyes, Alfonso. "Prólogo." In Antonio Mediz Bolio, *La tierra del faisán y del venado*, 7–14. Mexico: Editorial Mexico, 1934 [1922].

Rich, Adrienne. *Adrienne Rich's Poetry and Prose*. Selected and edited by Barbara Charlesworth Gelpi and Albert Gelpi. New York: W. W. Norton Company, 1993.

Riley, Denise. *'Am I That Name?' Feminism and the Category of 'Women' in History*. Basingstoke: Macmillan, 1988.

Rivera Cusicanqui, Silvia. *Oprimidos pero no vencidos: Luchas del campesinato aymara y qhechwa 1900–1980*. La Paz: HISBOL/CSUTCB, 1983.

———. "La raíz: Colonizadores y colonizados." In *Violencias encubiertas en Bolivia*. Vol. 2, edited by Silvia Rivera Cusicanqui and Raul Barrios Morón, 27–142. La Paz: CIPCA/Aruwiyiri, 1993.

Robles, Marta. "Rosario Castellanos." *La sombra fugitiva: Escritoras en la cultural nacional*, 147–91. Mexico: Universidad Nacional Autónoma de Mexico, 1985–86.

Rocha, Martha Eva. *El albúm de la mujer*. Vol. 4: *El porfiriato y la Revolución*. Mexico: Instituto Nacional de Antropología e Historia, 1991.

Rodríguez, Ileana. *House/Garden/Nation: Space, Gender and Ethnicity in Post-Colonial Latin American Literature by Women*. Translated by Robert Carr with the author. Durham, N.C.: Duke University Press, 1994.

Rodríguez Chicharro, César. *La novela indigenista mexicana*. Xalapa: Universidad Veracruzana, 1988.

———. "Reseña a *Balún Canán*." *La Palabra y el Hombre* 9 (1959): 61–67.

Rodríguez O., Gustavo and Humberto Solares S. *Sociedad oligárquica, chicha, y cultura popular*. Cochabamba: Editorial Serrano, 1990.

Rosario Castellanos: Homenaje Nacional. Mexico: Consejo Nacional para la Cultura y las Artes/Instituto Nacional de Bellas Artes, 1995.

Rowe, William. "El lugar de la muerte en la construcción del sujeto." In *Arguedas y el Perú de Hoy*, edited by Carmen María Pinilla, 131–38. Lima: SUR Casa de Estudios del Socialismo, 2005.

———. "Introduction." In José María Arguedas. *Los ríos profundos*, edited by William Rowe, vii–xxxiii. Oxford: Pergamon Press, 1973.

———. *Mito e ideología en la obra de José María Arguedas*. Lima: Instituto Nacional de Cultura, 1979.

———. "Sobre la heterogeneidad de la letra en *Los ríos profundos*: una crítica a la oposición polar escritura/oralidad." *Heterogeneidad y literatura en el Perú*, edited by James Higgins, 223–51. Lima: Centro de Estudios Literarios Antonio Cornejo Polar, 2003.

Roys, Ralph L. *The Book of Chilam Balam of Chumayel.* 2nd edition. Introduction by J. Eric S. Thompson. Norman: University of Oklahoma Press, 1967 [1933].

Said, Edward W. *Orientalism.* New York: Vintage Books, 1979.

Salmón, Josefa. *El espejo indígena: El discurso indigenista en Bolivia 1900–1956.* La Paz: Plural, 1997.

Sanjinés C. Javier. *Mestizaje Upside Down: Aesthetic Politics in Modern Bolivia.* Pittsburgh: University of Pittsburgh Press, 2004.

Sichra, Inge, and Adolfo Cáceres Romero, editors. *Poésie quechua en Bolivie.* Geneva: Editions Patiño, 1990.

Sommer, Doris. *Foundational Fictions: The National Romances of Latin America.* Berkeley: University of California Press, 1991.

Sommers, Joseph. "Literatura e historia: Las contradicciones ideológicas de la ficción indigenista." *Revista de Crítica Literaria Latinoamericana* 10 (1979): 9–39.

Soto, Shirlene A. *The Emergence of the Modern Mexican Woman.* Denver: Arden Press, 1990.

Spitta, Silvia. *Between Two Waters: Narratives of Transculturation in Latin America.* Houston: Rice University Press, 1995.

Spivak, Gayatri Chakravorty. *Critique of Postcolonial Reason: Toward a History of the Vanishing Present.* Cambridge, Mass.: Harvard University Press, 1999.

———. "A Literary Representation of the Subaltern: A Woman's Text from the Third World." In Gayatri Chakravorty Spivak. *In Other Worlds: Essays in Cultural Politics,* 241–68 .New York: Routledge, 1988.

———. "Three Women's Texts and a Critique of Imperialism." In *The Feminist Reader: Essays in Gender and the Politics of Literary Criticism,* edited by Catherine Belsey and Jane Moore, 148–63. 2nd edition. London: Blackwell, 1997.

Stabb, Martin S. "Indigenism and Racism in Mexican Thought: 1858–1911." *Journal of Inter-American Studies* 1, no. 4 (1959): 405–23.

Steele, Cynthia. "The Fiction of National Formation: The Indigenista Novels of James Fenimoore Cooper and Rosario Castellanos." In *Reinventing the Americas: Comparative Studies of Literature of the United States and Spanish America,* edited by Bell Gale Chevigny and Gari Laguardia. Cambridge: Cambridge University Press, 1986.

———. "María Escandón y Rosario Castellanos: Feminismo y política personal en el 'profundo sur' mexicano." *Inti: Revista de Literatura Hispánica* 40–41 (1994): 317–25.

Stepan, Nancy. *The Hour of Eugenics: Race, Gender, and Nation in Latin America.* Ithaca, N.Y.: Cornell University Press, 1991.

Stoler, Ann Laura. *Carnal Knowledge and Imperial Power: Race and the Intimate in Colonial Rule.* Berkeley: University of California Press, 2002.

———. *Race and the Education of Desire.* Durham, N.C.: Duke University Press, 1995.

Stephenson, Marcia. *Gender and Modernity in Andean Bolivia.* Austin: University of Texas Press, 1999.

Taller de Historia Oral Andina. *Ayllu: Pasado y futuro de los pueblos originarios.* La Paz: Aruwiyiri, 1995.

Tamayo, Franz. *Creación de la pedagogía nacional.* La Paz: Juventud, 1996 [1910].

Tapia, Luis. "La reforma moral e intelectual en el discurso del nacionalismo revolucionario." Segundo Congreso Internacional de Estudios Bolivianos. Auditorio Palacio de las Comunicaciones. La Paz, Bolivia. July 22, 2003.

Taylor, Charles. *Sources of the Self: The Making of the Modern Identity.* Cambridge, Mass.: Harvard University Press, 1989.

Thompson, Ginger. "Star Rising, Mexican Populist Faces New Tests." *New York Times,* May 5, 2005, A2.

Valcárcel, Luis E. "Garcilaso y la etnografía del Perú." In *Nuevos estudios sobre el Inca Garcilaso de la Vega: Actas del Symposium realizado en Lima del 17 al 28 de junio de 1955,* 137–64. Lima: Banco de Crédito del Perú, 1955.

———. *Tempestad en los Andes.* Lima: Editorial Universo, 1972 [1927].

Vargas Llosa, Mario. "Primitives and Creators." *Times Literary Supplement,* November 14, 1968.

———. *La utopía arcaica: José María Arguedas y las ficciones del indigenismo.* Mexico: Fondo de Cultura Económica, 1996.

Vasconcelos, José. "La raza cósmica." In *Obra selecta,* edited by Christopher Domínguez Michael, 83–115. Caracas: Biblioteca Ayacucho, 1992.

Vich, Cynthia. *Indigenismo de vanguardia en el Perú: Un estudio sobre el Boletín Titikaka.* Lima: Pontificia Universidad Católica, 2000.

Villoro, Luis. *Los grandes momentos del indigenismo en México.* Mexico: Fondo de Cultura Económica, 1996 [1950].

Wade, Peter. *Race and Ethnicity in Latin America.* London: Pluto Press, 1997.

Walcott, Derek. "A Frowsty Fragrance." In review of *Caribbeana: An Anthology of English Literature of the West Indies, 1657–1777,* edited by Thomas W. Krise, *New York Review of Books,* June 15, 2000, 57–61.

Warman, Arturo, et al., editors. *De eso que llaman antropología mexicana.* Mexico: Editorial Nuestro Tiempo, 1970.

Weil, Simone. *La pesanteur et la grâce.* Introduction by Gustave Thibon. Paris: Plon, 1948.

Williams, Gareth. *The Other Side of the Popular: Neoliberalism and Subalternity in Latin America.* Durham, N.C.: Duke University Press, 2002.

Wise, David O. "Vanguardismo a 38000 metros: El caso del Boletín Titikaka (Puno, 1926–30)." *Revista de Crítica Literaria Latinoamericana* 20 (1984): 89–100.

Yáñez, Agustín. "Estudio preliminar." *Mitos indígenas.* Edited by Agustín Yáñez. Mexico: Ediciones de la Universidad Nacional Autónoma, 1942, vii–xxv.

Yashar, Deborah J. *Contesting Citizenship in Latin America: The Rise of Indigenous Movements and the Post-liberal Challenge.* New York: Cambridge University Press, 2005.

Zamora, Antonio. Letter to Jesús Lara. July 24, 1942. Jesús Lara Personal Archive. Cochabamba, Bolivia.

Zavaleta Mercado, René. *Bolivia: El desarrollo de la conciencia nacional.* Montevideo: Editorial Diálogo, 1967.

Žižek, Slavoj. *The Sublime Object of Ideology.* London: Verso, 1989.

Index

Estelle Tarica is associate professor of Latin American literature and culture at the University of California, Berkeley.

CULTURAL STUDIES OF THE AMERICAS

(*continued from page ii*)